D1707583

Struble, Philip W.
Zebedee and sons
fishing co. : business a
r2017
333052
gi   05/23/18

Zebedee and Sons
Fishing Co.
Business Advice from the Bible

PHILIP W. STRUBLE

WESTBOW
P R E S S°
A DIVISION OF THOMAS NELSON
& ZONDERVAN

Copyright © 2017 Philip W. Struble.

All rights reserved. No part of this book may be used or reproduced by any means, graphic, electronic, or mechanical, including photocopying, recording, taping or by any information storage retrieval system without the written permission of the author except in the case of brief quotations embodied in critical articles and reviews.

WestBow Press books may be ordered through booksellers or by contacting:

WestBow Press
A Division of Thomas Nelson & Zondervan
1663 Liberty Drive
Bloomington, IN 47403
www.westbowpress.com
1 (866) 928-1240

Because of the dynamic nature of the Internet, any web addresses or links contained in this book may have changed since publication and may no longer be valid. The views expressed in this work are solely those of the author and do not necessarily reflect the views of the publisher, and the publisher hereby disclaims any responsibility for them.

Any people depicted in stock imagery provided by Thinkstock are models, and such images are being used for illustrative purposes only.
Certain stock imagery © Thinkstock.

Scripture quotations are from the ESV® Bible (The Holy Bible, English Standard Version®), copyright © 2001 by Crossway, a publishing ministry of Good News Publishers. Used by permission. All rights reserved.

THE HOLY BIBLE, NEW INTERNATIONAL VERSION®, NIV® Copyright © 1973, 1978, 1984, 2011 by Biblica, Inc.® Used by permission. All rights reserved worldwide.

Scripture taken from The Message. Copyright © 1993, 1994, 1995, 1996, 2000, 2001, 2002. Used by permission of NavPress Publishing Group.

ISBN: 978-1-5127-8334-6 (sc)
ISBN: 978-1-5127-8335-3 (hc)
ISBN: 978-1-5127-8333-9 (e)

Library of Congress Control Number: 2017905523

Print information available on the last page.

WestBow Press rev. date: 4/6/2017

This book is dedicated to
Virginia Lee Struble
September 29, 1928–April 2, 2003

Great is the Lord, and greatly to be praised;
and his greatness is unsearchable.
—Psalm 145:3

Contents

Acknowledgments

As with any big project, there are always many thanks to be passed around. First, I will always be grateful to my lovely wife, Stephanie. Her enduring support and partnership over the past thirty-seven years has carried me through many valleys and over many mountains. Of course, my children are my sense of joy and pride—and thanks to Adrienne who helped edit and is working to teach me the nuances of social media.

Second, I must thank my business partners and fellow employees at Landplan Engineering. They have given me the latitude to divide my time between my business responsibilities and my writing. I'm not the easiest boss to work for, and I hope that what I have learned from developing this book will pay multiple dividends throughout my company and my immediate business world.

Finally, I've got to thank my friends at Velocity Church for their unending encouragement and much needed prayers. God is good.

INTRODUCTION

Zebedee and Sons Fishing Co.

Truth be told, I know nothing about fishing. When our children were young, my wife and I took a family vacation to a Minnesota resort called Five Lakes. We like to try new adventures and go places we've never been, so this great state seemed ideal for ten days of pure fun. Our rustic lakeside cabin came with a small boat and various fishing supplies, so we fished in the morning, at noon, at suppertime, and at dusk. We caught fish like it was going out of style. If I knew more about fishing, I would brag about the kinds of fish we caught, but that is way beyond my meager expertise. It was the perfect fishing vacation until one morning when we were picking up bait. The gnarled old-timer behind the counter pointed out that the fish were really biting on leeches. One look at the container full of leeches and my kids decided they were done with anything that could be caught using a leech. Yuck. So much for fishing; fortunately, Minnesota has a million things to do other than fish.

I'm a small business owner who fortunately doesn't have to rely on fishing for a living. I have an engineering consulting business that employs twenty-five to thirty-five people, depending on the economic climate and our success in convincing people to hire us instead of our competitors. It's a good, hardworking way to make a living. With it comes a lot of financial and emotional risks, but the rewards offset them. I'm involved in projects that have an immediate impact on people's lives. Even today, I enjoy driving through neighborhoods we designed years ago and seeing yards full of swing sets and bikes. I like going to shopping centers we designed that are thriving with eclectic shops and great places to eat. And I enjoy going to meetings in office parks in which we played a significant role.

As I matured in my business career, however, I became driven to operate as a Christian business. I joined Christian businessmen's groups, went to workshops, and read about applying principles from the Bible to my business life. This borderline obsession resulted in my going back to college to study theology, which taught me my first of many valuable lessons: studying for a master's degree and running a business are full-time jobs. One or the other will suffer, and in my case, both suffered to a certain degree. But in the end, I came away with a new perspective on both my business and my faith that I want to share with businesspeople, leaders, and Christians to provide support for people searching for guidance just as I was.

Zebedee and Sons Fishing Co.

This book is a story about a man named Zebedee from the Bible. As opposed to me, Zebedee knows everything there is about fishing. He is the epitome of a fisherman. He lives and breathes fishing; it is both his passion and his occupation. This passion for fishing has also been passed on to his children. But before I tell you the story of Zebedee, let me be clear. Most of what I know about Zebedee is conjecture. There are only two references about him in the Bible. The first is from the Gospel of Matthew.

> And going on from there he saw two other brothers, James the son of Zebedee and John his brother, in the boat with Zebedee their father, mending their nets, and he called them. Immediately they left the boat and their father and followed him. (Matthew 4:21–22)

The other reference to Zebedee is in the Gospel of Mark (1:19–20), which is the same story as above but told by the author, Mark. Both are the story of Jesus calling His first disciples to travel with Him as He fulfills the prophecy of the Old Testament.

The story of Zebedee, as I have discovered, is typical of the Bible. It's a seemingly innocent story, Jesus calling His disciples to follow Him, and also includes the incidental participation of other minor characters—in this case, Zebedee. These other characters often become a parallel or a secondary lesson along with the main story. Every story is in the Bible for a reason. Although we don't have a lot of information about Zebedee, that doesn't mean he doesn't have a lot to teach us.

The way most Christians see this scripture (and rightly so) is about Jesus's calling His first four disciples to "follow me, and I will make you fishers of men" (Matthew 4:19). The way I see this scripture, however, is through the eyes of Zebedee as a business owner. What I read is this: "Immediately they *left the boat and their father* and followed him" (Matthew 4:22, emphasis added). Zebedee was the proud owner of a small fishing company that operated several fishing boats on the Sea of Galilee and employed at least four men. Zebedee was an owner-operator who labored side by side with his employees, not because he did not trust them, but because he was, after all, a fisherman. And fishermen fish. Like most small businessmen I know, he worked hard to attain some level of wealth and respectability. He and his family were personally known to the Jewish high priest (John 18:15), so they were a faithful family and were active in the community and synagogue.

From scripture, we know Zebedee had four business partners in his fishing business. Two of his partners were brothers named Simon Peter and Andrew, and they were the first two called by Jesus to follow Him. Zebedee's other two partners were two of his sons, James and John. All four of these young men became apostles who followed and learned from Jesus over the three-plus years He traveled the earth. All became highly respected in the Christian community, and all were viciously persecuted for their faith in Jesus Christ. And all four of these young men walked away from Zebedee and their fishing business to follow Jesus.

I know I'm supposed to love the story of how Jesus called these four men and how they all obediently gave up everything to be with Christ. But the small business owner in me grieves for Zebedee. I can picture him sitting in one of his boats with a torn fishing net in his hand and fatigue etched into his face from a night of fishing. I imagine him smelling of fish and sweat while staring off at the backs of five men walking away. No one looks back, waves good-bye, or says anything—let alone a simple "See you later." Zebedee realizes his business succession plan (probably not what he called it) just walked off into the distance.

Until that day he thought he had his future all figured out. His two boys had partnered with two of the hardest-working, honest young brothers from the village, and they would slowly take over his business. Zebedee could ease into old age. He would have grandchildren to take to the beach in the morning to watch their fathers come in from a night of fishing. Each morning he would meet his boats to help mend and hang the nets and hear the stories of where the fishing was good, what the weather was like, and how they needed to invest in some new equipment. If all went well, Zebedee could limit his work to focusing on customers—keeping them happy—and getting the best price for the fish. Maybe he could branch out and get into new markets, such as smoked fish that they could sell farther from their village. Or maybe they could buy more boats and he could oversee maintaining them while the boys focused on fishing. Zebedee had big plans. Now the foundation for all those plans just got off their boats and walked away.

I've been in the position of having my well-thought-out plans just evaporate into nothingness. One day business is good, and the next I'm scratching my head, lost and confused. Have you ever had a bank call your note, a key manager quit, or a trainee leave with your list of contacts? Maybe an associate who was to take over your medical practice chose to work for the local hospital instead. Or perhaps your son decided he did not want to spend the rest of his life working the family farm. Or your business partner decided she would rather focus on designing clothing instead of websites. I think we can all sympathize with Zebedee. Of course, he would hire more men to help him and continue his business as before—just like we would do. But his original plan included his two sons. As a father, it is difficult to imagine any job could be better than working side by side with your children. It's special to be able to teach them, watch them grow, and be a partner and friend in addition to a father. And he lost the two other brothers, who he also thought of as sons. Everyone was gone. Jesus saw something special in these four young men to pick them as His disciples. And Zebedee, who worked with them every night, knew firsthand they were special.

Not too much later in the Gospel of Matthew, Salome, Zebedee's wife, is identified as "the mother of the sons of Zebedee" (Matthew 20:20), which indicates Zebedee had died. Zebedee did not get to sit in the shade of their house and hear from his sons about Jesus's death on the cross. He did not get to hear about His resurrection, all the excitement about the Holy Spirit, and venturing to foreign lands to spread the Gospel. Zebedee was a special guy. We did not hear him complaining or chasing after his boys while telling them they were on a fool's errand. He was not upset that Jesus did not ask him to be a disciple. He was a simple businessman whose plans had changed, and like most businesspeople, he adapted. As a practicing Jew, I think Zebedee knew God was directing the change in his own plans. He knew God's word from the laws, the prophets, and the writings. I'm sure he knew he was not in charge, but He was in charge.

This brings me to this book's purpose. The story of Zebedee is a biblical story with many business applications for today's world. It is humbling that we can find great business advice from a two-thousand-year-old book that is just as applicable today as advice from any trendy, self-help, business leaders workshop. This is not to demean other sources of knowledge, but after buying the latest business advice books for years, it finally dawned on me that the same advice is in the Bible. Even better, it is great business advice paired with life lessons and moral stories that are all relevant and necessary today. I find it more rewarding to read about King Solomon building the temple than about yet another CEO who turned around a Fortune 500 company. Neither story, in a pure business sense, is directly applicable to my small business. I cannot relate to billion-dollar budgets and technology that I will never access. But I can relate to King Solomon and his life as found in Ecclesiastes, Songs of Solomon, and 1 Kings. And as a bonus to the good business advice, the King Solomon stories include lessons in compassion, humility, integrity, honesty, and trust in God.

Most people with a nominal exposure to the Bible know that Christ came and died for our sins, and by believing and trusting in him, we will have everlasting life. But *Zebedee and Sons Fishing Co.* is going to explore a different side of the Bible. The Bible is a story of a nomadic people who lived during a brutal time in history when human life had little value. Yet, when you look closely, the level of commerce in the Bible is remarkable. The Israelites, for example, started out as sheep and goat herders. This meant someone had to tend the sheep, shear the sheep, and make the fabric that became the final product. To complicate matters, this product often was transported a great distance through hostile territories to reach its final market. This product was then sold or bartered for money or other goods. So just the making of fabric involved many people, each who relied on their small part to earn a living.

The world of commerce in the New Testament is not just about the Israelites or individuals making a living. Although there were slaves doing some of the work, much of this revenue went to hired hands and other non-primary jobs (i.e., non-product manufacturing). These tent makers, carpenters, fishermen, vintners, and olive oil producers had payroll, taxes, and miscellaneous expenses, as well as set-asides for business expansion. Sound familiar? If you read the Bible closely, their world of commerce is not all that different from today's world of commerce. By using the Bible as our guide for maneuvering our business world, we learn how the Israelites handled similar situations, how we can apply those lessons today, and best of all, how we can also live with hope, integrity, and faith.

My method of conveying business lessons from the Bible is to tell Bible stories. And with a story, you need to know the context surrounding it so the application will be appropriate. I believe knowing the entire story is important. As John R. Erickson, author of the Hank the Cowdog series says, "A good story satisfies the appetite for entertainment, but it can also reveal truth, structure, justice, humor, and beauty."[1] I have taken the time to include as much of the details about each story as possible. The background, the environment, the surroundings, and the history of the individual characters make each story unique to the problem it's addressing. Knowing the story and its context is how we relate the Bible to our twenty-first-century business world. Furthermore, following how the stories are used here will show you how to use the Bible as your own source of business advice on issues not covered in this book.

Housekeeping

First, some housekeeping rules. Unless otherwise noted, all Bible quotes are from the English Standard Version (ESV). For those who are not biblical enthusiasts, the Bible was written in several ancient languages and subsequently copied numerous times for synagogues and other believers. It was originally written by forty-four different authors over a fifteen-hundred-year period. No Bible is a word-for-word reproduction of the original text, so there are many versions of the Bible that have varying degrees of interpretation of that text.

Second, although knowing a story's context is important, I have only included a portion of most stories. These portions will help guide you through each topic, but if there are more particular issues you are dealing with, I recommend you read the entire story. In fact, you may find it easiest to have a Bible available while you are reading this book. This book was not designed to be read just once. It is a book to be used to remind you how the Bible addresses business issues and to guide you to your own conversations with God in solving your struggles and problems. For example, next time you find yourself negotiating a new contract, open the chapter on negotiations and review how Abraham and Jacob achieved it. That will help mentally prepare you to negotiate in a biblical fashion.

Third, this book contains many biblical verses. I am guilty, when reading books referencing the Bible, of skipping over verses I think I already know. I would suggest you try not to do that. The way this book looks at the business aspect of scripture is not how most verses are traditionally viewed.

Fourth, I have included a page for notes at the end of each chapter. This book is a reference book. If I am dealing with a human resources issue, I can read or reread the chapters dealing with work benefits or employee discipline. I can make notes at the end of those chapters, and the next time I have employee issues, I can go back and see what I found useful before. Each time I can add anything new and build my own personal reference book.

This book is designed and written for everyone but specifically for businesspeople. Of course, if you think about it, we are all businesspeople. If you hire day care for your children, negotiate buying a car, settle an insurance claim, bargain with the home-repair guy, or take a new job, you're engaging in business. More specifically, this book is for men and women who run a small business and want to run it with integrity, have some level of rationality behind the myriad of decisions made, be proud of those decisions, and maintain a character that we, our family, and our friends will be proud of. If you are Christian, the stories found here will mean much more than if you are not. But, as I alluded to before, good advice is still good advice—and I want to share that with everyone, Christian or not. Don't worry if you do not know your way around the Bible or who many of the people I reference are. The point is these are stories of how the business circumstances we tackle today were answered by someone a long time ago—and they were answered by a God who has been around a long time and who loves us no matter what.

Enjoy.

CHAPTER 1

The Right People in Zebedee's Boat

Zebedee was speechless. The thought of losing his two sons and two key helpers had never occurred to him. These young men were his future, and he always assumed fishing was theirs. *What do I do now?* thought Zebedee. *I guess first things first; I need to find some new employees.* The city of Capernaum was known for producing hardworking men so that shouldn't be a problem. The real problem was replacing these specific four men. They were exceptional, they knew what to do, they listened, they asked the right questions, and each had strong leadership potential. "I guess it's not surprising that they are gone," murmured Zebedee. "It's hard to find and keep really great employees."

Just like many other businesspeople, in 2003 I purchased the Jim Collins book *Good to Great* and read it searching for the pearls of wisdom that would allow me to move my small company to a higher level. For those of you who are unfamiliar with this book, it is a compilation of stories detailing what makes some companies "great" while their peer companies continue to languish in the "good" category. One of the principles of getting from good to great is hiring the correct people and placing them in the correct job. In the Collins vernacular, this is known as the "right people in the right seats."[2]

As Collins elaborates, "The good-to-great leaders understand three simple truths. First, if you begin with 'who,' rather that 'what' you can more easily adapt to a changing world ... Second, if you have the right people on the bus the problem of how to motivate and manage people largely goes away ... Third, if you have the wrong people, it doesn't matter if you discover the right direction: you *still* won't have a great company."[3] These are powerful comments and have, as evidenced by the prolific use of "right people, right seat" throughout business literature, transformed the thinking of much of the business world. Of course, this concept is something we always intuitively knew from paying attention to sports, where the best teams were the ones with the right guys in the backfield or playing forward or pitching. But Collins was able to show it was true through his interviews with both good and great companies.

All that is presented in *Good to Great* is fantastic advice. The difficulty, in my experience, is twofold. First, who are these "right" people to put on the right seat on the bus? Second, how does a small company—where the HR department is also the office manager and the marketing coordinator—compete against major employers with staff and budgets to follow the employee recruitment philosophies expounded in *Good to Great*?

My experience at small companies over the years in the recruitment and retention of employees is often unconventional. The recruitment process may consist of placing notices on trade websites, association bulletin boards, and employment websites, as well as through word of mouth. We send employment notices to colleges and universities in areas of the country that are experiencing some level of economic downturn, assuming that potential employees may be interested in geographical relocation. When thus idea fails, we turn to professional employee recruiters. When we do find a capable candidate, our process is to have two or three existing employees meet the candidate and spend enough time to develop an opinion of the person. They are looking to see if the candidate has an acceptable level of technical competency and if the candidate's personality is compatible with our existing staff. When we've decided to offer a job, it becomes one of the senior management people's responsibilities to "go out and get them hired." Occasionally we check employment references, but since most of the time these responses are so noncommittal, even for the outstanding applicant, that effort is often deemed a waste of time.

There is no question this process is fraught with problems and could stand a significant amount of improvement. But remember, we are talking about employers who are entrepreneurs and have gotten to where they are under their own steam. Most are simply continuing a process that has worked well for them in the past.

Truth be told, the unconventional process used by numerous small businesses is not that unconventional. Geno Wickman, in his book *Traction: Get a Grip on Your Business*, outlines a slightly more sophisticated process. Wickman promotes a simple yet powerful system called the Entrepreneurial Operating System,[4] and one component of this system is to first identify the core values of your company. If you're like me, at first I envisioned this as a lengthy process that entails serious soul searching and potentially therapy after it's completed. Not so with Wickman's process. Pick your top three employees and list what is special about them, which you want to replicate and be the image of your company. Shorten this list to a handful of characteristics and you're basically done. Well, maybe there is a little more than that, but not much. Simplicity is the key. With this list of core values in hand, you use it to make all your personnel decisions. When deciding if someone may not be the right fit for your bus (or Zebedee's boat), use the list to evaluate him or her, give the employee tangible measurements to improve, and if ultimately necessary, use it as a determination for dismissal.

What is startling about this process is the traction system yields more personal characteristics as opposed to technical capabilities. While *Good to Great* talks of the rigorous nature of working for these types of companies and the need for them to always hire the brightest and the best, *Traction* is about getting people who are compatible with the nature or character of the company. Of course, everyone wants the right people, so the question is (and always will be): who are these right people? Geoff Colvin's book *Talent Is Overrated* takes a different angle on the concept of right people.[5] For Colvin, the right people are not the ones with an innate ability or the ones who work extra hard, they are the ones who have developed a habit of deliberate practice that makes them great. Colvin says you as the employer can make the right people.

Of course, the premise up to this point is we all want to make sure we hire the right people. Unfortunately, we also know that no one is inherently the perfect employee and that it is the prevailing business culture, whether at our place of business or at a previous employer, which develops that person into being the right person. So now the question is what characteristics make an employee a right person, and what can our workplace environment do to develop those characteristics in an employee? But instead of looking at Fortune 500 companies or other twenty-first-century business studies that evaluate employee impacts on business success, I will look at that twenty-first-century issue through the lens of the Bible to answer that question.

To examine the implications of having the right people on a team, I have selected two examples of teams God used in the Bible and one parable of right people and wrong people. The first team is that of God and his prophets who ministered to the Old Testament Israelites. Specifically, we will look at how Jeremiah, Ezekiel, and Daniel formed a team to minister to the Israelites in exile. The second example is that of Jesus and His disciples. We will begin with Jesus's defined mission, how He selected the apostles, look at the diversity of the apostles, and finally how He used the apostles' potential to train them. For the third example, I have chosen the parable of the ten minas to elaborate on the significance of having the right people versus the wrong people.

God and the Prophets

Right people are created by their environment, which includes their supervisors and mentors, the type of work they do, and the atmosphere of their surroundings. My first example of right people as found in the Bible is a group rarely considered a team. This team I'm thinking about is God and His Old Testament prophets, who all worked together for one purpose. Most of us know the story in a general sense. God selected, for some unknown reason, a man named Abraham to be the father of His favored nation. This favored family, called the Israelites after Abraham's grandson, was just like all of us—rebellious, opinionated, and prone to the occasional lack of good judgment. God's agreement with this family was that in return for worshipping Him and following His none-too-rigorous commandments, He would bless them. Being blessed in the ancient Near East four thousand years ago was a big deal. But the Israelites, now large enough to be a legitimate nation, could not consistently hold up their end of the agreement. So God assembled a team to be their advisors and be thorns in the sides of the rulers of this new nation. They were to remind the Israelites of their shortcomings and the potential ramifications if they did not start holding up their side of the agreement with God. This team of prophets was not your typical group. They made up a diverse group, each endowed with certain skills or traits that made them unique to the tasks for which they were called.

So as the Israelites continued a downward spiral of not adhering to their agreement with God, God began to have these prophets warn of their punishment. Beginning in about 660 BC, the southern tribes of Judah (Abraham's descendants were divided into twelve tribes, two of which comprised the southern tribes of Judah and the remaining ten tribes comprised the northern tribes of Israel) were led by a series of particularly nasty kings who practiced many of the acts forbidden in their agreement with God. God sent the prophets Zephaniah, Nahum, and Jeremiah to warn them. But the Israelites did not change their behavior, so God then called on the prophets Habakkuk, Obadiah, Daniel, and Ezekiel to advise His people of the consequences of their actions. Their prophecies are detailed in the books of the Bible, but for our purposes here, the three most notable prophets are Jeremiah, Ezekiel, and Daniel.

Jeremiah

Jeremiah was born between 650 and 645 BC in a small village just outside of Jerusalem. He was groomed from the beginning for holy service in the priesthood.

> Now the word of the Lord came to me, saying,
> "Before I formed you in the womb I knew you,
> and before you were born I consecrated you;
> I appointed you a prophet to the nations."

> Then I said, "Ah, Lord God! Behold, I do not know how
> to speak, for I am only a youth." But the Lord said to me,

> "Do not say, 'I am only a youth';
> for to all to whom I send you, you shall go,
> and whatever I command you, you shall speak.
> Do not be afraid of them,

for I am with you to deliver you,
declares the Lord." (Jeremiah 1:4–8)

Jeremiah was obviously reluctant from the beginning of his role as part of God's service but quickly understood its importance. The next verses laid out God's plan for Jeremiah.

Then the Lord put out his hand and touched my mouth. And the Lord said to me,

"Behold, I have put my words in your mouth.
See, I have set you this day over nations and over kingdoms,
to pluck up and to break down,
to destroy and to overthrow,
to build and to plant." (Jeremiah 1:9–10)

From the beginning, Jeremiah knew his job was to go to the Israelite rulers to proclaim the destruction and the subsequent rebuilding of a nation that would eventually be the Kingdom of God. King Josiah was the first king to whom Jeremiah prophesied. Both Josiah's father and grandfather were kings who promoted idolatry, child sacrifice, and other vile practices, but this young king understood the need to obey God and began making efforts to return the people back to worshipping God (read 2 Chronicles 34 and 2 Kings 22 and 23). Unfortunately, Josiah died, and the next king, Jehoiakim, did nothing to continue Josiah's reforms. Jeremiah found himself alone, preaching the consequences of the wrath of God in a world where no one would listen. Jeremiah, however, was true to his calling from God, although at great personal sacrifice. His written prophecies were clear, consistent, and accurate. With God's mentoring, Jeremiah was an effective prophet and team member despite the harsh political climate of Jerusalem.

Ezekiel

As odd as it may seem, God's wrath for the southern kingdom of Judah was to have their enemies, the Babylonians, conquer them, destroy the Temple of God in Jerusalem, and exile them to Babylon. One of the Israelites exiled was a man named Ezekiel. Little is known about Ezekiel prior to the exile, but once in exile, God called on Ezekiel to become His servant.

Ezekiel was living with his wife and a group of other Israelites in rural Babylon when God called him to be His prophet. God had a special task for him. This period in Jewish history was one of the most difficult times, and Ezekiel's service was to minister to a particular group of Jews. These Jews were far away from their own land because their enemies had taken them to Babylonia. They were feeling hopeless, and they had concluded God did not care about them anymore. Ezekiel's task was to declare God's message to them and to tell them the reason why they were in Babylon: God was punishing them. To make Ezekiel's message even more difficult, he had to call them to lead a holy life. This meant they must continue to obey God's laws, despite living in a foreign land. After delivering this difficult message, Ezekiel could give them the good news: God had a better future planned for them.

It's hard to imagine a more difficult task for Ezekiel. This group of Jews found themselves in exile by their own God. They were without hope, and it was Ezekiel's responsibility to convince them God still loved them. As with Jeremiah, Ezekiel's abilities to accomplish God's tasks thrived because of God's supervision and the environment in which Ezekiel prophesied. God made Ezekiel into the prophet He needed him to be.

Daniel

Jeremiah's job was to forecast the destruction of Jerusalem and then stay behind in Jerusalem after the conquering by the Babylonians to minister to the remaining people. Ezekiel's job was to minister to the Jews who were in exile, get them to turn back to God, and be ready for the day when they would get to return to their homeland. The prophet Daniel had a different mission. He was taken into captivity by the Babylonians at a young age. While Ezekiel lived in a community of Jews on the outskirts of Babylon, Daniel was taken into the king's palace to be trained as a civil servant in the Babylonian government. The Babylonians' strategy is obvious: put the cream-of-the-crop captives into public service and train them in the Babylonian ways, so these new servants will help control the remaining captives. Because of his circumstances, Daniel became an unconventional prophet. He did not write the type of prophecy found in Jeremiah or Ezekiel. The first half of his book tells how he would remain true to his Jewish faith and customs yet still be an invaluable servant to the Babylonian rulers. This is where you may have heard his famous stories about his fellow believers being thrown into the fiery furnace or Daniel being placed in the lion's den. The second half of his book is about his prophetic dreams and how God helped interpret them. Yet, despite the differences between Daniel's circumstances and those of Ezekiel and Jeremiah, he was a team player. Daniel 9:2 says:

> I, Daniel, perceived in the books the number of years that, according to the word of the Lord to Jeremiah the prophet, must pass before the end of the desolations of Jerusalem, namely, seventy years.

Daniel knew what his contemporaries were doing and based his ministry on what Jeremiah had prophesied. Jeremiah said the exile was to last only seventy years. Daniel believed him and was preparing his heart for his fellow Jews to return to Jerusalem.

When we examine all three prophets in light of their calling by God, it becomes obvious they constitute a perfect team to accomplish His will. They all proved to be the right people in the right seats. All were supervised by God, and although they each had their own individual skills and personalities that qualified them for their given tasks, the environments in which they worked strengthened these skills. They did their jobs to the best of their abilities, albeit sometimes reluctantly. All three exhibited characteristics that are found in successful teams. They were active participants who were reliable, respectful, able to effectively communicate, and committed to the team's mission. They indirectly coordinated with each other to complement the other's responsibilities but did not attempt to assume any responsibilities outside of their given roles.

In my business I need team members with a range of skills, who understand that their role is to excel in their assignment. I do not need anyone dabbling in someone else's assignment. Each team member needs to be accountable for his or her role first and foremost. They need to be committed to the project and willing to see it through to the end. Each team member understands the project's success is in his or her hands, and they are willing to meet that challenge. Each team member is committed to the team. As Jim Collins makes us aware, any one team member who does not fulfill his or her role sabotages the project's chance of success.

Jesus and the Twelve

The New Testament describes how Jesus's work on this earth was done with the assistance of his disciples. These disciples came from among His followers to believe in Him and followed the messages He taught (Matthew 16:24; Luke 14:26, 27, 33). When He healed people and was popular in a worldly sense, Jesus's followers were great in number (Matthew 15:30). When He talked about the hardships of being His follower and of how His blood was a symbol of His life, the numbers shrank (John 6:60–65). He did have, however, a core group that lived with Him. This was the handpicked group of twelve we refer to as the apostles. I would like to suggest this group not only as a team of the right people in the right seats on the right bus, but also as examples of Geoff Colvin's ideas about the development of world-class performers.

Jesus's Mission

Jesus initiated his ministry by announcing a mission statement, as found in the book of Luke. It seems Jesus had a custom of always going to the synagogue on the Sabbath, which was Saturday. Sabbath worship was typical of first-century Jewish life and was where members congregated to pray and to study scripture. Devout men of the community were often expected to read, interpret, and further explain the weekly Torah (first five books of the Bible) reading. Occasionally they also read from either the historical or prophetic books (such as Samuel, Kings, Chronicles, Psalms, Isaiah, Jeremiah, and Ezekiel). Evidently Jesus was considered one of the leaders of the synagogue and therefore had the responsibility to read and teach. On this particular day, Jesus read not from the Torah but from the book of Isaiah.

> And the scroll of the prophet Isaiah was given to him.
> He unrolled the scroll and found the place where it was
> written,

"The Spirit of the Lord is upon me,
because he has anointed me
to proclaim good news to the poor.
He has sent me to proclaim liberty to the captives
and recovering of sight to the blind,
to set at liberty those who are oppressed,
to proclaim the year of the Lord's favor."

And he rolled up the scroll and gave it back to the attendant
and sat down. And the eyes of all in the synagogue were
fixed on him. And he began to say to them, "Today this
Scripture has been fulfilled in your hearing." (Luke 4:17–21)

Jesus's mission statement was to proclaim liberty to the captives and
to those who were oppressed, to recover sight to the blind, and to proclaim
the year of the Lord's favor. Jesus's overall ministry had many priorities.
He ministered to the sick, called out for justice, provided compassion to
the poor, and still found time to preach the good news of the Kingdom
of God. Although he was fully human and fully God, and probably could
accomplish all that needed to be done by Himself, he decided to use earthly
help to accomplish his priorities.

Selection of the Apostles

Jesus's help came in the form of twelve apostles. Jesus did not ask for résumés
or use an employment agency to find these apostles. His first source for
finding the right people was to look at those around Him. Early on, Jesus
had developed a following of men and women who absorbed His every
word and action. These were His early disciples who recognized Him for
being something special. From an employment standpoint, this group of
candidates was passionate about Jesus's message, willing to learn at any
cost, and ready to make sacrifices for the good of the mission. Technically,
however, none of these people had any of the skills needed for the job of an
apostle. None had any experience in the mission of Jesus Christ. But some
of them had something better; they had a passion that led to a commitment
seldom found in employment studies.

One of these first disciples was a man named Andrew, who started as a disciple of John the Baptist. After spending time with Jesus, Andrew's instinct was to get his brother Simon Peter involved.

> One of the two who heard John speak and followed Jesus
> was Andrew, Simon Peter's brother. He first found his
> own brother Simon and said to him, "We have found the
> Messiah," which means Christ. He brought him to Jesus.
> Jesus looked at him and said, "You are Simon the son of
> John. You shall be called Cephas," which means Peter.
> (John 1:40–42)

You might remember these two brothers who were partners with Zebedee. Jesus knew them before He came to the shores of Galilee. Jesus called many to follow Him as disciples, but He was selective about this core group that would live with Him for the next three years. He recognized the significance of getting the right people to be apostles, so Jesus went to His source of power and inspiration for counsel.

> In these days he went out to the mountain to pray, and all
> night he continued in prayer to God. And when day came,
> he called his disciples and chose from them twelve, whom
> he named apostles: Simon, whom he named Peter, and
> Andrew his brother, and James and John, and Philip, and
> Bartholomew, and Matthew, and Thomas, and James the
> son of Alphaeus, and Simon who was called the Zealot,
> and Judas the son of James, and Judas Iscariot, who became
> a traitor. (Luke 6:12–16)

What is significant is that Luke's description of Jesus's praying uses the only occurrence of the Greek word *dianuktereuo*[6] found in the Bible. This word means "spend the whole night." Jesus wanted to make sure He got His instruction correct about whom to select as an apostle. We all know that a bad hiring decision has lasting impacts. First, as an owner or manager, your time spent looking for, interviewing, negotiating with, and hiring a new employee is unrecoverable as are the early training costs of the new employee. Second, the morale and physical costs of a bad hiring decision can have deep impacts on existing staff. Finally, the emotional and financial costs of terminating an employee and then starting the hiring process over are draining.

Obviously, Jesus understood the importance of selecting the right people. Although we don't have the same level of direct communication to our omniscient God that Jesus had, we should always use prayer when making important decisions. Because of the significance of choosing the right people, we need to develop other sources for reliable advice. I'd suggest any interview process include as many other individuals as possible, and allow for an open line of conversation where others feel able to express their observations and concerns. Using hiring professionals and others outside of the normal business activity should always be considered. Finally, we need to learn how to divorce our emotions from the hiring process and objectively consider all applicants.

Diversity

What is fascinating is the diversity of this group of twelve apostles that Jesus's selection process was able to assemble. As you can imagine, the historical records about each of the disciples are somewhat sketchy. We know Simon Peter, Andrew, James, and John were in a fishing business together. This by itself says that they were hardworking, accustomed to living and working outdoors, and used to taking risks. They were blue-collar but not uneducated. They were willing to gamble on catching fish, negotiate prices, invest in improvements (boats, nets, etc.), and search for new markets. All these men were Galileans who, per tradition, were fond of innovation, by nature willing to change, and delighted in rabble-rousing. Many references indicate Galileans were quick tempered and given to quarreling. In a group where everyone was known to be quick tempered, Simon Peter had the reputation of being even more impulsive and hot-tempered. The Gospels often report he had outstanding leadership skills, but his impulsive nature needed much tempering.

John, who wrote the Gospel of John, 1 John, 2 John, 3 John, and Revelation, and his brother James appear to have come from a more well-to-do family since their father could hire servants in his fishing business

(Mark 1:20). John was a man of action and ambition, with an explosive temper and an intolerant heart. His second name was Boanerges, which means "son of Thunder." John's brother James, known as the Elder, is not well known, but it seems he lived out his life of extraordinary faith in the shadow of his younger brother, John.

In contrast to the fishermen in the group, another apostle was Matthew, who was a publican or tax collector. Matthew is often referred to as Levi (maybe you have noticed it was customary for men in the Middle East during the time of Christ to have more than one name). A tax collector in first-century Judea was considered wicked and corrupt, and was consistently classified with harlots, Gentiles, and sinners. Their scam was to charge high duty taxes and then loan money at exorbitant interest rates to those who could not pay. It is no wonder they were hated. What's unique about Matthew is he knew how to write. He was the first man to present to the world in the Hebrew language an account of the teachings of Jesus Christ.

Two other examples of the apostles' diversity are that of Simon the Zealot and Judas Iscariot. All we know about Simon the Zealot is his name. The zealots were crazed with their hatred for the Romans and fanatical in their "pure" religious practices, but they also were extravagant and reckless in the demonstrations of their faith. Judas Iscariot was the only apostle who was not a Galilean; he was a Judean. Judas was the treasurer of the group and had a difficult time with Jesus's ministry. He could not understand why they were not raising money to fund an army. It is hard to understand how a man who had a front-row seat to the teaching, ministry, miracles, and healing of Jesus could ultimately betray Him to His enemies as Judas did.

Guided by prayer, Jesus selected an extremely diverse group of men to be his apostles. It almost defies most business studies to think that Jesus selected a group of hot-tempered Galileans, one reformed tax collector, and one Judean to be the future of Christianity. None had real leadership experience, team-building skills, or any management aptitude beyond what they learned in their simple daily lives. They had no experience in the tasks defined by Jesus's mission statement. But what Jesus knew was the potential each apostle carried. Who would have guessed a despised tax collector would articulate to the world the life of Jesus, or the hot-tempered, impulsive Peter would be the one many Christians believed to be the rock on which the church would be built.

13

The Apostles' Potential and Training

As employers looking to complete our own teams, we need to look hard at our prospective employees and think of their potential—not just the future employees' potential for themselves but the potential each new employee brings to the company. I love to read the success/failure stories where people apply for jobs numerous times before finally getting an opportunity to prove themselves. And when given that opportunity, they exceed everyone's expectations. My contradictory take on these stories is they are not about the potential employee's success in getting the job and excelling. It is more about the companies who failed to see the potential in the candidate they passed on. Jesus saw potential in each apostle, and as employers, we need to learn to look for potential in our prospective employees. Prayer, reliable advice from others, open-mindedness, and a search for diversity will help open our eyes to the potential in prospective employees.

It is not as if the apostles did not bring any attributes that Jesus could build on. First, the twelve apostles brought with them passion as well as compassion. They were all passionate about the mission of Jesus. Although to a lesser and human degree, they all felt what Jesus felt, wanted what Jesus wanted, and worked for what Jesus worked. You can imagine the apostles crying when Jesus cried and laughing when Jesus laughed. They were the right people in the right seats on the right bus, but not because they understood or were skilled in the work of Jesus Christ. Quite the contrary, they were the right people because they had the right emotion for the mission. They hurt for the right reasons, understood what they were expected to understand, and did not understand because they were all too human. When it was time to travel and move on, that is exactly what they did without hesitation.

Second, in addition to being passionate, the twelve apostles were trainable, although some of the teachings did not become apparent until Jesus had died, was resurrected, and finally went to be with the Father. Training the apostles, however, was not always easy or pleasant. Jesus was a tough teacher; do not think for a moment traveling and living with Jesus was all about Him performing miracles of making a few loaves of bread feed thousands of people and making water barrels into the best house wine. The Old Testament said this long before Jesus walked the earth:

My son, do not despise the Lord's discipline
or be weary of his reproof,
for the Lord reproves him whom he loves,
as a father the son in whom he delights. (Proverbs 3:11–12)

The Bible is full of stories of God rebuking His people. Jesus is often found admonishing his disciples for seemingly innocent mistakes. But He is teaching and preparing them for their mission once He departs to be in heaven. One example of Him rebuking His team of followers is in the ninth chapter of Luke. In twenty verses, Jesus has cause to correct His disciples five times.

The story begins with Jesus encountering a man whose son is demon possessed. The man claims, "And I begged your disciples to cast it out, but they could not" (Luke 9:40). Jesus responds, "O faithless and twisted generation, how long am I to be with you and bear with you?" (Luke 9:41), pointing out that His disciples should be able to cast out demons. While everyone is marveling at Jesus's ability to remove the demon from the young boy, Jesus attempts to tell his close followers about the betrayal that will lead to His death. Today we know these clues about Jesus's death, burial, and resurrection are important, but at the time His disciples were unable to comprehend what He was telling them. In growing frustration, Jesus says, "Let these words sink into your ears: The Son of Man is about to be delivered into the hands of men" (Luke 9:44). After two obvious comments about His Father, His disciples still do not understand. Instead they think it's an appropriate time to bicker over which one of them is the greatest follower of Christ. To teach the disciples, Jesus pulls a young child to his side and rebukes their pride, saying, "Whoever receives this child in my name receives me, and whoever receives me receives him who sent me. For he who is least among you all is the one who is great" (Luke 9:48). Instead of hearing Jesus's message, the apostle John speaks up, telling Jesus of a person who is not part of their group of disciples invoking the name of Jesus and trying to cast out demons. You can hear the angst in Jesus's voice when he says, "Do not stop him, for the one who is not against you is for you" (Luke 9:50). Shortly after, Jesus and the disciples travel to Jerusalem through Samaria. To make a long and interesting story short, the Samaritans and the Jews did not care for each other. Jesus and His disciples encountered the

Samaritans, and the Samaritans became inhospitable toward Jesus. "And when his disciples James and John saw it, they said, 'Lord, do you want us to tell fire to come down from heaven and consume them?'" Shaking his head in disbelief, "he turned and rebuked them. And they went on to another village" (Luke 9:54–55).

Let's take a moment to think about Jesus and his followers. Jesus prayerfully selected a diverse group of apostles not because of their qualifications but for their potential. He was in the process of turning them into the right people. But training is not easy. Have you ever been in an important meeting where you are trying to kick off a new project or having a strategy session to counteract some recently received bad news? The topic of the meeting should be the most important thing on everyone's mind. Then, from nowhere, someone asks a completely irrelevant question. Maybe it is about another project, gossip about a competitor, or some non-business-related news. You realize you do not have everyone's undivided attention. You would like to scream, grab their shirt collars, get in their face—do something to get their attention. Not so with Jesus. He displayed an unimaginable level of patience in understanding that every moment was a teaching moment no matter how frustrating.

We see in this drawn-out encounter between Jesus and his followers a rather juvenile level of understanding of Jesus and His mission on earth by his apostles. The disciples could not cast out a demon from a young boy but were ready to call down lightning bolts to destroy a village. They argued over who was the greatest disciple, yet they were embarrassed that someone, who was not part of their clique, was trying to cast out demons using the very methods Jesus taught. No, they were not ready for the task they were called to do. They needed the stern corrections and rebukes from Jesus. They needed a firm hand, and Jesus gave it to them. To ultimately have a staff of "right people, right seats," we need to exhibit the same level of patience with our employees.

Now picture this same group five, ten, twenty, or thirty years later. Peter was the rock of the church, and although he preached mostly to the Jews, he defended taking the message of Jesus to the Gentiles. James was the first to be martyred for preaching the Gospel. John, who wrote five books of the New Testament, was the last to die but fulfilled his promise to Jesus and took care of Jesus's mother, Mary. All apostles had similar impacts on the future of Christianity. Clearly, Jesus selecting twelve unlikely characters to be His apostles worked because He had the ability and patience to lead and train them to be the right people in the right seats.

Parable of the Ten Minas

Our final example is one of the parables of Jesus called the parable of the ten minas, found in Luke 19:11–27. It is the story of a rich and soon-to-be powerful man who goes on an extended trip to be crowned king. Many people in this nobleman's home country didn't like him so they sent a delegation to oppose the coronation. As the man prepared to leave, he called ten of his servants and gave each ten minas ("pounds" in some Bibles). "Put this money to work," he said, "until I come back" (Luke 19:13). The parable only reports on what three of the servants did with the wealth. Two of them invested their minas; one of them earned ten minas in return, and the second earned five minas. The third servant did not invest the minas but wrapped them up in a handkerchief to keep them safe.

Upon the nobleman's return, he asked for an accounting. The new king rewarded the two who invested the minas and received a good return with promotions to high positions of responsibility. The third, who received no return on his minas, was severely punished. The parable concludes by noting that the new king punished those who opposed his coronation.

To understand how this parable fits into our examination of teams and getting the right people in the right seats, each character of the parable will be individually studied. The first character is the nobleman turned king. This character could be a boss, a company CEO, a supervisor, or even a faceless industry or trade. Regardless, it is an entity that can make demands of those who answer to it and deserves some level of respect due to its position either in the company, the industry, or by legitimate regulations.

The second character in our consideration is the servants who did what they were supposed to do; they invested the minas and received a return. All servants in this parable are affected by the character identified as the king. They could be direct reports to a supervisor, divisions in a company that answer to a home office, subconsultants who are prime suppliers to a parent company, or a company that as part of their business answers to governmental regulations. And all that the servants who received a return on their investment did was execute their job as the king directed. I picture them as model employees who prided themselves in following instructions and being proud of a job well done. Clearly they were the right people in the right seats.

The third character is the servant who did nothing with the minas because he feared doing something wrong. On several occasions, I've given instructions and followed up later only to find nothing had been done because the employee did not understand or had more questions, or something else "more important" came up. Just as the people I gave instructions to, the servants would not have been given the minas had the nobleman not thought they could perform their responsibilities. The perception was they could handle the job and not fail. I picture this servant as someone who could do the job, but he was the wrong person in the seat because he did not have the intangibles to take the initiative and finish the job. Something was keeping this servant from charging ahead. It could have been the need for more training, the change of leadership style, or immaturity (meaning not enough years on the job). It is up to the manager to determine if this servant can be salvaged.

Finally, the fourth character in this parable is the group of people who opposed the coronation of the nobleman. As we heard, they too were punished, which on the surface seems harsh. But in thinking more about them, they remind me of the surrounding throngs of employees who, although not involved in the actions or decisions, still want to include their input. They want to voice an opinion regardless of whether they have any involvement or not. I see this as a style of office politics where an outside group, a department, or a competing company may have a chance to improve its own circumstances if someone else fails. This action is seldom helpful and often makes achieving great results more difficult than it otherwise would have been. I can think of the times when business partners were throwing roadblocks in the way of progress by using phrases like "the devil's advocate" to interject opposing and negative attitudes without acquiring supporting data. Teams of right people, right seats are often affected by outside influences. Certainly objective ideas and opinions should always be welcome, but ideas and opinions that are structured as obstructionist and opposing should always be resisted.

Although my summary of the parable of the minas is based on a business perspective, it is important to also understand the theology of the story. Jesus tells this parable as he is getting ready to go the Jerusalem for the last time. He will ride in on a colt and be heralded by many as the king (Luke 19:38). Soon thereafter, his people will reject him, and he will be crucified and buried. The two servants who received the minas and earned a return on their investment are examples of the people who did not misjudge who Jesus was and understood they needed to work hard while waiting for His eventual return. The king's return in the parable is Christ's return in the future. Jesus also instructs us to work hard with the gifts we have been given so that upon His return we will be able to proudly account for our actions. Upon Jesus's return, we will know that we are really the right people in the right seats.

Zebedee

Zebedee wasn't concerned about finding the right young men to be the right people on his boat. For starters, he knew he was in the right seat on the right boat—he had God and his faith. He also knew how to mentor and train young boys to be responsible young men. He could be stern and harsh; he could also be caring and kind. And he knew when to be one or the other.

Summary

Let's recap what we know about how the Bible instructs us to have the right people in the right seats.

1. Without question, having the right people to do your work is directly tied to your success. The right people are found in many places and from varying circumstances. When considering a list of potential candidates, think of the prophets of the Old Testament. They came from circumstances that enabled them to interact with the people to whom they were prophesying, but more importantly, they brought zeal to the job that made them stand out. I'm not sure you could say they loved their job, but they brought a passion to see the job done regardless of public opinion and pushback. They all saw the job through to the end. As with the prophets, good team

members effectively communicate, are respectful, are committed to the team's mission, complement other team members, and will not attempt to assume any responsibilities outside of their given roles.

2. The right people are made. Nobody shows up with an amazing genius for finance, designing dresses, writing software, or playing music. Jesus's leadership made the disciples the world-changing evangelists they were. He took a group with strong potential and molded them through teaching, as well as through chastising, to be the best they could be. Studying Jesus's patience in working with his disciples is a great pattern for us to follow in developing our future business leaders. In looking for new team members, we need to prayerfully consider our applicants, look for potential and diversity, rely on others for advice, and be prepared for extensive training.

3. In nearly all circumstances, we have four parties involved. First, we have the authority figure we answer to, whether it is a boss, a board of directors, a parent corporation, an investment group, or a set of regulations. Second, we have those employees who make our business machine run. These employees are the right employees in the right seats. Third, there are those who fail because they cannot understand their job—not the mechanics of their job but the overarching role they fill within the company. They have the skills and the know-how but do not see that they sooner or later need to take some risks and get the job done. These are the wrong people in the seats. Finally, we have the group of people not directly involved but who indirectly may benefit from your actions. Great teams of the right people are often affected by outside influences. Make sure you know if these outside groups are for you or against you.

Notes

CHAPTER 2

Workplace Benefits at Zebedee and Sons Fishing Co.

"Why would anyone want to work for me?" mused Zebedee as he thought through the names of the young men in Capernaum, likely candidates for his fishing crew. In the ancient Near East, getting paid was about the only benefit needed to find workers. But Zebedee knew that to get the best helpers he needed to have something more than just pay. Of course, they would get the benefit of Zebedee's vast knowledge of fishing, such as how to cast the nets, where to look for fish, and where to sell the fish. But what else could he offer them that his competitors could not? What could he offer that would entice these young men to make a career of working on Zebedee's boats?

It seems once a year or so business magazines devote an entire issue to recognizing local businesses that are the best places to work. It's often presented as a contest in which employees are encouraged to submit their own workplace for consideration. Various methodologies are used to evaluate companies that are presorted into varying classifications, such as companies with under twenty-five employees, nonprofit organizations, companies less than five years old, restaurants, etc. Some contests have a team of celebrity judges, some have a complex set of metrics, and some have the "smoky dark room" (not really) that produces the lists of winners. Of course, being a cynic, I also believe that how much money you spend in advertising with the sponsor of the "best place to work" contest plays a role in the decision. Aside from the fact that it does sell advertising, many of the efforts to promote local businesses as great places to work are legitimate. We spend most of our waking hours at work, so where we spend that time should be a great place. Recognizing the best of the best should help others to improve their working conditions.

To a certain extent, if a company only wants to win the great-place-to-work contest, all it needs to do is spend money. For example, some of the companies who win the contest win because the top-performing employees get a paid vacation to Fiji or some other desirable destination. I do not want to be unfair because I have never worked at the best place to work, nor have I ever been to Fiji, but rewards given to the top few do not recognize the efforts of the entire company. Fortunately, many companies want their establishment to be great for all employees and not just win a contest. These companies are creative in coming up with benefits, such as childcare pickup and drop-off, ergonomic office designs, and an equitable profit-sharing equation that represents an honest effort to benefit all employees from bottom to top.

From a business perspective, there are better reasons to be a great place to work than winning the local best-place-to-work competition. Tony Schwartz wrote in the *Harvard Business Review* about "The Twelve Attributes of a Truly Great Place to Work."[7] The premise of this short article is to create a win-win scenario for the employer and employee, which results in an increase in the employees' engagement in their work. The sad fact is more employees in today's workforce are more unengaged in their work than engaged. An engaged employee is someone who wants to come to work every day, knows what's expected of him or her, and understands how his or her work contributes to the success of the company.[8] The employer's task is to create an environment where the focus is not about working to receive a paycheck, but creating an environment for workers who are committed to the purpose of the organization and are willing to own the results of their work. The organization must tailor all its benefits to increase employee engagement, which in turn drives up the efficiency and productivity of the business.

As always, this is easier said than done. Most small business owners cannot afford to offer a one-year paternity leave (Netflix), freeze the employee's eggs (Apple), provide "baby cash" (Facebook), or provide unlimited vacation time (many companies). But those restrictions do not mean we cannot be creative to be competitive. What we need to do is back up and consider why we are providing employee incentives and what incentives the employees actually want. Patrick Lencioni recently wrote, "If you want the best out of your employees, you'd better take a real interest in who they are."[9] Many resources suggest you audit your employees to see what perks would be beneficial. There is no reason to offer day care if most of your employees are single or older. If most of your employees are active, maybe a health club membership would be beneficial. Look at what is distressing the employees, and see if you, as a company, can ease the difficulties they are experiencing. These difficulties may include long commutes, too much sitting, the occasional need to be home during working hours, and family circumstances that make getting to work problematic. Benefits must be useful in improving the business attractiveness. They need to be designed to entice new employees and retain existing employees. They need to add to the employees' sense of pride in the place where they work. In summary, employee benefits need to limit your turnover rate, improve morale, help keep employees healthier, and improve your corporate appeal, which should result in increasing your employees' job performance.

Zebedee and Sons Fishing Co. never had much of a chance to compete as a great place to work. They worked at night, most likely all night, and not just the graveyard shift. Conditions on the boat were not ergonomically designed. Bathroom facilities were, shall we say, primitive. They offered no day care, no insurance of any kind, no casual Fridays, no dry cleaning pickup/drop-off, and no 401K or any other retirement plan. But that did not mean Zebedee did not have to try to present working with him as a great opportunity. He still had to compete for hired help, and he still had to make the nights working with James, John, Andrew, and Peter tolerable if not enjoyable. It is not a recent discovery that people produce better if they enjoy where they work.

While thinking through all the potential benefits we could offer employees as both an employer and a Christian who wants to remain obedient to the God we serve, I began to wonder what the Bible says that we as Christians must do to equip our employees and workers. The Bible is vocal about the responsibilities of employees to the work they perform and to their employer. 1 Thessalonians 4:11–12 says:

And to aspire to live quietly, and to mind your own affairs, and to work with your hands, as we instructed you, so that you may walk properly before outsiders and be dependent on no one.

Unfortunately, there is no parallel set of instructions for the employer. So to understand what the Bible says about employers, we need to dig a little deeper. Our examination of biblical employee treatment is divided between the Old Testament and the New Testament. In the Old Testament, we will look at slavery and how King Solomon regarded treating employees. In the New Testament, we will think through how the apostle Paul considers employees and what Jesus has to say as well. We will see that while we can offer all kinds of amenities as part of a material benefits package, those amenities become of little value if the treatment of employees and the relationship between the employee and employer is not positive.

Old Testament

Slavery

The first difficulty in evaluating employment customs in the Bible is that much of the workforce in the Old Testament, as well as the New Testament, is made up of slaves. Doug Vander Lugt[10] notes:

Old Testament laws regulating slavery are troublesome by modern standards, but in their historical context they provided a degree of social recognition and legal protection to slaves that was advanced for its time (Exodus 21:20–27, Leviticus 25:44–46). We must keep in mind that on occasion it was an alternative to the massacre of enemy populations in wartime and the starvation of the poor during famine.

The mandates from the Bible on how slaves are to be treated set a baseline or minimal standard of care that is applied to anyone working for someone else throughout biblical times. We need to avoid focusing on the word *slave* and understand that this custom of the times represented the entire workforce and not simply people forced against their will to work for another. Remember, the Israelites were slaves in Egypt for centuries before being set free by Moses.

This brings us to Deuteronomy 16:13–15 where God describes the Festival of Tabernacles:

> Celebrate the Festival of Tabernacles for seven days after you have gathered the produce of your threshing floor and your winepress. Be joyful at your festival—you, your sons and daughters, your male and female servants, and the Levites, the foreigners, the fatherless and the widows who live in your towns. For seven days celebrate the festival to the Lord your God at the place the Lord will choose. For the Lord your God will bless you in all your harvest and in all the work of your hands, and your joy will be complete.

This passage sets one of the baseline treatments of male and female servants—they were to enjoy the celebration with the family just as if they were part of the family. This treatment of slaves was unique to Christianity since in most ancient civilizations the manservant and handmaids never received a day off.

King Solomon

A classic example of employment in the Old Testament is found as Solomon begins to build the great Temple of God as described in 2 Chronicles 2. For this project Solomon selects seventy thousand men to bear burdens, eighty thousand to quarry stone, and thirty-six hundred men just to oversee them. Louis Ginzberg relates some of the legends surrounding the building of the temple: "During the seven years it took to build the Temple, not a single workman died who was employed about it, nor even did a single one fall sick. And as the workmen were sound and robust from first to last, so the perfection of their tools remained unimpaired until the building stood complete. Thus the work suffered no sort of interruption."[11] Furthermore, Solomon contacted Hiram, king of Tyre:

Send me, therefore, a man skilled to work in gold and silver, bronze and iron, and in purple, crimson and blue yarn, and experienced in the art of engraving, to work in Judah and Jerusalem with my skilled workers, whom my father David provided.

Send me also cedar, juniper and algum logs from Lebanon, for I know that your servants are skilled in cutting timber there. My servants will work with yours to provide me with plenty of lumber, because the temple I build must be large and magnificent. I will give your servants, the woodsmen who cut the timber, twenty thousand cors of ground wheat, twenty thousand cors of barley, twenty thousand baths of wine and twenty thousand baths of olive oil. (2 Chronicles 2:7–10)

For an employer, this scripture offers several important employee-related examples. First, Solomon focused on getting the best talent for his project. In today's catchphrase world, it would be akin to getting the right people on the right bus. Solomon was looking for the most skilled people for the task at hand. It would not have been acceptable to do with only the skill level of the people he currently had available in Jerusalem. He looked for the best and would settle only for the best. If the temple was to be the best ever built, it demanded the best craftsmen to complete the job.

Second, Hiram was not an Israelite; he was a Gentile (to use a New Testament term). But Hiram had the best craftsmen, and they were all Gentiles. To build the greatest temple ever built, King Solomon understood he needed to get the best craftsmen even if that meant going "outside of the family," so to speak. The same was true of the cedars of Lebanon. These trees were notorious for their quality as were the Sidonians who were the best timber craftsmen available.

Third, Solomon was willing to pay handsomely for the skilled labor brought in to build the temple. I have never attempted to pay any of my employees in cors of barley or baths of wine, but most commentaries note these yearly amounts were not insignificant.

Finally, throughout the descriptions of building the temple is a theme of pride and respect for the skills of the laborers and craftsmen. "I know your servants have the skill to cut timber in Lebanon; and indeed my servants will be with your servants …" (verse 8). And the woodsmen were "endowed with intelligence and discernment …" (verse 12). Solomon was in effect saying, "I know your woodsmen are very skilled, smart, capable, and trustworthy in what they do, and my servants are able to be with them and assist them."

All the methods used by King Solomon are not only used today but also are emphasized to enhance employee engagement. We pay our talent well, and we allow them to grow and excel in the specialties they are known for. Although King Solomon in much of the text is saying "I built …," based on 2 Chronicles 2 he is saying he brought in the best and brightest to accomplish his project. Great leaders throughout time have always used the best to accomplish their goals and have gone out of their way to recognize them. Who in your organization has a comparable reputation of working in "gold and silver, bronze and iron, and in purple, crimson and blue yarn, and experienced in the art of engraving" (2 Chronicles 2:8)? Do you recognize them, promote them, and allow their reputation to grow as a representative of your business? Do they know you are proud of them and brag about them?

Wisdom Literature

The book of Proverbs contains wisdom attributed to King Solomon. Just as he showed in building the temple, King Solomon has something to say in Proverbs about how we treat our employees and boost morale. First, he comments on providing for our employees. Proverbs 13:4 says, "The soul of the sluggard craves and gets nothing, while the soul of the diligent is richly supplied." As employers, we need to focus on supplying the right people and not waste time trying to appease employees who are not engaged in their work. I like the concept of *supplying* employees, which emphasizes amenities other than just pay.

Additionally, King Solomon emphasizes how we are to honor our employees' talents. Proverbs 22:29 says, "Do you see a man skillful in his work? He will stand before kings; he will not stand before obscure men." Like the skilled craftsmen Solomon recruited, we will be proud to have our skilled employees represent us and our companies. Their work is our biggest advertisement.

Finally, from the book of Ecclesiastes, also attributed to King Solomon, we find one of the all-time, most popular Bible verses, which says, "There is nothing better for a person than that he should eat and drink and find enjoyment in his toil" (Ecclesiastes 2:24). This verse, when viewed from the employees' vantage, emphasizes the requirement for their employer to ensure each employee has the time and ability to eat, drink, and find enjoyment. Overbearing work hours and poor working conditions take away from the time and ability to enjoy life. If we know and understand our employees, we will know what benefits they desire and will be able to use these benefits to allow them to be more engaged in their work, which will increase their value to the company.

New Testament

First-century Judea was a brutal time for the Christians. They were in a spiritual battle with the Jewish community, and the Romans were not tolerant of any sect of people who challenged their status quo. The disparity between the upper class and the working class was massive. Most Christians were in the working class, and many were slaves. The apostle Paul's calling was to the Gentiles in Asia, where he experienced persecution by the Jews, the non-Christians, and the Romans. Despite this persecution, Paul continued to deliver a message of love and respect, even in the face of severe adversity. Many of the Gentiles he was preaching to were employed by non-Christians who could make their lives miserable. Paul's message was not to reciprocate that kind of treatment.

Ephesians

In the apostle Paul's letter to the church in Ephesus, he specifically wrote about how we are to treat each other. Although not specifically about the employer/employee relationship, his first dialogue is in Ephesians 5:15–21:

> Be very careful, then, how you live—not as unwise but as wise, making the most of every opportunity, because the days are evil. Therefore do not be foolish, but understand what the Lord's will is. Do not get drunk on wine, which

leads to debauchery. Instead, be filled with the Spirit, speaking to one another with psalms, hymns, and songs from the Spirit. Sing and make music from your heart to the Lord, always giving thanks to God the Father for everything, in the name of our Lord Jesus Christ. Submit to one another out of reverence for Christ.

Being filled with the Holy Spirit means being guided by Him and letting Him accomplish His will in our lives. As employers and employees, we are first and foremost the children of a gracious and loving God, and we are to present that love to the secular world. When we think of ourselves as business owners or employees of a business, we lose sight of the concept that God owns us. So, for the employer, all treatment toward any and all employees is found in the fact that we are guided by the Word of God and by the Holy Spirit. Employers and employees alike are to submit to one another out of reverence to God.

As for specific direction on employer/employee relationships, we must listen to Ephesians 6:5–9. Like what we found in the Old Testament, we are faced with the issue of slavery in that this portion of the apostle Paul's letter to the Ephesians is focused on the relationship between masters and slaves.

Slaves, obey your earthly masters with respect and fear, and with sincerity of heart, just as you would obey Christ. Obey them not only to win their favor when their eye is on you, but as slaves of Christ, doing the will of God from your heart. Serve wholeheartedly, as if you were serving the Lord, not people, because you know that the Lord will reward each one for whatever good they do, whether they are slave or free.

And masters, treat your slaves in the same way. Do not threaten them, since you know that he who is both their Master and yours is in heaven, and there is no favoritism with him. (Ephesians 6:5–9)

For clarification, Paul is not discussing the morals of slavery. He wrote in 1 Corinthians 7:20 that God has called people to different stations of life, and they are to live out the Christian life in any situation. As urged in Ephesians 5, Ephesians 6 says masters must treat slaves with Christian charity. Our twenty-first century understanding of this verse says employers are to treat employees with Christian charity. Simply said, employers or supervisors have a choice to make. They can be a boss and act like a boss who lords their authority over those under them, or they can set a Christian example and lead through respect and love. In the workplace this will be manifest by showing respect, promoting two-way communication, being open minded, and holding each other accountable.

Corinthians

Paul also wrote to the church in Corinth, where he included advice about workplace morale and the employer/employee relationship:

> The one who plants and the one who waters have one purpose, and they will each be rewarded according to their own labor. For we are co-workers in God's service; you are God's field, God's building. (1 Corinthians 3:8–9)

From an employer or supervisor's position, this passage is about delegation. The two different tasks listed each indicate a responsibility. Watering is no more important than planting, nor is planting more important than watering. Watering is not responsible for seeing that the planting is done, and planting is not responsible for seeing that the watering is done. We are all coworkers. In a healthy workplace environment, everyone is on the same team to complete the project, which means everyone will focus on his or her own small part and ensure it is completed. Most importantly, employees will receive their reward for their part based on their labor. Rewards are not given according to gifts, talents, or even success but to the individual's labor. We need to remember some parts of all projects are more glamorous and visible, and more profitable, than other parts. Those identities should not be part of the rewarding structure. Frequently, the most critical part of a project is the most obscure yet labor intensive. All coworkers know who worked the hardest, so it is imperative that the reward-sharing plan genuinely reflects the efforts of everyone on the team.

Paul and Timothy

A third example by the apostle Paul about the relationship between employees and employers is between Paul and Timothy. Much of what is written in 1 Timothy and 2 Timothy can be interpreted as great advice to employees. As an example, 2 Timothy 2:1–7 (NIV) reads:

> You then, my son, be strong in the grace that is in Christ Jesus. And the things you have heard me say in the presence of many witnesses entrust to reliable people who will also be qualified to teach others. Join with me in suffering, like a good soldier of Christ Jesus. No one serving as a soldier gets entangled in civilian affairs, but rather tries to please his commanding officer. Similarly, anyone who competes as an athlete does not receive the victor's crown except by competing according to the rules. The hardworking farmer should be the first to receive a share of the crops. Reflect on what I am saying, for the Lord will give you insight into all this.

Think of this letter as written from a superior to a subordinate or employee. The instructions were not given in private but in the presence of other employees, so there is no favoritism. This passage gives three metaphors for the relationship between the supervisor and the subordinate. First, Paul likens work to that of a military life—a life of order and regiment. While we first think of soldiers, we must not forget the commanding officers and the influence they have over their entrusted troops. History books are full of great stories of the leadership skills of commanding officers whose presence and encouragement changes the tide of a single battle that eventually changes the outcome of a war. And the same is true of the stories in the Bible. Second, the athletic metaphor is different in that while we all compete, it is our teammates and leaders (coaches) who provide the encouragement to continue competing, finish the race, and win. Regardless of the leadership hierarchy, we are all to support and encourage our teammates to successfully fulfill our obligations. Finally, with the farmer, the key word is *hardworking*, and it is the hardworking farmer who first receives his share. Employers are to remember it needs to be the hardworking employees who first receive credit, praise, respect, and a share of the profits from their endeavors. All three metaphors collectively point out the importance of the relationship between the employer and the employee. This relationship is not static, but it is a dynamic and evolving relationship to which the employer must always pay attention. Leading employees may require a strong presence at one point, a cheerleader at another point, and an understanding coworker at a third point.

Benefits of Jesus

So far we have seen that the Old Testament requires Christians to treat employees with Christian charity and that King Solomon used many of the same methods to encourage his workers that we use today to increase employee engagement. The apostle Paul followed the Old Testament advice and recommended in his letters to various churches and followers that they submit to God and allow Him to guide us in how we treat our employees. We need to obey our earthly masters, but our real Master is in heaven and is the one we follow. We need to support our employees, encourage our employees, and allow our employees to prosper; all these will allow our companies to prosper and grow. The benefits package we offer to employees needs to include not just material amenities but also a healthy and constructive relationship between the employer and employee.

But let's change gears for a moment and consider not the benefits of being an employee, but the benefits of being a believer in Jesus Christ. Psalm 103:1–5 says:

> Bless the Lord, O my soul,
> and all that is within me,
> bless his holy name!
> Bless the Lord, O my soul,
> and forget not all his benefits,
> who forgives all your iniquity,
> who heals all your diseases,
> who redeems your life from the pit,
> who crowns you with steadfast love and mercy,
> who satisfies you with good
> so that your youth is renewed like the eagle's.

Verse 2 specifically says "and forget not all his benefits." Up to this point we have been discussing the tremendous advantages of having a great benefit package for our employees. With a great benefit package, our employees will be more engaged, more productive, happier, and healthier, and they will be employees for a longer time. Psalm 103:1–5 says this is also true for those who understand the great benefit package God has for us. Just like the effect a great benefit package has on employees, understanding God's benefit package for us will have the same effect. Knowing God's benefit package will make us more engaged, more productive, happier, and healthier, and we get eternal life as a bonus. God's benefit package far exceeds any benefit package available from even the best employers who can afford the most over-the-top, out-of-this-world, unbelievable benefits ever. It is no wonder the number of workplace chaplains is on the rise.[12]

Combining the power of our own company-provided benefits with the power of God's benefits will produce better results than we can accomplish on our own. Employees still will have issues and problems that we, as employers, cannot answer. Employer-provided benefit packages can help with commuting, working at home, and noontime naps. But issues such as divorce, cancer, accidents, and legal problems affect our employees' work engagement, and none of our employer-provided benefit packages can adequately address those problems. "Who forgives all your iniquity, who heals all your diseases, who redeems your life from the pit, who crowns you with steadfast love and mercy" (Psalm 103:3–4). Adding God to our list of what we provide as a benefit will produce results beyond anything we can individually provide. If our sole goal is to improve employee engagement because we understand its powerful implications on our bottom line, God needs to be part of our benefit package.

Zebedee

Zebedee did not have to think long about finding new help. "I did pretty well the last time getting Peter and Andrew to come to work with me. I can do that again." He knew his reputation for being honest, fair, and hardworking was well known. Having his four best helpers lured away to follow Jesus should be a positive for anyone looking for a new job. Sometimes your best reputation is the quality of the competition that steals away your workers.

Summary

1. Don't let the idea that the Bible includes discussions of slavery impair your ability to see the value of its advice regarding employer/ employee relationships. The message of treating slaves as if they were family is counsel for us to treat our employees, coworkers, and subordinates likewise.

2. King Solomon, the wisest and richest man ever, knew the value in getting the best people for the job and treating them extremely well. Brag about your employees, know what they want, and provide everything you can so they can prosper.

3. Remember that we are all children of God (read Ephesians 5 and 6). God is ultimately our master; therefore, we have no right to lord our earthly responsibilities over those we work with. Treat everyone with Christian charity. In the workplace, Christian love and respect will be manifest by showing respect, promoting two-way communication, being open minded, and holding each other accountable.

4. 1 Corinthians reminds us to delegate and to make sure our part of each project is completed. If our job is to plant, do not worry about watering. If we all focus on our individual tasks, we all will be successful and the rewards will be distributed accordingly. As employers, we need to make sure our rewards for project success are distributed based on effort given.

5. Paul's friendship with Timothy, as found in the two letters he wrote to him, describe the perfect working relationship between an employer and an employee. As an employer, at times we will need to provide strong leadership, at times we will provide encouragement, and at times we will be a coworker.

6. God provides us with a benefit package that far exceeds the benefit package that any earthly employer can provide (Psalm 103:1–5). It doesn't have to be mandatory, but allowing our employees to lean on God's benefits exponentially increases the potential for employee engagement and satisfaction.

Notes

CHAPTER 3

Zebedee and Accountability

Zebedee, slowly shaking his head back and forth, was left alone on his boat. His crew, business partners, and sons had just walked away, a mutiny of sorts. Zebedee was consumed with his thoughts, which ran from pity to anger to indifference. He wondered why those boys—maybe he should start thinking of them as men—walked off and did not express any sense of responsibility to the company. Where was the sense of accountability they should have had toward Zebedee, or at least the business?

It's thought-provoking to consider the business aspect of accountability in relation to the Bible. Essentially the entire Bible is a story of accountability, or more importantly the lack of accountability. God cut a deal with His chosen people, and in this deal God would be responsible for certain things like setting standards to live by and providing them with eternal life. His people were to simply obey and worship Him. God never faltered on His side of the deal, and His people never failed to fail. As strange as it sounds, that is good news for us because in those stories of failing is where our life lessons are found. The Bible would be a boring story if the Israelites were obedient as they promised. Unfortunately, in today's world, we are just as disobedient as the Israelites were in the Old Testament.

Henry Evans starts out his book *Winning with Accountability*[13] by stating, "Successful teams cannot exist without accountability—high performance and accountability go hand in hand. Accountability starts with understanding the truth and continues with the thoughts, words and actions of everyone involved in your organization. It is the key to long-term, sustained organizational success." We work hard to get people in our organizations to be accountable, yet we place on their shoulders the added burden of "understanding the truth." One online business resource[14] states the definition of accountability is "the obligation of an individual or organization to account for its activities, accept responsibility for them, and to disclose the results in a transparent manner. It also includes the responsibility for money or other entrusted property." This definition is more reasonable yet still lacks any indication of why we should be accountable and how specifically we are to learn to be accountable.

I understand the drive to define what it means to be accountable, but the problem is we are overthinking what accountability is. To be accountable is simple, given the right mind-set and foundational training. Everyone has always been called to be accountable for the actions he or she takes. Children are called to be accountable for their disobedience to their parents. Students are to be accountable for their homework assignments. Team members, whether involved in sports, debate, work, or volunteering, are accountable for their specific assignments. Spouses are accountable to their partners by being faithful to marriage vows taken in devotion. The downside of not being accountable is total chaos. Just imagine, for example, the results on a Sunday afternoon when the linemen on a football team do not follow their responsibility to block for the quarterback. Or imagine if we do not obey the traffic laws and instead drive on whichever side of the street we choose. The results of not being accountable are never good.

Most business attempts to institute and reinforce accountability are built around doing a better job of communicating and establishing a better organizational structure. Communication is used to better convey job performance and define expectations. The organizational structure is how businesses establish and accomplish specific goals that define success for their business. While these recommendations are great, they do not teach accountability; they simply build on the employees' natural accountability instincts that they acquired prior to entering the business world. If we are to improve accountability in the workplace, we need to look at where we get training in accountability in the first place. While there are inherently accountable people, the best written resource and manual for teaching accountability is the Bible. My premise here is the proper mind-set and training in accountability are not found in schools, self-help books, or the workplace. Proper training comes from a lifestyle of obedience to the Gospel of Christ as found in the Bible. So let's look at what the Bible says.

Old Testament

When I think of accountability, I immediately think of Ezekiel and his prophetic writings. Ezekiel was a Hebrew prophet who authored the book of Ezekiel. He was one of several Old Testament prophets responsible for revealing the prophecy of God's planned destruction of Jerusalem, the restoration of the land back to the Israelites, and specific visions of a future third temple. He personally experienced the fulfillment of several of his prophetic visions as an exile in Babylon, so he had firsthand knowledge of people being held accountable by God.

Inequity of the Father

Ezekiel wrote on several occasions specifically about accountability. One of these occurrences is in chapter 18 of the book of Ezekiel, verse 20:

> The soul who sins shall die. The son shall not suffer for the iniquity of the father, nor the father suffer for the iniquity of the son. The righteousness of the righteous shall be upon himself, and the wickedness of the wicked shall be upon himself.

In this rather harsh declaration, Ezekiel is commenting on the reason the Israelites were in exile. The sins of earlier generations caused God to have the Israelites become Babylonian captives, who were removed from their promised land and exiled in Babylon. Many of the exiles complained that it was unfair they were suffering the sins of previous generations. Although they were complaining, the current generation could not deny that they too had sinned and thus were being punished for their own sins. Ezekiel lists the sins of both generations and emphasizes the point that God was holding each one accountable for his or her own actions and not those of others. Everyone is either rewarded or punished according to whether he or she has done good or evil, regardless of how anyone else (in this case the father or previous generation) had acted.

In our business world, we need to ensure our policies and actions promote a culture where everyone is responsible for his or her own actions. It is often a delicate balance to encourage employees to take self-initiative within the limits of their job, yet hold them accountable for the results. The rewards of such action must significantly outweigh the reprimand for failure. Being accountable must always be more rewarding than either inaction or taking inappropriate action.

The Watchman

A second verse and an important metaphor by Ezekiel is in chapter 33, verses 7–9:

> So you, son of man, I have made a watchman for the house of Israel; whenever you hear a word from my mouth, you shall give them warning from me. If I say to the wicked, O wicked man, you shall surely die, and you do not speak to warn the wicked to turn from his way, that wicked man shall die in his iniquity, but his blood I will require at your hand. But if you warn the wicked to turn from his way, and he does not turn from his way, that person shall die in his iniquity, but you will have delivered your soul.

The beauty of these verses is the metaphor of the watchman, which everyone in the ancient Near East intimately understood. There is no clearer image of accountability and responsibility than the watchman. The watchman's responsibility lies in sounding the alarm and pronouncing danger from outside the walls. This sentinel is stationed in a strategic lookout position and is to sound a trumpet upon the sight of any potential threat. But the watchman's real responsibility lies deeper than just sounding an alarm. First, everyone sees the watchman both from within the protected enclosure and from the outside. He is in full public view, and everyone knows if he is standing his post or shirking his duties. The people he is protecting, as well as the enemies he is protecting against, know if the watchman is on the wall. His visible conduct on the job is an obvious message of his competence and trustfulness—that he is accountable.

Second is the sheer responsibility of the watchman to be ever vigilant, steady, intelligent, and cautious. People can sleep soundly because they know the watchman is on duty. The enemy, on the other hand, is more cautious knowing that the watchman is looking and anticipating danger. The watchman is not just visible at his post but also mentally engaged in his job. Ezekiel does not allow any room for failure in this verse. The enemy is watching the watchman for an opportunity to exploit any weakness, and such an event would be catastrophic. When the alarm is sounded, it must be sounded loudly and confidently.

Third, while the watchman is accountable to everyone, he is also accountable to himself. He carries a great amount of responsibility. The personal responsibility Ezekiel describes is to warn the wicked. If they are not warned and they die, their death is on the hands of the watchman. The challenge is that it is the wicked the watchman is to warn and not just the nice, friendly people. For the watchman, accountability is not easy.

For the businessperson, accountability also is not always easy. Can you stand the scrutiny of your peers, your employees, your competition, and the public? Are you vigilant of your actions and your words in every circumstance? As leaders, we are always on display. How we talk and act at work, at home, in our leisure time, and with our pals directly reflect our level of accountability. We are the watchmen; and to be accountable, we must be ever vigilant of all our actions and words.

A Threefold Cord

One final Old Testament story about accountability is in a familiar line from Ecclesiastes 4:9–12:

> Two are better than one, because they have a good reward
> for their toil. For if they fall, one will lift up his fellow; but
> woe to him who is alone when he falls and has not another
> to lift him up. Again, if two lie together, they are warm;
> but how can one be warm alone? And though a man might

prevail against one who is alone, two will withstand him.
A threefold cord is not quickly broken.

This verse is interpreted many ways. To begin to understand it, we need to recognize the writer is not stating that having two of something is always better than having one of something. We think we know two hundred dollars is better than one hundred dollars, two cars are better than one car, two televisions are better than one, and so forth. To keep this passage in context, however, we need to remember that the writer of this passage is King Solomon, who was the richest and wisest king of his day. He never just had two of anything. He had hundreds of concubines, numerous wives, and multiple stables, each with hundreds of the best horses, and he owned pieces of gold too many to count. I believe the "two" that King Solomon speaks of is about a relationship and not a simple number.

Furthermore, the two is not just a couple, such as a married couple, but represents the minimum number to create a sincere and honest relationship. A team, if you will, consists of more than one person, and winning teams are not made up of individuals but a cohesive group working in concert with one another to achieve a single goal. This is evidenced by King Solomon's reference to being able to lift each other up and to keep each other warm. A team of three working in unison is stronger than a team of two. Four working in unison is even better.

The key to this verse, of course, is working in unison or concert, which is at the heart of accountability. King Solomon begins this lesson from a financial standpoint: "because they have good reward for their toil" (Ecclesiastes 4:9). Being in a relationship pays off, and being on a true team pays off. In today's world and throughout the Bible, we will find stories of individuals who quit the team and broke off the relationship to achieve their personal goals. Sometimes these individuals were successful for a while, but they could never achieve what the team could accomplish. Sports teams are easy examples of how a team working together can overcome an opposing team that has one superstar player trying to win for himself. This outcome is true in the business world, although there are always extenuating circumstances that impact this situation as is the case in some athletic games. Recent studies show star performers, such as investment bankers, who change teams are only able to retain their star performance half the time. It was the supporting teammates who gave them their star performer status in the first place; they just did not realize or recognize it.

Of course, we need to remember not every group of people is a team. What King Solomon speaks to is the synergy that is created by a group of people who are all in a relationship with one another. That's what makes the group a team. Each individual is not only committed to the common goal of the group, but also committed to working with and valuing the contributions of the other teammates. Occasionally a team's lure of success can help people overcome their self-centered desires, but more frequently than not, the team as a group needs to adopt the attitude of being accountable to each other. This is exactly the attitude exemplified by the teachings of Jesus Christ.

In our business world, accountability builds the kind of teams with the synergy to succeed. We need to promote team building at all levels in our organizations. But our team building is not just to improve the relationships between our employees but also to emphasize the need for accountability. Great teams are not identified by how well they get along, but by how well they cooperate, coordinate, and function to achieve the same goal—how strongly they are accountable to each other.

New Testament

As with the Old Testament, the New Testament is full of great advice about being accountable. Most Christians have taken this advice to the level of creating accountability groups to foster character building and hold each other personally accountable. In the business environment, we are interested in fostering a culture of accountability that leads to an improvement in the bottom line—not just in overall revenue but also in product development, character growth, increase in market share, accounts receivable, etc.

With that in mind, there are two related parables that speak to being accountable. In first-century Judea, as Jesus told these parables, not everyone understood them. Occasionally His own disciples had to ask Him for clarification. God selected those He wanted to understand the parable. Those He did not want to understand, such as the Pharisees, remained in the dark. Even today, the messages of some parables are still subject to discussion. The danger in reading and understanding a parable is to read too much into the story. Parables are almost always simple in their message with only one or two significant points.

Parable of the Wise Servant

The first parable is in Luke 12:41–48:

> Peter said, "Lord, are you telling this parable for us or for all?" And the Lord said, "Who then is the faithful and wise steward, whom his master will set over his household, to give them their portion of food at the proper time? Blessed is that servant whom his master when he comes will find so doing. Truly, I say to you, he will set him over all his possessions. But if that servant says to himself, 'My master is delayed in coming,' and begins to beat the menservants and the maidservants, and to eat and drink and get drunk, the master of that servant will come on a day when he does not expect him and at an hour he does not know, and will punish him, and put him with the unfaithful. And that servant who knew his master's will, but did not make ready or act according to his will, shall receive a severe beating. But he who did not know, and did what deserved a beating, shall receive a light beating. Every one to whom much is given, of him will much be required; and of him to whom men commit much they will demand the more.

When studied in depth, this parable is contrary to the thinking of our modern world. I'm not speaking so much about the physical beating promised in the parable as I am talking about the strong message of moral obligation and duty in the absence of any oversight. This parable is a message for all those in leadership roles in the church, and as such, I think it is also an excellent lesson for all those at every level of leadership in the business world.

This parable has three main characters. The first is the faithful and wise servant or manager. This is the one whom the master puts in charge of the other servants and the household or estate. The interpretation of the word describing the first manager in the original Greek is *pistos*, which is defined as "pertaining to being worthy of belief or trust, trustworthy, faithful, dependable, inspiring trust/faith."[15] Another adjective used is *phronimo*, which means "pertaining to understanding associated with insight and wisdom; sensible, thoughtful, prudent, wise."[16] In other words, the first manager is the ideal employee. These are the ideal qualifications we should all give our HR director when we search for a new employee (of course, for most of us, the HR director title is just one more hat we wear). The reward for this amazing employee is even more responsibility—and the only thing he did was his job.

The second character in the parable is the opposite of the first character: an unwise and unfaithful servant. Notice what circumstances put the unwise manager on the wrong path. The master is delayed in coming. Something is not as anticipated, the normal routine is disrupted, and unforeseen circumstances have occurred, and the unwise manager somehow sees that as an opportunity to abandon his self-discipline and allow his selfish desires to take over. The actions taken by this manager were all detestable in the first century. In the twenty-first century, similar actions might include drug usage, exploitation of expense accounts, sexual abuse, Internet shopping abuse, and online pornography. This servant was living for himself and not for the team, not for his relationship with the household, and not for the master. What is more amazing is he seemed to be surprised that the master returned at all.

The third character in this parable is the master. Theologically, the master is Jesus Christ and the overarching message is that Christ will return one day and we need to be ready. For our use in the business world, however, the master is any authority to whom we answer upon completing our work. Examples of the master could be an immediate supervisor, and the return of the supervisor is a simple change in management where you now have a new boss. It could be a change in governmental administration, which means a new interpretation of existing laws and administrative orders. Or it could be your company was sold and the new owner wants to know all there is to know about your job, your department, and your accounts. As the saying goes, it's time to pay the piper.

The reward for the wise manager was more responsibility. The reward as described for the unfaithful manager is unimaginable in our world, but typical in first-century Judea. Prison time, disgrace, unemployable reputation, etc. all might fit better today. The point is, as managers we need to do our job. And for whatever level we are not doing our job and are not prepared, we need to be ready and willing to accept the consequences. We do not know if the unfaithful manager pleaded and begged, created excuses, or simply accepted his punishment. But we do see the punishment was swift and just.

Which brings us to the last line of the parable: "Every one to whom much is given, of him will much be required; and of him to whom men commit much they will demand the more" (Luke 12:48). This is true accountability. As a manager, an employee, a president, or a janitor, we have all been given a certain set of skills, and it is our responsibility to use those skills to the best of our ability (therefore giving glory to God). When we know we could have done better, tried harder, and included more of our teammates, the penalty is doubled. When we try hard, build others up, and use the synergy of the team, the reward is also doubled.

The takeaway from this parable for the employer is the reinforcement that accountability is important. We need to do all we can to reinforce accountability. And when we find employees who act in an accountable and responsible manner, it is imperative we do all we can to reinforce that attitude and support these employees.

Before going on to the second and final parable from Jesus, I want to cover several other New Testament verses that relate to accountability in the workplace. The first verse has to do with the question if we are good or bad.

Good or Bad

> Either make the tree good, and its fruit good; or make the tree bad, and its fruit bad; for the tree is known by its fruit. You brood of vipers! how can you speak good, when you are evil? For out of the abundance of the heart the mouth speaks. The good man out of his good treasure brings forth good, and the evil man out of his evil treasure brings forth evil. I tell you, on the day of judgment men will render account for every careless word they utter; for by your words you will be justified, and by your words you will be condemned. (Matthew 12:33–37)

If you are looking for one verse to remind you of accountability in the workplace, this is a likely candidate. Your work is either good or bad, your product is either good or bad, and your reputation is either good or bad. The marketplace will buy good products, employers will hire good workers, and clients will use those with good reputations. A poor employee, a company with a bad reputation, or a business with a poor product line will not survive. Are there employees and companies out there that are substandard? Sure. But if we are concerned with accountability, then accountability should be our complete focus. At the end of the day, we are accountable to our Creator "for every careless word" we utter. Notice the reference is simply a *careless* word. It is not just the blasphemous, profane, malicious, false, slanderous, or reviling words; it is understandable they are to be avoided. But it is even the careless words that God cares about. The same is true for our performance at work. It is not just the cheaters and liars who deceive their employer or the abusive and demeaning employers who are condemned. It is also those who do not give full attention and effort, who look the other way, and who are always looking out for just themselves and not their employer or other employees. The bar to meet the standards of accountability as found in the Bible is set extremely high. But as employers, bosses, and managers, it is up to us to start displaying the example of how to meet that bar.

James 3:1

A second verse I find that relates to accountability is in James 3:1:

> Let not many of you become teachers, my brethren, for you know that we who teach shall be judged with greater strictness.

This section in James is talking about "taming the tongue," which also has strong accountability implications. But here the focus is on training, teaching, and mentoring. At some point in your career, you are going to teach someone else. It may be your replacement because you are retiring or promoted (or even dismissed). It may be a new company and you are tasked with training all your new employees in areas you also are unfamiliar with. Maybe you have sold a product and now you need to train its new users.

Maybe your company is growing and you need to train coworkers to take the workload off your shoulders. Whatever the case, you are now a teacher and that responsibility rests on your shoulders.

In the business world, that responsibility is greater than most realize. Large corporations can afford training programs and allow periods of inefficiency while new employees learn the nuances of their job. For those of us with small business operations, training and teaching is problematic. We have our own jobs to do, deadlines to meet, and other responsibilities to fulfill. Taking on the job of training someone is just another task squeezed into a day with too few hours.

But what we need to understand is, despite the added effort, teaching someone his or her new job must be the highest priority. In the long run, the new employee being able to do a great job will relieve some of our own responsibility. James also talks about conveying wisdom (James 3:13), which is something deeper than teaching or training. It is a lifelong message and a career-making lesson that results in developing a great employee who understands the mission of the company. This wisdom starts employees on a path of accountability. Many times, that kind of wisdom cannot be imparted by a corporate training program; it is only passed on shoulder to shoulder just as Zebedee taught his sons and Andrew and Peter each night on the Sea of Galilee. We should always take training and mentoring seriously.

Obey Your Leaders

A third verse emphasizing accountability is in the book of Hebrews 13:17:

> Obey your leaders and submit to them; for they are keeping
> watch over your souls, as men who will have to give account.
> Let them do this joyfully, and not sadly, for that would be
> of no advantage to you.

I have chosen to write about this verse because it is misused, yet the correct understanding of it has a significant application for accountability. The original word translated into "obey" is *peitho*, which also means being convinced, gives assent [agreement], believe, trust, and yield to.[17] As you can see, the intent of the verse is dependent on which definitional word you choose. Most English replacement words carry less strength and dominance than the word *obey* conveys in the twenty-first century. A better interpretation is "Listen to the warnings of the leaders who watch over you."

A better understanding of this verse, therefore, indicates we are not called to mindless submission and conformance. We have a mind, but we are also given the instructions to listen to our leaders (for further study see Mark 10:42–45, 1 Peter 5:1–3, Matthew 6:24, and Matthew 23:8–12). Our bosses are accountable to a higher authority, that being our God and Savior, but also accountable to those they answer to in the performance of a specific job. You also must be accountable to your boss and your boss's boss. Notice the last line: "Let them do this joyfully, and not sadly, for that would be of no advantage to you" (Hebrews 13:17). An alternative way to say the same thing is "It is to your advantage to make your supervisor's job easy." Most of us learn this lesson the hard way and endure many run-ins with our boss until we realize we are seldom in a position to win. At some point, we learn it is about being accountable to the mission of your business and your boss. Until we learn this lesson, accountability will be impossible to achieve.

Parable of the Unjust Steward

This brings us to our final verse, which is the second parable explaining the biblical concept of accountability. The parable of the unjust steward (or manager) is found in Luke 16:1–13 (NIV):

> Jesus told his disciples: "There was a rich man whose manager was accused of wasting his possessions. So he called him in and asked him, 'What is this I hear about you? Give an account of your management, because you cannot be manager any longer.'
>
> "The manager said to himself, 'What shall I do now? My master is taking away my job. I'm not strong enough to dig, and I'm ashamed to beg— I know what I'll do so that, when I lose my job here, people will welcome me into their houses.'

"So he called in each one of his master's debtors. He asked the first, 'How much do you owe my master?'

"'Nine hundred gallons of olive oil,' he replied.

"The manager told him, 'Take your bill, sit down quickly, and make it four hundred and fifty.'

"Then he asked the second, 'And how much do you owe?'

"'A thousand bushels of wheat,' he replied.

"He told him, 'Take your bill and make it eight hundred.'

"The master commended the dishonest manager because he had acted shrewdly. For the people of this world are more shrewd in dealing with their own kind than are the people of the light. I tell you, use worldly wealth to gain friends for yourselves, so that when it is gone, you will be welcomed into eternal dwellings.

"Whoever can be trusted with very little can also be trusted with much, and whoever is dishonest with very little will also be dishonest with much. So if you have not been trustworthy in handling worldly wealth, who will trust you with true riches? And if you have not been trustworthy with someone else's property, who will give you property of your own?

"No one can serve two masters. Either you will hate the one and love the other, or you will be devoted to the one and despise the other. You cannot serve both God and money."

I'm sure you are wondering how this story about an incompetent, corrupt, and lazy steward can be a good example of accountability. The deliberate actions of this steward and the inexcusable decisions by the rich man in handling his employment and dismissal present a textbook case study for all employers and managers.

On first reading it is easy to see how this parable can be incorrectly interpreted. We need to remember we are reading the Christian Bible and a parable told by Jesus is intended to make only one or more narrowly defined points. As always in reading the Bible, context is everything. This parable is one of four consecutive stories that Jesus told about money and material possessions. All of these parables have accountability implications, and I would suggest you read and study them at some future point in time. As for the parable of the unjust steward, many are quick to think Jesus is commending the illegal actions of an unworthy employee. But that interpretation is incorrect, and to understand the meaning and the implications of workplace accountability, we need to examine the parable in detail.

To understand this story, we need to look at the individual characters, so let's start with the steward (or manager). He may at one time have been competent since the rich man felt secure in hiring him and keeping him in his employment. Unfortunately, human nature took over and temptation got the best of him. In today's world, we could see this person padding his or her expense account, playing golf when he or she should be working, and attempting to profit from inside information known only to company employees. He used his employer's wealth, possessions, and knowledge for personal gain, but produced little for his employer. He was greedy and lazy (as evidenced by being caught), and he was given notice that in some near-future time he would join the ranks of the unemployed.

Next, let's look at the rich man. Many commentaries think this person is a typology of God. I do not think that's accurate. The rich man apparently was unaware he was being taken advantage of for a long period of time. His actions were rather weak, and he failed to provide close oversight of the now short-term employee. Remember the actions of God in the first parable from a few pages back where the punishment was swift and painful; those characteristics do not show up in this parable. Furthermore, God will not commend unethical actions regardless of whether he appreciates shrewdness or not—we will get to this point in a moment.

The parable abruptly ends where Jesus's teaching begins by saying, "The master commended the dishonest manager because he had acted shrewdly.

For the people of this world are more shrewd in dealing with their own kind than are the people of the light" (Luke 16:6–7 NIV). Both the manager and the rich man are "people of this world"; they live for worldly things and think worldly thoughts as opposed to the teachings of Jesus, who said, "I have given them your word, and the world has hated them because they are not of the world, just as I am not of the world" (John 17:14). The manager and the rich man think alike, which is why the rich man could appreciate the manager for being shrewd albeit illegal, unethical, unjust, and unrighteous. The phrase "it takes one to know one" applies here.

Before going on to what we are to learn from this parable, think about those you have worked with, worked for, or employed, or maybe even some of your own actions. Do they reflect the kind of rationalizations used by the unjust manager to "feather your own nest"? Money, knowledge, and reputation that were not yours were used for personal gain all the while those same assets were not used for the employer's gain. Where is the accountability on both the employee's part and on the employer's part? Is it the employer's job to provide total oversight of the employee, or should the employee deserve the respect and freedom to do his or her job independently? The immediate business application of this parable is accountability is a two-way street. As employers, we need to show accountability to gain the respect and trust of our employees. As employees, we need to demonstrate our understanding of accountability to receive trust and responsibility from our employer.

To understand this story from a biblical standpoint, we need to recognize two important concepts. First, "worldly wealth" is money, and it is temporal, meaning you cannot take it with you when you die. You cannot buy true friends; or better said, the kinds of friends you can buy are not the ones you need. Second, it is only these true friends you can take with you when you pass from this temporal world. Helping those people to find Christ, helping heal them, and allowing them the opportunity to achieve eternal life is the only way to true friendship.

So the accountability lessons from this parable are:

1. Be wary of financial offers for favors or friendship. Buying clients or influence is always temporal, and it is a short-term solution often with disastrous results.

2. Faithfulness to your employment responsibilities should be your number one priority. As Christians, we know that God is true to faithful believers and being faithful in even the small responsibilities will be rewarded at some point. In our workplaces, we are given the opportunity to display that faithfulness to the secular world.

3. As an employer, recognizing faithfulness among your employees is critical. If it is not part of your employee review process, find a way to spot and reward faithful employees.

4. Do not be afraid of shrewdness, but be cautious of it. There are many stories of shrewd teachers finding creative ways to teach unwilling students, of construction workers finding innovative solutions to difficult construction situations, and of managers finding creative ways to motivate employees to reach challenging deadlines. As believers, we need to apply shrewdness without sacrificing righteousness and ethics.

Zebedee

Zebedee started the day questioning whether his partners acted in a responsible and accountable manner by walking away from their business. When Jesus showed up, they had a choice to make. One choice was to continue to fish each day for the rest of their lives and be part of "this world." Zebedee easily understood that meant a hardworking yet routine life, and the only impact and influence they would ever have would be on those immediately around them. Although he did not easily understand, Zebedee could see the eternal nature of Jesus Christ and know that His work would go well beyond anything he and his fishing business could have influence on, on their own. Any influence they might have while being part of this world would end when they died. All influences on this world while traveling with Jesus would last forever. The first choice was to be accountable to Zebedee and the fishing business. The second was to be accountable to our Creator and His work among all people. Zebedee had to smile once he understood that it was not a difficult choice.

Summary

1. Ezekiel 18:20 reminds us we are all liable for our own decisions and always need to be ready to accept the ramifications of our actions.

2. Do not miss the opportunity to imagine our accountability as a watchman on the wall. While we are looking outwardly and inwardly, everyone is watching our actions so make sure they are those of respect, honesty, integrity, and trust.

3. Are you a wise servant who focuses on doing your job, or are you falling victim to this world and will not be ready when the Master returns?

4. Matthew 12:33–37 reminds us to be a good tree with good fruit so we can speak good words and bring forth good treasure. Good products sell, good service brings repeat business, and honest and reputable help and advice is appreciated. There is no excuse to be anything less.

5. Make teaching your employees and your subordinates a top priority. Be aware that you are an employer or supervisor who respects authority. If you do not provide respect, how can you expect it in return?

6. What kind of business friend are you? The parable of the unjust steward is a platform for managing employees; we must use our resources and influence in a way that respects our business and glorifies God.

Notes

_____

_____

_____

_____

_____

_____

_____

_____

_____

_____

_____

_____

_____

_____

_____

_____

CHAPTER 4

Zebedee's Employee Discipline

"If there has ever been a time to discipline employees, it's now. Do they think they can just stop whenever they want and walk off? It's completely disrespectful on their part. Don't they realize whom they are dealing with? I'm the senior member of this partnership, I'm highly respected around here, I carry a lot of influence, and if they think I'm going to ever give a good reference to them for a future job, they better think twice. Either you come right back here or you're fired."

These may not be Zebedee's words as he watched the boys walk off into the distance, but I am sure some of them would go through my mind. With losing his workers, Zebedee found himself in a position to consider disciplining his employees. He may or may not take any action, but what does the Bible say he and we should do?

To quote numerous articles and books on employee discipline, "there is not a more difficult decision than firing an employee." From my experience that quote is only partially true. I have had the pleasure to fire employees who, for whatever reason, decided they were no longer happy and were not willing to perform their job as required. Fortunately, like many employers, I have followed the prudent advice to create and maintain an employee manual that spells out the dos and don'ts of managing a workforce. It was this manual that directed me to which actions I should consider against these nonperforming employees. So, considering the amount of work that goes into discussing and documenting employee performance (or lack thereof) leading up to his or her dismissal, it feels good to finally get it over with.

I'm far from an expert in the legalities and details of employment relations, so I frequently rely on experts and consultants for their guidance. My company has a detailed employee handbook, and every employee gets a copy. We follow this handbook and frequently refer to it as we make decisions related to our workforce. Our actions (and reactions) in disciplining our employees, unfortunately, have little to do with biblical care and everything to do with the laws adopted by our government. For this chapter, I'm going to stay away from discussing those laws and focus on what I think the Bible tells us about disciplining our employees.

In all my years of employing people, I have never had an occasion where an employee needed discipline for a stand-alone action. Employees do not wake up one morning and decide, "Starting today I'm going to lie on my expense account so I can make my car payment." In all cases, there is a series of incidents and changes pointing to a problem on the horizon. These are easy to see looking back after firing the employee but are difficult to notice as they occur. These incidences and changes are important to pay attention to, as they represent opportunities to intervene in a way that is far more productive than firing the employee.

I have divided the cycle of employee discipline into four parts:

+ The first part is noting a change in the employee's *attitude* and what actions we can take.
+ The second part is the actual *act* that required, per the employee handbook, some type of discipline.
+ Third, we look at our potential actions following the incident to discover if the employee can be *saved* or not.
+ The final part is the actual act of *firing* or dismissing the employee.

In all four of these parts we will rely on stories from the Bible to help guide us in determining our appropriate choices and actions.

Workplace Attitude

Tell me if you have heard this before: "My business would be great if it weren't for the employees and the clients." The attitudes we experience internally from our employees and externally from our clients shape our perspective of our business. How we as employers receive, encourage, respond, and reflect those attitudes determines how successful we will be in managing our business. Although this book touches on the employee's attitudes in several places, the focus of this section is the attitude of both the work environment and the employee at the time the infraction occurred, creating the need for discipline. More specifically, what caused the employee to act the way he or she did that was contrary to good workplace behavior?

Workplace attitude is more important than most employers think. Over the years I have received industry-based HR training and continue to receive several HR newsletters that help keep me current on industry trends. I admit I am biased when reading studies and reports about the right attitude in the workplace. My jaded thinking hears that the employer did not communicate well enough, the employee did not completely understand the rules, and the office environment that led to the infraction was a byproduct of the business owner's attitude toward the workplace. The basic assertion is the owner/manager was too cavalier, standoffish, unapproachable, not involved, hard-hearted, and detached from the day-to-day workings to create the friendly, fatherly, learning, fostering, and loving environment, which is what all ungrateful employees need to be successful.

I don't believe I'm the only one who, after being in business for many years, develops this skewed attitude toward employees. To see how the Bible can be effective in thinking about and modifying these attitudes in our places of work, I've selected a scenario in which the employer has caught an employee stealing. The question to start with is what is it in the workplace that makes an employee think it is reasonable to steal from his or her employer? I know stealing is a rather harsh example, but the forms of stealing we are talking about could include financial theft (padded expense accounts, fraudulent sales, direct cash theft, etc.) and hourly theft (incorrect time cards, personal computer usage during work hours, personal activities during work hours, etc.), as well as backing up a truck to the loading dock and making off with a truckload of product. In all its forms, taking what is not yours and not earned is theft, plain and simple.

I have chosen Ephesians, chapter 6, as a study in workplace attitude. The first five chapters of Ephesians assure us of our rock-solid position as part of the body of Christ. In chapter 6, it is Paul's intent to give practical instructions on how to relate well with others in whatever position you are in life. It is here we find his instructions on what our workplace attitude should be. Ephesians 6:5–9 reads:

> Bondservants, obey your earthly masters with fear and trembling, with a sincere heart, as you would Christ, not by the way of eye-service, as people-pleasers, but as bondservants of Christ, doing the will of God from the heart, rendering service with a good will as to the Lord and not to man, knowing that whatever good anyone does, this he will receive back from the Lord, whether he is a bondservant or is free. Masters, do the same to them, and stop your threatening, knowing that he who is both their Master and yours is in heaven, and that there is no partiality with him.

Servants and Slaves

Before we discuss employee attitudes, we need to clarify the issues of servants and slaves. In this passage Paul is addressing slaves and those they serve or work for. Technically, the word *bondservant* is *doulos*,[18] which means bond slave, bondservant, minister, and one pledged or bound to serve. Paul frequently referred to himself as a bond slave to God (1 Corinthians 7:21–24, Colossians 3:22–4:1, 1 Timothy 6:1–2, Titus 2:6–10). In Roman times men and women became slaves by being captured in war, being kidnapped and sold into slavery, or by selling themselves into slavery to pay debts. They were nonpersons and treated as one would an animal. The slave's life was in the hands of his or her owner or master.

The Bible does not condone slavery nor does it authorize it. Slavery was a way of life in many eastern countries for thousands of years before the coming of Christ. It was a part of the culture, not a pretty part but a reality nonetheless. What Paul is recognizing is slaves are people too, and part of God's plan. Paul does not address the morals of slavery and was not opposed to the freedom of slaves if the opportunity arose. In Corinthians 7:20, Paul wrote, "Each person should remain in the situation they were in when God called them." Paul taught that God called people to different stations in life and that they were to live out the Christian life in whatever situation they were in.

In Ephesians 6 Paul addresses those slaves who are Christians and instructs them how to conduct themselves. The issue of slavery is a civil matter for governments, but the issue of their conduct as Christians is a spiritual matter. The principles of this passage are the same as the relationship between subordinate and supervisor or employee and manager. Furthermore, Paul is also addressing slaves or those who work for or are owned by non-Christians, which would represent the most difficult working conditions. In all circumstances, we are to render "service with a good will as to the Lord" (Ephesians 6:7).

Attitude

Following Paul's use of slavery as our current employee-employer analogy, he wrote in 1 Timothy 6:1–2 (NIV):

> All who are under the yoke of slavery should consider their masters worthy of full respect, so that God's name and our teaching may not be slandered. Those who have believing masters should not show them disrespect just because they are fellow believers. Instead, they should serve them even better because their masters are dear to them as fellow believers and are devoted to the welfare of their slaves.

And in Colossians 3:22–25, 4:1 (NIV):

> Slaves, obey your earthly masters in everything; and do it, not only when their eye is on you and to curry their favor, but with sincerity of heart and reverence for the Lord. Whatever you do, work at it with all your heart, as

> working for the Lord, not for human masters, since you know that you will receive an inheritance from the Lord as a reward. It is the Lord Christ you are serving. Anyone who does wrong will be repaid for their wrongs, and there is no favoritism … Masters, provide your slaves with what is right and fair, because you know that you also have a Master in heaven.

In both verses Paul is addressing slaves as forced labor. They are not willing workers, and as such their effort is only to do the minimum work to get by. When the master is not around or additional work is required, most slaves will not put forth any extra effort. This, in Paul's terms, is the "flesh" of the slave; it is only the outward manifestation of being a slave. Outwardly a slave may appear eager, helpful, and trustworthy ("eye-service, as people-pleasers," Ephesians 6:6). Inwardly the slave is seething with contempt, hating his or her master, and is begrudging every effort he or she is required to perform in service to the master. This inward attitude is the "spirit" of which Paul is addressing.

Paul's point is that if the slave is a believer, then it is incumbent on the slave to go above and beyond the minimum required effort. A Christian slave is to have an attitude different from that of typical slaves. The authority of the master is limited to the slave's flesh, but the extent of the slave's submission to Christ goes far beyond the outward. There is a spirit of submission in the slave to which Christ calls the slave to work as if working for the Lord ("doing the will of God from the heart," Ephesians 6:6). Obedience will be the outflowing of a spirit of submission that is the manifestation of a sincere heart. When a slave obeys his or her master, he or she is to do so with a sincere motive to praise and please God. Christian slaves were to be set apart because they acted and worked differently from non-Christian slaves.

The application of Paul's message to employees in the workplace is clear: work should be completed not in an outward fashion but with an inner sense that you believe in what you are doing. Do not work just to please your boss; work as if you are working for God and it is Him you want to please. We all are a sort of slave; we have agreed to sell part of our time each day in return for labor. This includes both the employee and the owner/manager.

Granted, we get to go home at night and we get paid well. But in the end, we must work whether we like it or not. Just like first-century Christian slaves, we need to be set apart because we act and work differently.

Our goal as employers should be to foster a healthy workplace attitude like that of the first-century Christian slaves. The Bible provides tools to help in developing the healthy workplace attitudes that are discussed throughout this book. These tools include team building, treating employees as family, and developing and maintaining integrity. For encouragement, I suggest you read two Old Testament stories that reveal how this attitude works. One is the story of Joseph (Genesis 37–45), and the second is that of Daniel (book of Daniel). Both were slaves who rose to high levels of prominence because of their integrity, which they received as a gift from God.

The message about slaves also relates to the masters (or bosses, employers, and owners). A master has the same responsibility as the slave: to honor God. Ephesians 6:9 says:

> And, ye masters, do the same things unto them, forbearing threatening: knowing that your Master also is in heaven; neither is there respect of persons with him.

Masters are to submit themselves to God and should subordinate self-interest to serving others. Masters should use their position to serve the best interests of those who are their slaves. In the secular world, there is a double standard—one standard for masters and one standard for slaves; one for owners/bosses and one for workers; one for husbands and one for wives. With God there is only one standard for masters, slaves, bosses, workers, husbands, wives, adults, and children. We are all slaves of Christ and are called upon to submit to one another in the fear of Christ (Ephesians 5:21).

The question now is how to implement that strategy. The first step, and quite possibly the only step needed, is to adopt a new you. As an owner or manager, leading by example is a remarkable tool. Learn from Joseph and Daniel; read Ephesians, 1 Timothy, and Colossians; and begin practicing the art of believing in what you are doing. Demonstrate honesty and integrity every minute of every day. This attitude will catch on. Current business leadership resources reinforce this management style. Michael Hyatt and others frequently emphasize the need to connect the employees to the vision of the company and connect the employees to you as the company leader.[19] Also look to hire people who already understand what it means to be a bondservant and know how to be committed to a job and a mission. Remember, I started with a jaded opinion about the workplace attitude, but I discovered the power to change this attitude rested completely within me.

The Act

Not all workers, unfortunately, will develop the workplace attitude as taught by the apostle Paul to first-century slaves and masters. I am also aware that not everyone recognizes God's authority as a source for handling employee discipline issues. It is, however, interesting that those who do not follow God's teachings often continue to handle employee discipline issues just as prescribed by the Bible. These methods are time tested—at least for the past two thousand years. But because there are many opinions on how to treat workers, employee discipline issues have evolved into a $20 billion per year industry. In the United States, governmental scrutiny of employment relations is everywhere, from federal, state, and local statutes to administrative regulations to common law. Personnel policies and employee management decisions cannot be considered without close examination of numerous laws and regulations. According to the Equal Employment Opportunity Commission, employment discrimination charges rose about 120 percent during the 1990s. Regardless of the government's intervention, the concept to treat employees fairly is a biblical principle.

Proverbs 14:18 says, "The simple inherit folly, but the prudent are crowned with knowledge." In considering an action that might result in disciplining one or more employees, it is always helpful to know the facts. Unfortunately, many of these instances are "he said, she said" situations where the truth is impossible to ascertain. Prudence, patience, and prayer are always tools to use in meeting privately (but not alone) with employees to get to as much of the truth as possible. In the United States, the basic structure of the law is that an employer has the freedom to discharge an employee for any reason unless the employer is constrained by some law, court case, or contractual arrangement. This is called "employment at will," which does not require the employer to have a performance-related reason or just cause to dismiss an employee. The only requirement is that the termination cannot be motivated by criteria prohibited in antidiscrimination laws, common laws, or contracts. As a Christian, however, our higher level of care should cause us to consider our actions and weigh those actions on the impact to the employee and the company.

Despite our feeling for a higher level of care, we need to remember we live in the secular world and that world revolves around documentation. Just because we are believers and we prayed for advice about the situation does not preclude the affected employee from taking some type of action. This is where the industry of professional HR consultants can help. While we place our trust in God, we must make sure we always follow applicable employment laws.

Saving the Employee

In the secular business world, there are many legitimate reasons to work diligently not to dismiss or fire an employee. You have gone through the effort to advertise, interview, check references, negotiate, hire, and train an employee, so why would you willingly fire him or her just to do that all over again? Maybe somewhere in the process you missed a message or warning sign, but can you salvage, retrain, and reorient the employee in question? Can you afford the lost productivity and direct expenses of starting over? What is the effect on the remaining staff?

Of course, the other side of the coin is can you afford to have the wrong person as part of your team in the long run? What are the indirect expenses of an employee of questionable loyalty and marginal productivity on the other team members? Is this person the right person in the right seat on the right bus?

My experience is that saving an employee is not geographical. Moving him or her to another team, another project, another type of client, another cubical, or another office never solves any problems. The issue is internal, and the change must be internal—it is an issue of the spirit. Before going into what the scripture says about saving a questionable employee, let's look at a story where Jesus changed someone's spirit and that person became a key "employee."

This story is about a guy named Levi. Levi was a tax collector or a publican, as he was referred to in the King James Version of the Bible . Tax collectors in first-century Jerusalem were not liked any more than IRS agents are liked today. Levi's job was to sit in a booth along a road in Capernaum near the Sea of Galilee and collect a toll on any goods transported past him into the region ruled by Herod Antipas. With a name of Levi, it is likely he was a descendent of the tribe of Levi, from whom the Jewish priests and Levites descended. But instead of a holy ministry of serving in the temple, this Levi instead engaged in a most unholy trade: collecting taxes.

Jesus was teaching along the Sea of Galilee at Capernaum, and when he finished, He walked over to a small tax office alongside the highway. Sitting inside was this despised man, Matthew Levi, whom Jesus had seen several times in the crowds as He was teaching. Jesus looked at him and said, "Follow me" (Matthew 9:9). Levi had just been called from a life of wealth to one of poverty. He was invited to leave his lucrative tax collection business to follow this itinerant rabbi and live a life of begging for food and contributions. Even though Levi had been ostracized from respectable society, Jesus cared enough about him to stop by his tax collector's shack. Jesus accepted him. Jesus loved him—the most unloved man in Capernaum.

Now we are not Jesus and do not have His insights into people and their motives, but I doubt I would have hired Levi. Lest I forget to mention, Levi is also known as Matthew, who wrote the first book in the New Testament and was one of the twelve apostles. Clearly his spirit changed. When I think about working with a problem employee, I immediately think of Matthew 10:16:

> "I am sending you out like sheep among wolves. Therefore
> be as shrewd as snakes and as innocent as doves."

It is in this act of working with problematic employees that we find ourselves in a well-known yet difficult balancing act. The verse comes from the Gospel of Matthew when Jesus is sending out his disciples into the world to spread His message. He is warning them that it will be difficult and that they will suffer many trials and persecutions. The sheep and dove metaphors refer to Jesus's message that we do not bear witness to the world as dominant and strong, but as defenseless and weak. Sheep and doves are innocent, meek, and gentle. Serpents, on the other hand, were thought to be wise in the ways of the world. The balancing act is how to survive in the world and preach the good news of Christ, yet survive to spread the message another day.

How do we witness to a difficult employee and show the love of Christ, yet not allow this issue to detract from the mission of our ongoing business to compete in and with the secular world? As mentioned previously, we as Christians operate at a higher standard of conduct that has been set by God. The Old Testament provides the virtues of forgiveness and patience with those who have offended us. Proverbs 19:11 says, "A person's wisdom yields patience; it is to one's glory to overlook an offense."

Both the Old and New Testaments urge believers to rid their relationships of those whose behavior is offensive. Proverbs 22:10 says, "Drive out the mocker, and out goes strife; quarrels and insults are ended." And Proverbs 25:4–5 says, "Remove the dross from the silver, and a silversmith can produce a vessel; remove wicked officials from the king's presence, and his throne will be established through righteousness." Both verses give us license to oust the irritants and scorners who disrupt the workplace. From the New Testament, Paul says in 1 Corinthians 5:6–7, "Your boasting is not good. Don't you know that a little yeast leavens the whole batch of dough? Get rid of the old yeast." In context, Paul was taking to task the believers in Corinth for tolerating an unrepentant, immoral church member, which is not dissimilar to our issue of a problem employee.

So, in a nutshell, the Bible has some tension between a forgiving attitude on one hand and a disciplining action on the other. For me, this is the part I love about being a Christian. There is no cookie-cutter solution. We get to wrestle through the circumstances and finally hear God's voice about our next steps. To get to this point, we must exercise patience and forgiveness; we cannot act impetuously and induce knee-jerk reactions. We learn that the decision to fire or salvage an employee is not our own decision. God will deliver the decision, and you need to be prepared for a surprising recommendation. God's ways are not ours, and He just might have other plans for this problematic employee. Did you ever think this employee might have been given to you to save, not from your work environment but for eternity?

I think we can all agree the choice to salvage an employee or release him or her is a big decision. For me, it's too big of a decision to be made on my own, and often I am not sure about the message I'm receiving during my prayer time for what God wants me to do. Proverbs 11:14 recommends, "Where no counsel is, the people fall: but in the multitude of counselors there is safety." I suggest you cultivate a group of other like-minded business leaders who are Christians with whom you can discuss these types of issues. These relationships become a two-way street in the exchange of ideas and mutual support. My experience shows the benefits will go way beyond talking about business.

Firing the Employee

Nowhere does scripture support the notion that it is sinful or uncharitable to fire an employee. We have even seen the Bible support terminating problem employees (Proverbs 22:10). Furthermore, we have seen that being a Christian carries with it a higher standard (yes, it is a double standard). Christians who do not recognize that higher standard need Christian mentoring, and that mentoring process may involve losing their job. I'm a Christian boss and I will, without question, expect more from my fellow believers who are employees.

Let's review the one story in the Bible where someone who was a follower of Christ was fired. Acts 15:36–41 reads:

> Some time later Paul said to Barnabas, "Let us go back and visit the believers in all the towns where we preached the word of the Lord and see how they are doing." Barnabas wanted to take John, also called Mark, with them, but Paul did not think it wise to take him, because he had deserted them in Pamphylia and had not continued with them in the work. They had such a sharp disagreement that they parted company. Barnabas took Mark and sailed for Cyprus, but Paul chose Silas and left, commended by the believers to the grace of the Lord. He went through Syria and Cilicia, strengthening the churches.

The apostle Paul and his friends Barnabas and John Mark's first missionary trip was to southern Asia Minor. This was a particularly arduous journey; Paul was beaten several times, and in many instances the group was not especially welcome (Acts 13 and 14). Toward the end of the trip, John Mark had enough and left the group to go home. After a brief time in Jerusalem, Paul and Barnabas decided to go on their second missionary trip, and it is in this verse where they discuss their companions journeying with them. Paul and Barnabas were a team, and Barnabas wanted to again take John Mark. Paul wanted nothing to do with John Mark because he quit the team once before.

It is easy to see this same type of conversation occurring many times throughout the working world. "Come on, give the guy a chance; it's his first DUI." "Yes, he's not detail oriented and makes some mistakes, but he has a family to feed." "I know her attitude is bad, but yours would be too if you were married to her husband." Barnabas probably put up a similar argument and felt that John Mark would stick with them this time. Paul would not budge.

Paul took a man named Silas on his second missionary trip, and they made two more historic mission trips that are documented in twelve chapters of the book of Acts. We never hear any more about the mission work of Barnabas and John Mark. The beautiful ending to the story is John Mark is the Mark who wrote the Gospel of Mark, the second book of the New Testament, and who impacted the world with his story of the life of Jesus Christ. Would he have written this important book had he continued to travel with Paul, who ultimately ended up in a Roman prison?

The takeaway from this story, following Jim Collins's bus analogy, is we need the right people in the right seats on the bus. We also need the wrong people off the bus. An employee who is a problem for management is a known problem to other employees. Employees know more about workplace antics, shortcomings, deceptions, and lies than management will ever know. When it is time to fire an employee, hesitation is not an option. Be like the apostle Paul and be firm in your decision and action.

Once the decision is made to fire an employee, the next step is to notify the employee. It is universal to notify the employee in a private conference, and it should be attended by at least one other person. To draw from a baseball truism, once the decision is made to pull the pitcher from the game, never change your mind. The coach cannot let the pitcher talk him out of his decision, and the employer cannot let the employee talk him into changing his mind. This meeting should be short, to the point, and not debatable.

You may want to explain your rationale for the decision, but that is not a requirement; in fact, if not stated properly, it may be fuel for future actions against the company and supervisor. A scripture to keep in your mind during this meeting is Proverbs 15:1: "A gentle answer turns away wrath, but a harsh word stirs up anger."

Nowhere is humility more needed that during this contentious, explosive, emotion-filled time. You need to consider the time of the week, month, and year that you are dismissing the employee. Also consider severance pay and any other benefits you will extend to the now-terminated employee. Remember, you are a Christian, and it is during these times that the charity of Christ can shine through in an otherwise bleak situation.

Zebedee

Did Zebedee have cause to consider disciplining any of his employees who walked away with Jesus? I think not. Peter, Andrew, James, and John harbored none of the negative or destructive attitudes that are held by problem employees. There is no evidence they were stealing, had developed an attitude that caused strife among other employees, or created a problem for the management (Zebedee). How do you feel when a good employee finally finds the dream job he or she was looking for? Think of a physical therapist who wants to work exclusively with children and finally receives that job offer. Or an employee who lives in the middle of the continental United States whose dream is to design submarines. Or a receptionist who has graduated night school and finds it's time to move on to a better career opportunity. In those circumstances, you can only be happy for your now ex-employees, and Zebedee was likewise happy for his four former employees.

Summary

1. Workplace attitudes for both the employee and employer will improve if both understand they are working as if working for God. There is only one standard, and that is to work with the heart of Christ. Utilize biblical tools that reinforce team building, treat employees as family, and develop and maintain integrity.

2. Proverbs 14:18 says, "The simple inherit folly, but the prudent are crowned with knowledge." Follow all secular laws and rules once an employee is suspected of acting in a manner that might result in some form of discipline.

3. Think of Levi, the tax collector (Matthew 9), when considering if an employee can be salvaged or not. Levi's other name is Matthew, who wrote the first book of the New Testament. As business leaders, we need to look to our employees' character when considering disciplinary actions.

4. Mark, the writer of the second book of the New Testament, was fired from a missionary trip by the apostle Paul (Acts 15:36–41). Terminating an employee is a test of humility, compassion, and resolve. This action must be done decisively and must be in the best interest of both the employer and the employee.

Notes

CHAPTER 5

Zebedee and Sons' Marketing Plan

"Well, the old marketing plan worked fairly well," considered Zebedee. "A couple of boats and four of the hardest-working young men around, and all we had to do was get back to the shore by sunrise so we could sell all the fish we caught." No golf tournaments to sponsor, trade magazines to advertise in, trinkets with the Zebedee and Sons logo to pass out—being in business was simple in first-century Judea. All you needed to do was find a need and fill it. Things have not changed that much—or have they?

My personal lack of expertise in marketing and selling will quickly become evident as I expose my limited knowledge in this area throughout this chapter. I learned the basics about marketing while getting my MBA in the early 1980s, and the rest I accumulated over the years while growing a small engineering business. Marketing and sales are a couple of the areas that have developed a language of their own, but when you get to the basics, it's all about common sense and personal observations. I think of marketing and selling as two distinct activities, and as such, we will look at each independently as we compare them with what scripture says.

Marketing

I love when someone introduces themselves and states their occupation is marketing. My curiosity forces me is to ask what that means. Do they write, direct, and produce television ads showing famous celebrities? Are they responsible for the irritating full-page ads in local newspapers? Do they pick the names of cars? Just what does an occupation in marketing mean? Of course, I've learned the answers are as diverse as the examples I can make up, which explains why many people are enthusiastic about an occupation in marketing. The idea of marketing is widely different among industries and even within competitors.

Definition

One definition of marketing is "the management process responsible for identifying, anticipating, and satisfying customer requirements profitably."[20] A second definition is "an organizational function and a set of processes for creating, communicating, and delivering value to customers and for managing customer relationships in ways that benefit the organization and its stakeholders."[21] The "market" is a group of consumers who happen to be interested in your product and has the ability to buy the product. Definitions of marketing all sound rather broad, and many professionals like to make it even more complex, but the idea of marketing is simple. Find a group of people who need a product and develop a product to sell to them while not going broke before the first sale is made.

Traditional marketing is first about researching what products are needed that are within the mission and scope of a particular business. It does no good to discover a market that needs new accounting software if you are in the business of mowing lawns (although that is often the entry point for an entrepreneur to begin a journey on a new business venture). With a new product in mind, a communication strategy is implemented to inform potential customers about its availability, qualities, and pricing, as well as how this new product fits into the line of existing products and services. Finally, marketing involves follow-up in customer satisfaction to determine if promises made meet customers' expectations. In summary, marketing is universally known as the six Ps: product, place, price, promotion, people, and process.

So far, the theory of marketing is sound. For all business owners, the issue of marketing revolves around how we get our products or services sold to the consumer. More specifically, the issue is how we get someone who has been purchasing product X for years to decide to change and begin to purchase our product Y. Seth Godin, in his book *Purple Cow*,[22] makes his case that the difference maker is the ability to make your product "remarkable." We strive to discover how to make what we do or sell stand out so we can attract new buyers, thus increasing our market share—or as is often the case, we replace market share that we lost to someone else who is also working on being remarkable and taking away our clients. For me, marketing is a vicious cycle that requires constant attention.

Salt in Today's World

As strange as it may sound, when I think of marketing and its relationship to the Bible, I often think of salt. Although the people who sell it may disagree, salt is a boring product. There is no action or excitement. And just like many other boring products, such as aspirin, tires, plumbing, or kiwifruit, creative marketers find a way to convince you to buy their boring product instead of a competitor's by showing you the value that even a boring item can bring to your life.

Salt as a product has a long run of being a valuable commodity. What is amazing about salt is that it is both indispensable and invisible. When people salt their food, such as tomatoes, they do not say, "Wow, that salt really makes this taste good." They are more likely to say, "Wow, those are great tomatoes," and never mention the salt. Salt also has the ability to inflict pain. If you've ever been swimming in the ocean with a minor cut, the salty seawater causes significant pain as it disinfects the cut. Many people prefer to gargle with salty water when they have a sore throat. The multiple uses of salt are amazing. But salt is also a villain in today's world; too much salt in our diet has a negative effect on our kidneys, arteries, heart, and brain.

From a professional marketing standpoint, salt requires us to devise ways to market something that most people think they understand and know, and present it in an interesting, intriguing, or desirable way. Not too long ago, there were only a few major producers of salt, and most people had already decided on their favorite brand. Then along came sea salt. It's still salt, but I can now buy popcorn, for instance, with either regular salt or sea salt. I can buy different kinds of salt for my salt shakers, such as coarse salt, finishing salt, flake salt, French sea salt, organic salt, kosher salt, Hawaiian sea salt, smoked sea salt, and many more. The success of marketing salt is a great example to contemplate when considering your own dilemma of how to best present your product or services, present them in new ways, and hopefully attract new customers to your business. A product once perceived as boring was cleverly remade into a product that now requires thought, selection, and care when considering its purchase. And we can apply those same principles to whatever we sell—even if it's seemingly as boring as salt.

Salt in Ancient Times

Salt in the ancient times was not considered boring but an extremely valuable and useful commodity. The Greeks thought it contained something almost divine, and the Romans occasionally even paid their soldiers with salt—hence the phrase "not worth your salt." Scholars have identified many different functions of salt in the ancient world, such as preservatives, antiseptics, fire catalysts, and food seasonings.

To see the Christian aspect of salt in the ancient times, we need to turn to scripture for a quick biblical and historical lesson. Salt was procured by the Jews from the Dead Sea either from an immense hill of rock salt or from that deposited on the shore by natural evaporation. As I said, it was well known for its seasoning and antiseptic qualities, but it was also known to be used as a fertilizer and in animal fodder (Isaiah 30:24). Salt is also the symbol of perpetuity and incorruption. Numbers 18:19 says, "It is a covenant of salt forever before the Lord for you and for your offspring with you." Newborn children were often rubbed with salt (Ezekiel 16:4). It is the symbol of hospitality and of the fidelity due from guests and friends to those who receive them at their tables. It cemented friendships: "to eat bread and salt together" is an expression of mutual goodwill. To eat salt with someone was to be bound to look after his or her interests.

Salt also signified utter barrenness and desolation (Ezekiel 16:4), a condition often illustrated in the Bible by allusions to the regions of Sodom and Gomorrah with their soil impregnated with salt and covered with acrid, slimy pools. When Abimelech took the city of Shechem, he sowed the place with salt that it might always remain barren soil (Judges 9:45).

Lastly, salt was an important part of Jewish worship rituals. Salt was sprinkled over the sacrifices that were consumed on God's altar (Leviticus

2:13, Ezekiel 43:24) and was used as a sacred incense (Exodus 30:35). Elisha healed the waters of Jericho by casting salt into the spring that fed the city (2 Kings 2:20). To say salt served many necessary purposes in the ancient world is an understatement.

Salt and Jesus

In Matthew 5:13–16, Jesus called for his followers to be the salt of the earth:

> You are the salt of the earth, but if salt has lost its taste, how shall its saltiness be restored? It is no longer good for anything except to be thrown out and trampled under people's feet.

> You are the light of the world. A city set on a hill cannot be hidden. Nor do people light a lamp and put it under a basket, but on a stand, and it gives light to all in the house. In the same way, let your light shine before others, so that they may see your good works and give glory to your Father who is in heaven.

This quote from Jesus happened during his Sermon on the Mount, the great manifesto of the Kingdom of God. The Sermon on the Mount in general was addressed to Jesus's disciples and not necessarily to the multitudes. It wasn't intended to be a social gospel or to bring an end to suffering and wars. It was used to assure his followers that they mattered, and as a follower of Christ, you also matter. Just as salt preserves, it is the Christian's role to help preserve what is good in our culture.

Without a doubt, Jesus's reference to salt in Matthew 5 was no accident. No other mineral was intertwined in the Jewish life like salt. Jesus most likely referred to salt as a seasoning agent. Salt improves the flavor of food, and His usage means that being salty is to live out the eight beatitudes as listed in verses 3 to 12 just preceding His comment about salt. If we live out these beatitudes, we make Christian living "tasty" or attractive.

When Jesus says, "You are the salt of the earth," he is instructing us to be like salt and be an integral part of everyone's life. We are to be like salt and penetrate society and make a difference. You and I are to be the spice of life, and we need to live out our lives as Jesus instructed us through the beatitudes. For salt to be a preservative or an antiseptic, it needs to come into contact with that which we are treating. Food does not get a better flavor by just showing the salt to the food, and a sore throat does not heal because we pass a shaker of salt over your mouth. The salt must have contact, and we as Christians must have contact with the hurting world to make a difference. We are called to help preserve the earth from the evils of the world. We are called to disinfect a dying world from itself.

But Jesus goes on to say, "But if salt has lost its taste, how shall its saltiness be restored? It is no longer good for anything except to be thrown out and trampled under people's feet" (Matthew 5:13). Critics love this statement because technically salt cannot become unsalty and still be salt. What they are assuming is that the salt used in Jesus's day was perfect, just like many people want to be. Salt taken from the shores of the Dead Sea is not pure, and no one walking this earth today is pure. The small granules of rock that were used as salt became granules of anything except salt. The sodium chloride was used up, and the impure properties remained. The only thing left was gravel, whose only remaining use was to make a walkway, but because a small amount of the salt remained, this gravel made an excellent walkway. Walkways made of used salt are often as hard and smooth as concrete. No weeds or grass will grow in it, so it's maintenance free. Isn't this just like many believers and churches? They lose their fire for Christ and the passion to make disciples of men. They are still Christians and believers with their salvation promised, but they are not making a difference. They are not worthless and to be thrown away; they still have a use in God's kingdom. Even the believers with a loss of desire to campaign for God have a place in His plans.

Application

The marketing efforts in today's salt industry intentionally created a new interest in a product that was previously considered boring. Marketing made salt a remarkable product (a purple cow, as Seth Godin phrases it). In ancient times, salt was already a remarkable product. So Jesus took the image of that product and used it as a metaphor to show Christians how to be a remarkable product. The image first-century Christians understood was that they could be a seasoning, a preservative, fertilizer, the best walkway, a follower of the salt covenant, or an antiseptic. They just needed to discover what God was asking them to be.

From a business application, if through marketing, salt can become unboring and if through the Bible, we can become salty, then you as a businessperson can find a way to make your business remarkable while still following the teachings of Christ. We do not have to settle for selling status quo. The combination of making whatever we sell outstanding and our business practice of following the Word of God will lead to rewards beyond measure.

Selling

Selling is perhaps the most important function of marketing. In a broad sense, the success of a business is directly related to selling. If you are in business, whether it is retail or services, you are always selling. Although you had no experience, you got your first job because you sold yourself better than the other applicants who also had no experience. If you own a business, you are selling your ideas and yourself to investors and bankers to finance your venture. You motivate your employees by selling them on the premise that your ideas and methods are the right way to do business. You even sell your kids on the idea that doing homework will lead to future rewards, such as scholarships, good jobs, and a better life. To get married, you sold your spouse on the idea that life together would be grand. Selling is all about convincing others that your ideas and their dreams can come true.

For businesses, sales are a necessity. If no one bought cars, car dealerships would close, which would cause the automobile manufacturers to close, and then the tire manufactures, seat makers, windshield installers, etc. would all close. Then all the service industries that rely on maintaining and repairing automobiles would close. Selling is the one thing every business has in common: goods and services must be sold for the entire business world to exist.

At the individual business level, selling is the marketing function that involves finding out the client's needs and wants, and then responding to those needs through planned communications that influence their purchasing decisions. In today's world, every business has something to sell, and to succeed businesses must sell their product or service better than their competitors. It is no surprise that an entire subindustry exists to help businesses understand how to do a better job of selling. This industry provides market studies, looks at the packaging of products or services, and trains people who connect to the customer so the chance of a transaction will increase. Getting professional help to sell goods and services in industries like mine is often the difference maker between success and failure.

Commerce in the Bible

What we are interested in is the biblical perspective of selling. I was surprised to discover there is a remarkable amount of commerce occurring in the Bible. The first recorded transaction is in Genesis chapter 23. As the story goes, God had called Abraham to travel to a foreign land where God would make a home for his family. Abraham was to be the beginning of the people of God. After many episodes between Abraham, his family, and God, we are at a place in the story where Abraham's wife, Sarah, has died. Sarah passed away in a foreign land, and Abraham needed a burial place. After the traditional courtesies and customary negotiating, Abraham said, "That he may give me the cave of Machpelah, which he owns; it is at the end of his field. For the full price let him give it to me in your presence as property for a burying place" (Genesis 23:9).

Now this verse does not mean much on its own, but from the dialogue and the negotiations, it is obvious that buying and selling was already a long-established rite throughout the ancient Near East. Throughout the Old Testament and New Testament are passages of buying and selling animals (Luke 14:19), tracts of land (Genesis 47:20–22, Ruth 4:3, Jeremiah 32:9–10, Matthew 27:7, Luke 14:18, Acts 4:34), food and drink (Genesis 41:57, Deuteronomy 2:28, John 6:5, John 13:29, Revelations 6:6), other goods (Revelations 18:11–13), slaves (Genesis 17:12, Exodus 21:2, Leviticus 25:44–45, Hosea 3:1–2), and labor (Leviticus 25:39–40, Matthew 20:1–2). To complement the commerce recorded in the Bible are many verses on fairness, honesty, greed, exploitation, and worldliness. To specifically look at what the Bible says about selling, I have selected four topics that I have seen to be problematic in the selling process. The four topics are selling yourself, relationships, sowing, and deceit.

Selling Yourself —The Apostle Paul

In my thinking, selling yourself is (1) presenting yourself in a fashion that you want to be perceived, and (2) being convinced that what you are selling is something you believe in. Obviously, this topic could take one entire book to cover. Well, it's covered in the thirteen books of the Bible written by the apostle Paul. And through these thirteen books we learn that it was Paul's confidence in what he was selling that allowed him to better sell himself.

As a reminder, the apostle Paul was first known as Saul of Tarsus. He was born a Jew, and since Tarsus was under Roman authority, he was also a Roman citizen. He was well educated, well trained, and cultured in the ways of the world. He originally was a Pharisee, which meant he was orthodox in following what the Jews of the day considered the right way to be faithful to scripture. As a Pharisee, Paul had the task of hunting down Christians and bringing them to the Jewish authorities for punishment. One day, on the road to Damascus, he met Jesus in the spirit, the same way we can meet Jesus today; the physical Jesus had already been crucified, had died, and had risen. When he met Jesus, he was asked, "Saul, Saul, why are you persecuting me?" (Acts 9:4). Thus began the conversion and ministry of one of the greatest apostles.

Paul had limitless energy, personality, persistence, and drive. He was a psychologist and a student of motives and of the mental traits of men. He was the missionary to the Gentiles in Asia. He started churches in numerous cities and provided them counsel as found in his letters. Paul wrote thirteen letters to his churches and friends over a twenty-year period, and these letters have become thirteen books of the Bible. Within these letters there is no evidence of complaining about his travels or fatigue and no whimpering about his hardships and the beatings he had taken. He displayed no disappointment about wasted years, lack of family, and loss of wealth and fame. He continuously expressed joy in serving his Lord and for the blessing of a life yet to come.

Through the writings of Luke, Paul's frequent traveling companion, we know that Paul's courage was never questioned. During one of his initial missionary campaigns with Barnabas to the city of Lystra in Asia Minor, he encountered a man who had been crippled all his life. By God's power Paul healed the man, and the crowds who witnessed the event were enthralled, attempting even to worship the apostle and his companion. But Paul's followers restrained them; mere humans were not proper objects of worship. Unfortunately, not everyone was excited about someone being miraculously healed, and a group of Jews from neighboring cities decided to stir up the crowd and incite anger against Paul. He was stoned, dragged outside the city, and left for dead. Being stoned in first-century Asia was as bad as it sounds—they actually had written rules about the proper way to stone someone. Nevertheless, Acts 14:20 says, "But when the disciples gathered about him, he rose up and entered the city, and on the next day he went on with Barnabas." Note the words *rose up*, indicating a miraculous recovery, especially considering he was ready to travel the very next day.

But the most amazing thing about Paul was his commitment to the brand. The brand for Paul was his unwavering commitment to spread the Word of God through the teachings of Jesus Christ. In Romans 12:11 he wrote, "Do not be slothful in zeal, be fervent in spirit, serve the Lord." Paul suffered many hardships in serving the Lord and being a messenger of Christ. He faced persecution, scorn, beatings, and imprisonment. But despite all this hardship he still had the faith to write the following:

> Since we have the same spirit of faith according to what has been written, "I believed, and so I spoke," we also believe, and so we also speak, knowing that he who raised the Lord Jesus will raise us also with Jesus and bring us with you into his presence. For it is all for your sake, so that as grace extends to more and more people it may increase thanksgiving, to the glory of God. (2 Corinthians 4:13–15)

Let's look at this verse for a moment. The preceding verses in 2 Corinthians 4 are about the hardship Paul endured. The apostle Paul had just finished explaining to the Corinthian congregation how his weakness had released God's power—he was afflicted but not crushed, perplexed but not despairing, persecuted but not forsaken, and struck down but not destroyed (2 Corinthians 4:7–9). He then went on to tell his readers that his experience in God's power was being made apparent in his weakness. After all his troubles, he still gave all the glory and credit to Jesus Christ.

After having described to the Corinthians his situation, he transitioned to why these circumstances were important. "Since we have the same spirit of faith according to what has been written, 'I believed, and so I spoke,' we also believe, and so we also speak" (2 Corinthians 4:13). Here is the salesman in Paul. In this verse, he continues to explain to his readers why he chose to speak boldly even though in speaking this way he knew he would suffer. Paul told the Corinthians he spoke this way because of what he believed, or in other words, because of his faith. To further make this point, we need to consider the phrase "spirit of faith." This is not a reference to the Holy Spirit that caused Paul to speak as he did. Spirit of faith refers to the disposition or the impulse of faith. It was the disposition or impulse that caused him to speak boldly, proclaiming the Gospel of Christ. It was the same disposition or impulse that moved King David when in Psalm 116:10, he said, "I believe therefore I spoke." For Paul and King David, it was not a divine interaction or force that caused them to speak but a true belief in God.

We cannot force someone to sell with conviction a product or service that the salesperson does not believe in. Sure, salespeople can work hard and drum up sales for a while, but without completely believing in what they are selling, they will not be successful for long. If we are selling, or if we have people selling for us, as business owners we need to make sure our sales staff knows what they are selling and completely believe in it. Otherwise they will not be successful in the long run. If you have a successful salesperson, chances are he or she believes in the product, and your responsibility is to make sure the salesperson has your total support. On the other hand, if you have a salesperson who does not believe in your product, chances are he or she is not consistently successful and should be moved to another area of responsibility.

Business Relationships—Equally Yoked

One of the primary reasons for business relationships is to allow others to help you sell your products and services. When I think of relationships, I immediately think of a covered wagon crossing the plains of Kansas, carrying a family that is relying on two oxen yoked together to get them and their belongings to their dream destination. This image from paintings, photographs, movies, and the occasional Old Settlers Day Parade is the only reference I have to something being yoked. A "yoke" is a favorite image in the Bible. Matthew 11:29 says:

Take my yoke upon you, and learn from me, for I am gentle
and lowly in heart, and you will find rest for your souls.

A yoke is something that attaches two animals together so they move
in lockstep together. When one turns to the right, the other must also
turn to the right whether it wants to or not. When pulling on something
like a plow or a wagon, they must pull evenly or they will veer off course;
the two animals must cooperate. When the two animals (or people
metaphorically) are yoked, each is bound to whatever the other has chosen
to do. Deuteronomy 22:10 instructs, "You shall not plow with an ox and a
donkey together." Why? The two animals are of differing sizes, strengths,
and demeanor. The outcome will be a disaster. Rows plowed will not be
straight, and the notorious orneriness of the donkey will make the task
unbearable, as well as humorous.

For marketing our products and services, we are always faced with
building and entering into relationships. We may contract with outside
salespeople to sell our products, we may need someone to recommend our
services, or we may rely on an advertising company to promote our business.
In these situations, we are relying on others to represent us. They are to
become, for better or worse, an extension of ourselves. Situations such as
these are the purpose of 2 Corinthians 6:14:

Do not be unequally yoked with unbelievers. For what
partnership has righteousness with lawlessness? Or what
fellowship has light with darkness?

Many have picked this verse out of context to show that Christians are
not to work with non-Christians. But just prior to this verse, the apostle
Paul has discussed the importance of good relationships with all the people
with whom we work. Furthermore, in 1 Corinthians 5:9–10, he says that
we should work with non-Christians, and in 1 Corinthians 10:25–33,
he discusses how we are to work with non-Christians. So he cannot be
advocating working only with Christians since he states otherwise.

To understand what Paul is getting at in the above verse we need to
better understand the Corinthians. The church in Corinth was Paul's
problem child. Corinth was a city without any ethical foundations or moral

roots. Its nicknames included Sin City and Carnal Corinth. And in the middle of one of the darkest, most morally corrupt cities in the Roman Empire was Paul's Church of Corinth (Acts 18). There could not be a harder market in which to sell faith in Jesus Christ than in Corinth.

What Paul was trying to get across to the Corinthians in 2 Corinthians 6:14 was the need to set boundaries and not be *un*equally yoked. In Matthew 11:29, Jesus calls us to "take my yoke upon you." If we are already yoked to Jesus, we cannot be yoked to anyone or anything else. Just like the oxen, mules, or horses, we have a yoke that is in part around Jesus, and the other part is around us. Jesus is the one who is determining the direction, pace, and path that we are on. Through the use of His yoke, Jesus trains us to be part of a larger team of people who are also yoked to Jesus. To be unequally yoked, as Paul said in 2 Corinthians, would mean we are connecting ourselves to someone or something that would be contrary to the direction, pace, and path that Jesus has set for us. To be unequally yoked places you in situations or relationships that bind you to the decision or actions of others whose values are incompatible with biblical values.

We need to remember in all our relationships, business and personal, that we always need to consider if the person we are relying on for advice, a recommendation, or to sell and promote our product—and by extension ourselves—is yoked to the same belief we are. This is not a believer versus nonbeliever issue; this is about building true, lasting relationships with others in the business world who have integrity, values, purposes, and beliefs like ours.

Sowing—King Solomon

As we have seen, the first step in selling is developing a confidence in your brand that allows you to sell yourself. The next step is building great and honest business relationships that allow others to help sell your products or services. The third step is sowing seeds that lead to selling your products or services. In my business the activity of planting seeds is a top-of-mind activity. The question we always ask is how can we get our name out in the marketplace, so when people need what we sell, they immediately think of us? We want our name to always be on the top of everyone's minds. I cannot think of a better verse to reflect this than that written by King Solomon in Ecclesiastes 11:1–4:

Cast your bread upon the waters,
for you will find it after many days.
Give a portion to seven, or even to eight,
for you know not what disaster may happen on earth.
If the clouds are full of rain,
they empty themselves on the earth,
and if a tree falls to the south or to the north,
in the place where the tree falls, there it will lie.
He who observes the wind will not sow,
and he who regards the clouds will not reap.

What amazing selling advice from a man who had everything. King Solomon was the richest and wisest man in his day; in our day and age, the two do not necessarily go together.

These verses are often used to encourage investors to diversify. "Don't put all your eggs in one basket" is one interpretation of King Solomon's advice. Isn't the same true for selling? Having just one purchaser of your product or one client for your services is not good business planning. The more markets in which you can place your product and the more clients who need your service put you at less risk to the whims of the market and the demands of one client. It is our job as small business owners to be able to seize opportunities as they present themselves. Small business owners cannot be too cautious or too wary of opportunities. We need to take calculated risks. Some of my best business successes were based on taking risks, either in being bold by making proposals when proposals are not being asked for or by making suggested solutions in directions that were not obvious. A salesman friend often remarks, "You never know where your next sale is until you ask."

Deceit—Ananias and Sapphira

The fourth topic I have selected to look at through the lens of the Bible is deceit. The first three topics were about confidence in your brand, building trust and honest relationships, and being prepared to act when opportunities arise. While those three are about trust and integrity, we also need to remember that temptation is always lurking in our world and is frequently evident in the world of sales. Jeremiah wrote:

The heart is deceitful above all things,
and desperately sick;
who can understand it? (Jeremiah 17:9)

Ouch! This verse does not come with a trap door. It has no "except" clause that provides a way to exclude ourselves from the all-too-painful recognition that we all are inherently deceitful. Adam and Eve gave us this gift, and it is our relationship with Jesus that helps us overcome it.

A lie is a deliberate falsehood told with the intent to mislead or cause someone to believe in error. Lying is generally in spoken form. Deceiving is an action, either by word or deed, that will lead people into believing something that is not true. Outright lying is prohibited multiple times in the Bible, and I'm assuming that discussing such an elementary topic is not needed. Deceit, however, is so subtle that it has become pervasive in our culture.

There is a great story in the Bible (Acts 5:1–9) about a couple named Ananias and Sapphira that demonstrates the deceit we see today is not new. This couple was part of the church in its earliest days. It had not been that long since Christ had been crucified and buried, and then rose, and these faithful followers still felt the overwhelming presence of God. The believers had a unique kinship; they were of one heart and soul. Everything they owned was common property for the good of the group. Early Christians cared for each other and made decisions that reflected this mutual concern. Believers were not required to contribute anything, but they all gave from the heart. Acts 4 ends with a story of a man named Joseph, who sold a field he owned and brought the money, placing it at the feet of the apostles, as a contribution and a devotion to the church. This attitude toward each other became well known and resulted in a blessing on the church. They knew everything they had was a gift from God. Giving to and for each other was a reflection of their genuine expression of love for God.

Ananias and Sapphira were part of this caring and devoted group. Seemingly the two were in the right place. But as the prophet Jeremiah stated, we all have the sin of deceit in our heart. And as many of us know, it sneaks out at the worst times. Reading between the lines, it is possible that Ananias and Sapphira wanted more than to be members of this growing, powerful church. Maybe they wanted to be in the inner circle, or wanted notoriety or recognition. Maybe they wanted to satisfy their pride. They had seen the enthusiastic reception that others like Joseph received when they made sacrifices and brought forward large donations for the group, and maybe that's what they wanted. What we learn is that even believers sometimes fail.

Ananias and Sapphira wanted that same recognition, but they did not have the deep feeling of devotion and commitment the other early Christians had. So they devised a plan to sell some land, hide part of the proceeds, donate the rest of the cash, and then receive accolades as if they donated everything. If they made the donation announcement correctly, they would never technically lie; they would just let the others come to their own conclusion. This is fame without total commitment. Ananias and Sapphira thought what people assumed and thought was out of their control. And if nobody asked the right question, no harm done.

Many things happened during the time Christ walked the earth and during the early years of the church, but not all those things are told in the Bible. Everything that is told in the Bible, however, is included for a reason. Stories such as the one about Ananias and Sapphira seem incidental but are deep with messages about how we lead our lives, make relationships, and conduct our business. Ananias and Sapphira did not need to deceive anyone. No one would have cared if they told the truth that they wanted to keep some money for themselves. In fact, they did not have to sell the land at all. For all we know, this one deceitful event could have been the only time they allowed sin to perpetrate their heart. But it could have also been a common characteristic of all their relationships. We do not know. What we do know is the apostle Peter saw right through their scheme, and when he confronted them individually, they fell down dead. Biblical justice was swift for Ananias and Sapphira.

Whether deserved or not, salespeople have a deceitful reputation. I cannot count the times in making a purchase where I have conducted the necessary research and have asked as many questions as I could, only to discover there is some significant element I missed that no one volunteered to clarify. Thinking back to Jeremiah, how easy is it to be close to making a sale, signing a contract, or making a deal only to recognize the purchaser does not know all the facts? From the seller's side of the arrangement, you are aware that knowing all the facts might kill the deal. Should you speak up or remain silent? On one hand, we are all adults and experienced business professionals. On the other hand, I have not heard of anyone dropping dead lately like Ananias and Sapphira, but why risk it? When we find ourselves in a situation where silence is an option that will allow a prospective client or purchaser to draw his or her own conclusion, we need to stop for just one minute and think of Ananias and Sapphira. I think they gave their lives for us as an example of what happens when the sin of deceitfulness runs its course. Those sins are there and are always going to be there. It is at that moment we need to thank God for His Son Jesus who conquered sin and gives us strength to know the difference between right and wrong.

Zebedee's Marketing Plan

Before Jesus came along the shore of the Sea of Galilee, Zebedee had the best marketing plan for his business. He built his business on integrity, trustworthiness, honesty, and hard work, and he taught those qualities to his employees. Why else would Jesus have selected James, John, Peter, and Andrew to follow Him? Zebedee needed to remember that he still had those qualities and that there were four more young men who would enjoy the chance to learn how to market the fishing business from Zebedee.

Summary

1. In developing and managing a marketing plan, think of salt. Salt was once considered a boring commodity but was rejuvenated as a remarkable product (remember the purple cow). If it is possible to make salt exciting and interesting, only your imagination can limit how interesting and exciting you can re-create your business.

2. In ancient times, salt was already a remarkable product. But Jesus took that remarkable product and challenged us, His believers, to also be remarkable. We are to be a spice to the world, a preservative for the Word of God, and an antiseptic for those who are hurting.

3. The apostle Paul's commitment to the brand (the Word of God) teaches us how our commitment to what we are selling creates

self-confidence that allows us to sell ourselves. Regardless of the outside pressures to conform and change, God has called you to be you.

4. Always be conscious of to whom you are yoking yourself. If someone is to represent you and your business, make sure he or she is giving representation that reflects you and reflects your yoke to Jesus.

5. King Solomon told us nearly three thousand years ago to "cast your bread upon the waters" (Ecclesiastes 11:1). We need to diversify into markets and products and not rely on just one supplier or client.

6. Ananias and Sapphira paid the price to provide us with a vivid example of the impact that inherited deceit in our hearts leads us to. Even when they had no reason to lie or deceive, Ananias and Sapphira were compelled to try to deceive the other believers only for short-term, personal gratification. Resist any temptation to deceive anyone, even through silence.

Notes

_____

_____

_____

_____

_____

_____

_____

_____

_____

_____

_____

_____

_____

_____

_____

_____

_____

CHAPTER 6

Negotiating with Zebedee

The realization finally hit home; Zebedee was going to have to rebuild his business. "Well, if I'm going to rebuild, I might as well take a hard look at everything," Zebedee said to himself out loud. As he thought through his business, he realized the starting point was to renegotiate all his existing agreements. Starting over would provide a unique opportunity since hiring a new crew would require negotiating new employment contracts. With no employees, he wouldn't have any fish to sell, so he now had an opportunity to negotiate new agreements with his "retailers." It was also possible to add new markets. Maybe it was time for a new boat or to replace his worn-out nets. Whatever business transactions he prepared to undergo, he needed to get his mind ready to negotiate. And he had better, for he was living in a part of the world renowned for its negotiating skills.

An early business mentor of mine once said, "Remember, everything is negotiable." At that time, we were discussing his philosophy for dealing with banks and borrowing money, but I think the adage applies to everything in our business life. As far as a primer or tutorial on negotiating, there is no better source than the Bible, especially the stories found in Genesis and Exodus. In these two books are stories of negotiating that cover the gamut of experiences. Some stories are about people trying to buy assets, such as land and cattle; some are about people attempting to hire laborers for harvesting; and some are about people negotiating directly with God. What I want to examine here are three types of negotiations found in the Bible: negotiating with God, negotiating for God, and negotiating among God's people. In each section, we will use a story from the Bible, and by looking at the details behind the story, we will be able to identify several negotiating techniques from which we may benefit.

Negotiating with God

Just writing "Negotiating with God" seems more than a little odd. After all, God is God. He is the One who created the universe, told the oceans where to start and stop, spoke light into existence, and breathed life into all creation. And yet, in the Bible there are a few instances where people have tried to negotiate with Him and even fewer still who have been successful (at least as successful as God intended them to be).

Abraham and Lot

I think the most famous negotiation in the Bible is the one between Abraham and God. God called Abraham to leave his family home and travel to an unknown, faraway place that God would later show him. As he traveled, he and his family's livestock increased to the point that it became a problem for their nomadic lifestyle. The solution was to split the herds with his nephew, Lot. Abraham and his entourage would travel in one direction, and Lot and his people would go in another. Lot chose to move to Sodom and become a city dweller while Abraham maintained the nomadic lifestyle, traveling through the lands as guided by God. Abraham still cared for Lot as exemplified in one story where a rival king sacked Sodom and took Lot captive. Abraham marshaled a small army, caught the raiders unaware, defeated them, freed Lot as well as the people of Sodom, and earned the respect of Sodom's king. Through rescuing Lot, Abraham developed an awareness of the people of Sodom and knew that as time passed, Sodom would develop an unhealthy and nasty reputation. What Abraham did not know was that God had decided to act on Sodom's reputation.

The Visitors

Our negotiation story begins with Abraham resting in front of his tent when three visitors appear. As is custom, Abraham immediately begins preparing food for the visitors and seeing to their comfort. Through the story we learn the initial reason for the visit is to inform Sarah, Abraham's elderly wife, that she is to have a son who will be the father of a great nation. Of course, she laughs in disbelief but sometime later bore a son who they named Isaac.

But the real reason for the visit becomes apparent as the three visitors prepare to leave. Here we learn the visitors have been sent by God and are on their way to punish Sodom. At this point, one of the visitors (who is referred to as Lord) somewhat innocently says:

> Shall I hide from Abraham what I am about to do, seeing that Abraham shall surely become a great and mighty nation, and all the nations of the earth shall be blessed in him? For I have chosen him, that he may command his children and his household after him to keep the way of the Lord by doing righteousness and justice, so that the Lord may bring to Abraham what he has promised him. (Genesis 18:17–19)

I have been involved in many negotiations, as I'm sure you have, and this is a setup if there ever was one. Some visitors stop by to deliver some unrelated news (Sarah soon will bear a son) yet drop an outrageous hint of something else they are planning, which has a strong connection to Abraham. This is like stopping by your neighbors' house to give them their newspaper, which is lying at the end of the driveway, and just accidentally mentioning that you are thinking of selling your house, hoping the neighbors might know someone who would be interested in buying it—someone they would like as a neighbor. Or you have an idea for software that would benefit the front office of medical practices. It just happens you have a medical appointment where you also can talk about your software idea to both a potential user and a potential investor. In my experience these contrived occasions happen all the time.

Of course, because of the source of the comment (the Lord) and the polite references to Abraham and his future, Abraham is immediately interested as the visitors knew he would be. Abraham is curious about the visitors' intent.

> Because the outcry against Sodom and Gomorrah is great and their sin is very grave, I will go down to see whether they have done altogether according to the outcry that has come to me. And if not, I will know." (Genesis 18:20–21)

Ironically, this is God speaking and He knows everything. Again, God is setting up Abraham for the negotiations, and Abraham takes the bait. He knows this is God he is talking to and knows how evil Sodom is. He is aware of God's capabilities and knows his nephew is living in Sodom. He also knows he must do something:

> Then Abraham drew near and said, "Will you indeed sweep away the righteous with the wicked? Suppose there are fifty righteous within the city. Will you then sweep away the place and not spare it for the fifty righteous who are in it? Far be it from you to do such a thing, to put the righteous to death with the wicked, so that the righteous fare as the wicked! Far be that from you! Shall not the Judge of all the earth do what is just? (Genesis 18:23–25)

My interpretation of this verse is Abraham says, "Hold on just a moment. I'm not questioning your motives and intent, and I'm sure you are a fine, upstanding man, but let me just ask one simple question for you to think about. We have a common interest in destroying the wicked, but are we both not concerned about the righteous as well? Let's make sure we understand the ramifications of what you are thinking about, and maybe there is another course of action we should consider. But, no matter what, I'm sure whatever you do will be the right thing."

Negotiations

Abraham neither confronts the visitors nor does he state his personal interest. He is negotiating, and every statement and question are backed with compliments and reasoning. The universal negotiating strategy is to find a common interest and then work to find what the boundaries or limitations are from that common interest. Think about the last time you went to a garage sale or yard sale to see what bargains you could find. Even though you find something you are interested in, you start by discussing the weather, the lawn, and why they are having the sale (common interest) before ever starting to negotiate. "Say, that's a mighty nice kitchen table you have for sale." Then you work on the boundaries by using "if" phrases. "I don't know how interested I am or where I'd put it, but if I happened to offer five hundred dollars, would that be in the range you might accept for that oak table and chairs?" You have not made an offer, only asked an innocent question. The seller is in the same situation. He or she responds by not changing the price yet, but by asking, "If I happened to change the price to six hundred fifty dollars, would you buy it?" Another example would be buying a used car. You are not in the market to buy a car, but the notice online interested you. You work to find a common interest, such as why they are selling the car, what memories they have of owning this car, and what repairs it needs. Are there some emotional hurdles to get over, or are they just ready to be rid of a clunker? The conversation is tailored around finding the boundaries that inform you what price you can offer. A third example would be hiring a new employee. If you offered a certain annual amount to a potential employee, would he or she accept? No offer has been made yet. The employment candidate might respond with certain benefits that need to be added to make that amount work. The employer responds that he or she does not have those kinds of benefits but could sweeten the deal with a little more money, more paid vacation time, or a larger car allowance. The goal is to determine the boundaries and parameters before ever making an offer.

Abraham gets his answer:

> And the Lord said, "If I find at Sodom fifty righteous in the city, I will spare the whole place for their sake." (Genesis 18:26)

Since Abraham knows Sodom, he suspects there are not fifty righteous people there, so he continues his negotiations. How about if the Lord finds forty-five that are righteous, how about forty, how about thirty? Abraham understands he is negotiating for the life of his nephew and family. And then he gets to ten:

Then he said, "Oh let not the Lord be angry, and I will speak again but this once. Suppose ten are found there." He answered, "For the sake of ten I will not destroy it." (Genesis 18:32)

Abraham senses he is pushing the limits. He starts out with more compliments, assuring the visitors not to be angry with him; he is only talking. At this point the visitors leave, but Abraham has done his job and found out their limits. The negotiations are over, and it is time for action.

Win-Win Outcomes

So we see how Abraham negotiated with God and how that negotiation fits in a secular business world. It is important to be aware of the spiritual implications of this story. When I think of negotiations for purposes here, I'm not talking about the kinds of negotiations that are massive in size and well publicized. The buying of a downtown skyscraper, the salary of a talented professional athlete, or the discussions between a union and a particular industry are not what I have experience in or have in mind. While the same principles apply, when I am thinking of negotiations, I'm thinking of the agreement between my company and the clients for whom I want to perform work, the people I want to hire to work for me, and the daily business transactions that place me in front of the public as a representative of my company. I want a good deal, but I also want to complete more than one project for my clients. I want my employees to be happy in their jobs, and I want the public to think of me as a fair, trustworthy, and reliable businessman. It seems in these circumstances we need to always shoot for a win-win outcome. So did Abraham.

To see how God orchestrates a win-win outcome, we need to look at the negotiations with Abraham from God's perspective. There are several aspects of God that we need to be aware of. First, as mentioned earlier, God knows everything. Psalm 139:1–6 says:

O Lord, you have searched me and known me!
You know when I sit down and when I rise up;
you discern my thoughts from afar.
You search out my path and my lying down
and are acquainted with all my ways.
Even before a word is on my tongue,
behold, O Lord, you know it altogether.
You hem me in, behind and before,
and lay your hand upon me.
Such knowledge is too wonderful for me;
it is high; I cannot attain it.

There is nothing that Abraham is doing or thinking that God does not already know. He already knows everything about Sodom, and he knows how Abraham will negotiate with him.

Second, God has a special relationship with Abraham. He is the only person in scripture called God's "friend." Isaiah 41:8 says:

But you, Israel, my servant,
Jacob, whom I have chosen,
the offspring of Abraham, my friend …

And finally, God has entered into a covenant relationship with Abraham, as we have observed in verses 18 and 19 as stated earlier. But to make Abraham the father of God's people, Abraham will need training and will therefore experience many trials so he can pass that knowledge on to his offspring. Abraham is to "command his children and his household after him to keep the way of the Lord by doing righteousness and justice" (Genesis 18:19).

I think of this story in terms of God being the guy from our previous example, who is selling his used car but this time to the neighbor kid. The guy has seen how hard this young person has worked, how hard he tries to grow up. He knows what the family has experienced, what they can afford, and he feels a connectedness to this kid. He is going to take this kid through the negotiation process because he wants to impart a valuable lesson. He wants the kid to feel like they negotiated a good deal, and that in turn adds to the ownership of the car. But the guy is going to structure the negotiations so the kid will get a great deal in the end. In these negotiations, the guy and the kid develop a connectedness that might not otherwise exist and the interaction becomes more about imparting wisdom and experience than just negotiating.

God is forcing Abraham to negotiate with him, and in that process Abraham must go through a metamorphosis. Up to this point in history, the story was about Abraham and what God was going to do for him. All Abraham had to do was follow God's commands. Abraham and his offspring just had to worship God. Through the negotiations, however, Abraham becomes concerned with the well-being of others—not just himself or his family, but with people he did not know. Sure, he is trying to again save Lot and his family, but he is also interceding on behalf of the unknown few who were righteous. He is becoming the person God said he was to be in verse 19; he is concerned about righteousness and justice. God is allowing Abraham to take a stand that is outside of himself and bigger than himself. God subtly comments that he is going to Sodom to check things out, to see if the people there are as awful as advertised. Abraham knows full well they are awful (so does God), but he is willing to intercede nonetheless. And God allows Abraham to negotiate Him down to ten righteous people. Looking at God's response to each of Abraham's offers, God never says Abraham changed His mind or that God's plans were altered. God says, "I will not do it, if I find thirty there" (Genesis 18:30). I suggest you read chapter 19 of Genesis to learn the outcome of the story.

God achieved a win-win outcome in negotiating with Abraham. Abraham did not really negotiate with God—no one can do that. Negotiating with Abraham was designed to achieve specific results in Abraham's character. As believing businesspeople, our goal in negotiating should always start with what God has in mind for us as His people. Our negotiating should be about integrity, fairness, and relationships and not about just being a winner regardless of the process.

Negotiating for God

While the story of Abraham negotiating with God is not widely known, the selected story of negotiating on behalf of God is one of the most recognizable stories in the entire Bible. The story is that of Moses rescuing the Israelite people from the control of the Egyptian pharaoh. To get caught up to where the negotiating begins, let's start at the beginning. Jacob and his family, who were descendants of Abraham, moved from Canaan to Egypt because of a severe famine. Over the course of four hundred years, they grew in number to such an extent that the pharaoh of Egypt put them under bondage and slavery to keep them from rebelling against him. At one point, Pharaoh's concern was so great he ordered all male Israelite children killed to control their population growth. It was during this time Moses was born of an Israelite woman who hid her child for three months so he would not be killed. Fearing for his life, the mother placed Moses in a basket in the Nile River with the hope that someone would find him and raise him. That someone happened to be Pharaoh's daughter, so Moses grew up in a life of privilege. Of course, he found out he was an Israelite by birth, and as he grew older, he became concerned about the unjust treatment of his people. During a fit of rage, he killed an Egyptian who was beating a fellow Israelite, causing Moses to flee to the desert in fear of his life. For forty years Moses was content to live in the desert tending sheep and starting a family.

Pharaoh

Earlier in the Bible, God made a covenant with the forefathers of the Israelite slaves, and He decided it was time to act on the cries of His people under Egyptian bondage. God called Moses while he was living in the desert to be His intermediary, and through a negotiation between God and Moses, God convinced Moses that, despite his flaws, he was the right person to return to Egypt and ask Pharaoh to set the Israelites free. Moses would be the one to lead the Israelites out of captivity, and he would lead them to a "land of the Canaanites, Hittites, Amorites, Perizzites, Hivites, and Jebusites—a land flowing with milk and honey" (Exodus 3:17).

So Moses returns to Egypt and meets with Pharaoh. Think about this from a negotiating standpoint: Pharaoh holds all the cards. He rules Egypt, is thought of as a god, has total control over all the slaves, and has a massive army. By giving up his Israelite slaves, his ability to harvest crops and build buildings, temples, and pyramids would be completely lost. Moses has nothing Pharaoh does not already have or want, so there is no upside for Pharaoh to negotiate with Moses.

But Moses, who by this time is eighty years old, and his brother Aaron have their orders from God, and they meet with Pharaoh to begin the negotiations. In this first meeting, Moses asks Pharaoh to allow his people to take time off work to go into the wilderness to hold a feast honoring their God. As expected, Pharaoh turns down this request. Unexpectedly, Pharaoh makes life harder on the Israelites by increasing their workload. At the next negotiation and as a demonstration of their commitment to the slaves, Aaron throws down his staff that immediately turns into a serpent. In a tit for tat, Pharaoh's court magicians throw down their rods that also turn into serpents. Not to be outdone, Aaron's rod/serpent devours the other serpents before becoming a rod again. Unfortunately "Pharaoh's heart became hard and he would not listen to them" (Exodus 7:13). All the while, the slaves continue with their increased workload, so Moses knows he is not only negotiating with Pharaoh to free the Israelites, but he is also negotiating with the Israelites to believe and trust him. They had lost their faith that the God of Moses could help them, and unfortunately he could make things worse.

At this point in the negotiations, God sends ten specific plagues against Egypt. God first turns water into blood and then sends torrents of frogs across the land. Pharaoh agrees to release the captives if Moses will stop the onslaught of frogs, but he then retracts that decision and refuses to let the Israelites go despite the stinking piles of dead frogs. God next covers the land with lice and then flies at which points Pharaoh again agrees to release God's people and immediately retracts that decision. Talk about a battle of wills. Plague five is a pestilence on the livestock, plague six is boils and sores that break out on men and livestock, and plague seven is a massive fire and hailstorm breaking every tree and flattening every field. Finally Pharaoh relents and agrees for the third time, but true to form, the moment the fire and hail stops Pharaoh reneges and refuses to release the Israelites. Plague eight is a cloud of locusts, and nine is total darkness; both cause Pharaoh to give in only to harden his heart again and refuse to release God's people. Finally God issues plague ten, which is the death of all firstborn of each house. God tells His people, however, to sprinkle the blood of a blemish-free lamb on their doorposts to keep His angel of death from killing their firstborn. At midnight, this angel strikes, killing the firstborn of Pharaoh, his servants, his people, and his livestock. This last and final judgment finally breaks the Pharaoh, and he agrees to let the Israelites go.

Negotiating

So let's look at Moses's negotiations with Pharaoh. Moses comes to Pharaoh and asks him to let the Israelites go on a three-day holiday, despite the fact God had sent him to negotiate their freedom. This action irritates Pharaoh, so he makes life more miserable for the Israelites who in turn vent their anger on Moses and his brother Aaron. Through sheer persistence and determination, Moses continues to negotiate with Pharaoh until he relents. Of course, we know the hand of God is involved in all aspects, but let's also examine the roles of each party in the negotiations.

The first party is the role of Pharaoh. He is the hardheaded (hard-hearted per the Bible) person who thinks he holds all the cards. The person in this role thinks he or she is in control and is going to dictate any terms if the negotiations are to proceed. This person is not aware of any reason to be considerate or even care about the negotiation process. The second party to the negotiations is the role of Moses, who is frequently a reluctant participant. This party is at the negotiating table because of a compelling need outside of the negotiations. Finally, the third party in the process is the unnamed entity who will benefit from the negotiations yet is not involved in the actual discussions. In our Bible story, this would be the Israelite slaves.

A twenty-first-century example would be placing wireless transmitters on private light poles. The owner of the poles (first party) does not directly benefit and has no reason to agree to having the light poles modified. The wireless transmitter company (second party) has little to offer the first party to convince the owner to agree. And the third party is the public who will benefit from better Internet access but is most likely unaware of the negotiations.

A second example is operating a homeless shelter. The first party is the existing neighborhood that must approve of the homeless shelter being in or near the neighborhood. The second party is the homeless shelter, which can only offer the satisfaction of helping the homeless as a benefit to the neighborhood. And the third party is the homeless who are unaware of the negotiations going on between the shelter and the neighborhood.

The success in this type of negotiation as shown by Moses is persistence. While Moses had God to bring multiple miracles to the table to change Pharaoh's heart, in our negotiations, we need to be persistent and continue to prod, looking for the one or two details that will allow the unwilling party to sympathize. Unfortunately, sometimes it may take a miracle like those Moses needed to find the point of common interest that will allow for a successful outcome. In my experience, however, this common interest might be a mutual friend or someone at city hall who can speak on your behalf; maybe you like the same baseball team or you can offer some needed property improvements, such as replacing a neglected fence. Remember, even Moses started his negotiations with a small request to ease into finding a common interest. If you believe in your cause and are unrelenting in talking about your need, you will find that common interest.

Negotiating among People

My last example of learning negotiating techniques from the Bible involves one of the most colorful characters ever found in scripture. The story of Jacob (renamed Israel) is in Genesis chapters 25–36. Jacob, the father of our Christian heritage, is a testament to God's ability, and even desire, to use non-perfect people to be His people. As you will see, Jacob has more than a few flaws yet eventually comes around to be a man of God. I suggest reading these chapters, as they are full of the colorful stories and antics of Jacob's failed drive to be independent of God.

Jacob was born second in a pair of twins to Isaac and Rebekah in a world where the firstborn is favored in everything in life. While Jacob is portrayed as a homebody, preferring to tend his father's animals and hang around the tent, his brother Esau was a man of the outdoors, preferring to hunt and travel. Jacob was fair complexioned, and Esau was a hairy brute. Jacob was favored by his mother, Rebekah, and Esau was favored by his father, Isaac. Jacob was a schemer and a negotiator. Once when Esau came in from hunting and was famished (he must not have been a successful hunter), Jacob traded a simple meal in exchange for Esau's birthright—those benefits of being firstborn. He later tricked his father, Isaac, who was blind by that time, into giving him the blessing (which was a big deal in the ancient Near East) instead of Esau. Because of this trickery, Jacob had to leave home in fear of his life and travel to a new country. It was in this new country where he met his match.

Laban, Rachel, and Leah

A man named Laban had two daughters; one was beautiful and the other one wasn't. Jacob fell in love with the beautiful one, Rachel, and negotiated with Laban to allow him to marry her in exchange for seven years of working for Laban. On the wedding night, Jacob discovered the woman he married was not the beautiful Rachel but was instead her not-so-beautiful sister, Leah. Jacob had to work for Laban another seven years to finally marry Rachel.

At this point in our story, Jacob had two wives and was employed by Laban with presumably son-in-law status in the family estate. Somewhere along the line, Laban added several sons to his family either through his own wives or by adopting relatives. These new sons did not think very highly of Jacob. Whatever the case, Jacob now had competition for a share of Laban's estate of which Jacob, in his fourteen years of labor, was a significant contributor. As an employee, Jacob worked hard and was smart, and Laban was the direct beneficiary of those skills.

Knowing he was an outsider and his brothers-in-law were against him, Jacob decided it was time to return home. He had been gone for over fourteen years, and his obligation to Laban was completed. It was time to see his father, Isaac, and mother, Rebekah, again.

> After Rachel gave birth to Joseph, Jacob said to Laban, "Send me on my way so I can go back to my own homeland. Give me my wives and children, for whom I have served you, and I will be on my way. You know how much work I've done for you."

> But Laban said to him, "If I have found favor in your eyes, please stay. I have learned by divination that the Lord has blessed me because of you." He added, "Name your wages, and I will pay them."

> Jacob said to him, "You know how I have worked for you and how your livestock has fared under my care. The little

you had before I came has increased greatly, and the Lord has blessed you wherever I have been. But now, when may I do something for my own household?"

"What shall I give you?" he asked.

"Don't give me anything," Jacob replied. "But if you will do this one thing for me, I will go on tending your flocks and watching over them: Let me go through all your flocks today and remove from them every speckled or spotted sheep, every dark-colored lamb and every spotted or speckled goat. They will be my wages. And my honesty will testify for me in the future, whenever you check on the wages you have paid me. Any goat in my possession that is not speckled or spotted, or any lamb that is not dark-colored, will be considered stolen."

"Agreed," said Laban. "Let it be as you have said." That same day he removed all the male goats that were streaked or spotted, and all the speckled or spotted female goats (all that had white on them) and all the dark-colored lambs, and he placed them in the care of his sons. Then he put a three-day journey between himself and Jacob, while Jacob continued to tend the rest of Laban's flocks. (Genesis 30:25–36 NIV)

Negotiating

Here we have two skilled negotiators at work. Laban had little wealth when Jacob showed up. In exchange for permission to marry Laban's daughters, Jacob labored hard for fourteen years and Laban prospered. Now Jacob was ready to leave and needed something to show for his efforts other than two wives and a tent full of kids. Both began their negotiating with flowery salutations and gratitude, but with only themselves in their hearts. Each was out to get the better of the other. Laban, as he prepared for a hard bargain, said, "What shall I give you?" only to have Jacob respond that he did not want a gift; he only wanted the oddly colored sheep and goats from the flocks. Laban's audible sigh of relief could be heard, as he knew the oddly colored sheep and goats were a rarity and Jacob would receive very little for his negotiations.

So Laban and Jacob went through all of Laban's flocks and removed all oddly marked and colored sheep and goats and moved them to another pasture. Jacob would tend to the remaining unspoiled, unspeckled, and unstriped flock, and he would be the owner of all new animals that were oddly marked and colored. Laban thought Jacob was of questionable intellect and that he had just negotiated the greatest open-ended agreement ever, since unspoiled, unspeckled, and unstriped animals rarely produced speckled and spotted offspring.

Jacob, true to his nature, thought he also had just negotiated the best deal ever. See, Jacob was not yet a man of God on whom he would eventually rely. He had a ridiculous plan that would allow him to be the winner in this deal. In Jacob's thinking, he was not going to allow the offspring's markings from the sheep and goats he was responsible for to be left to chance. He had derived three techniques to control the outcome of the growth of the flocks. First, he reasoned, whatever the sheep and goats saw while they were mating would influence the offspring—sort of a prenatal influence. So, if the sheep and goats saw stripes while mating, the offspring would be striped. Since sheep and goats mated while at the water trough, Jacob placed striped wooden poles in front of the water troughs and the offspring of these sheep and goats amazingly were striped, speckled, and spotted. His second scheme was that if the first technique worked with striped wooden poles, it would work even better if they saw real striped animals. Jacob placed the striped, speckled, and spotted animals in front of the water troughs while the remaining animals watered. For his third technique, he placed the stronger animals at the watering trough so the resulting offspring were only from the stronger and better sheep and goats. Jacobs's striped and speckled flock thrived and grew exponentially. While Jacob thought his plan worked to perfection, we know it didn't because it couldn't. God is the only one in charge of determining the markings and color of the offspring. Jacob was prosperous but not because of Jacob.

Let's consider how these negotiations went. Both Laban and Jacob were out to get the best deal for themselves despite being father-in-law and son-in-law. You would think Laban would want to be generous with Jacob since whatever he gave Jacob would be used to take care of his daughters and grandchildren. In addition, Jacob had worked side by side with Laban for fourteen years. Didn't they develop any level of respect for each other's abilities and skills? Honestly, we only suspect Jacob went into the negotiations thinking about winning from his history of previous negotiations. Nonetheless, he was apprehensive about negotiating with Laban because of the way Laban tricked him into marrying Leah before Rachel. Jacob had to have a grasp of Laban's wealth and the condition of his estate, and he knew better than anyone what Laban could afford to give him. Both came out of the negotiations thinking they got a sweet deal—Laban because he thought the odds of the open-ended agreement were in his favor, and Jacob because he thought he could alter the outcome by trickery. Both were wrong. The end of this Bible story is most of the new goats and sheep were spotted, striped, and colored. Jacob prospered, and because of that, the rest of Laban's household developed such a strong resentment toward Jacob that he and his wives had to sneak away in the middle of the night.

Negotiating based on deceit and contrivances never ends well. In Jacob's case, the outcome was a blessing from God and not from Jacob; we never know if Jacob figures that out.

Honesty and forthrightness are the only attributes to bring when negotiating between men and/or women. God deals with His people with grace, and all the outcomes are a blessing from God. We may think negotiating in today's world is more sophisticated that in ancient times, but I'm not sure that's true. Negotiating with integrity is not that hard. We need to decide what we want in return for what we are offering, know at what point to walk away, and place the rest in the hands of God. We need to remember it is a perverse world we live in and we are forced to negotiate with Laban every day, but we are not called to this world to negotiate. We are called to "seek first the kingdom of God" (Matthew 6:33). We must negotiate in good faith and allow God to establish the outcome.

Zebedee

Zebedee did not have to worry about negotiating *for* God, and he did not have to negotiate much in the way of new contracts and employment agreements. I think he may have done a little negotiating *with* God, since it was God's Son who showed up on the shores of the Sea of Galilee and spoke a few simple words, enticing four young men to leave the life of fishing to become fishers of men. Maybe it was not a negotiation per se; it may have been more of a resignation. I see that in my life. I'm thrown a curveball that I could not hit, and I'm left wondering what to do next. I could think God put me in the situation so He owes me and I have something to negotiate. Ha! Negotiating *with* God is an act to fulfill what He has planned for you in the first place. Resignation is good. Zebedee allowed God to tell him what His will was, and he responded accordingly.

Summary

1. When you think you are in a position to negotiate with God, think of Abraham and what he accomplished. God was in charge, and the negotiations by Abraham were structured to cause him to grow and learn. When you have this sense that you are negotiating with God, the question to ask Him is "Okay, I know You are taking me through this negotiation for a reason, so what is it in my life that You want me to learn and how can I apply it to glorify You?"

2. Always be ready to negotiate on behalf of God. Be ready to find yourself where the only card you have in negotiating is having God on your side. There are endless needs in our world where God is waiting for us to represent Him to help the poor, disenfranchised, and the lost. If we do not negotiate for them, who will?

3. The story of Jacob's life is a "scratch your head," "laugh out loud," and "how could he think that" kind of story. He is always deceiving people to get what he wants. When it is what God wants, no matter the trickery, Jacob is blessed. It is so easy for us to just be honest and sincere, and despite that we are in a sinful world, God will bless us when it is part of His plan. Negotiating with that in mind makes life so much simpler and more enjoyable.

Notes

CHAPTER 7

Investing in Zebedee

Sitting in the bow of his boat with the early morning waves of the Sea of Galilee lightly beating against the hull, Zebedee's thoughts wandered to his investments. He had a fair amount invested in hard assets, such as the boat, sails, and nets, and those assets were still with him. But he dwelled on the investment in his crew, which he could still make out in the distance as they walked away. He had spent countless hours with these young men, teaching them where to fish, the importance of maintaining their equipment, and how to get the best price for their daily catch, as well as passing along the incidental life lessons that he hoped would pay dividends down the road. He knew the investment in these boys would not go to waste. They could always go back to fishing, and life lessons are good no matter where you find yourself. In retrospect, even with James, John, Peter, and Andrew leaving with Jesus, everything Zebedee had invested so far was still a good investment; unfortunately, it was one on which he might not get to see the ultimate return.

Most people seem to think investing is all about money and would only be essential to a business that deals with money, such as a bank, brokerage firm, or other financial institution. The prevailing thought is investing equates to money and rightly so, as this is the predominant definition. But the second, third, and fourth definitions of *investment* (the first is about money) from the Oxford Dictionaries website[23] are as follows:

- Devote (one's time, effort, or energy) to a particular undertaking with the expectation of a worthwhile result.
- Buy (something) whose usefulness will repay the cost.
- Provide or endow someone or something with a particular quality or attribute.

In applying these definitions with the teachings of the Bible, it is clear investing is not just something we do with money. In fact, despite many sermons and investment newsletters, the Bible is interested in investing, just not through using money. To address this topic, I am going to look at investing as three distinct activities in the order of least important to most important: money, spouse and children, and others.

Money

I have noticed, as I'm sure several of you have, that many writers and speakers like to start the topic of stewardship or tithing with quotes that lead you to believe the Bible wants us to think money is important. I have heard it said the Bible references *money* somewhere between two thousand and 2,350 times, yet only references *love* three hundred times. Sadly, the unsaid implication is money is about ten times more important than love. Or they point out the Bible talks more about money than hell. I'm not sure what the unsaid implication is there. Other than frequently being taken out of context, I find the Bible does not care all that much for money. The use and need for money is a common reference point. One example is the woman who loses a coin and lights a lamp so she can sweep the house until she finds it (parable of the lost coin, Luke 15:8–10). The real story is about the "joy before the angels of God over one sinner who repents" (Luke 15:10) and not about her losing one tenth of her wealth. Money just happens to be a common point of knowledge both in biblical times and now.

Consider the story of the rich young ruler who asks Jesus, "What shall I do to inherit eternal life?" (Mark 10:17). Jesus says to sell everything and give to the poor, and the young ruler goes away sad. The story is not about the young ruler's wealth that he has been asked to give away, but it is about the idols he places ahead of God. The story could have been about the owner of a bobblehead collection that was idolized ahead of everything else.

Everybody knows about money; not everybody knows about employment, home ownership, education, or bobblehead collections. If the Bible was about money, the message of the life of Abraham would have been told differently since his wealth accumulation in his day would be like that of Bill Gates or Warren Buffett today. But the Bible does not paint that picture of Abraham because his love of God and his faith completely block out any implication that wealth or money have anything to do with his life.

Having said all that, I do think the Bible has something to say about money because the concept of money and what it stands for is a spiritual matter. Money represents this world, and all attachments to money represent the friction between focusing on the here and now versus focusing on eternity with Christ. Consider 1 John 2:15–17:

> Do not love the world or the things in the world. If anyone
> loves the world, the love of the Father is not in him. For all
> that is in the world—the desires of the flesh and the desires
> of the eyes and pride of life—is not from the Father but is
> from the world. And the world is passing away along with
> its desires, but whoever does the will of God abides forever.

We are living as sojourners in this world, and we need to manage the gifts we are given. The first step to being a good steward with our money is to recognize our culture is built around the premise that accumulating money and possessions will make us happy. Fortunately the Bible reminds us that the accumulation of wealth is a lie, and only trusting in God will make us happy. Once we come to grips with the fact that everything we have— money, looks, talents, heritage, etc.—is a gift to us from God; God owns everything. Everything we have is on loan to us, and it is our responsibility to take care of it, nurture it, and to be a good steward of it up until our time on Earth is over.

To focus our discussion on investing money and the Bible, let's look at a parable we have already seen but this time in an unusual format. This is the parable of the talents as found in the biblical interpretation called *The Message*. This version takes the traditional readings of the Bible and characterizes them in a more current cultural language intended to cause us to reexamine how we may have previously understood scripture.

The Story about Investment (Matthew 25:14–30 MSG)

It's also like a man going off on an extended trip. He called his servants together and delegated responsibilities. To one he gave five thousand dollars, to another two thousand, to a third one thousand, depending on their abilities. Then he left. Right off, the first servant went to work and doubled his master's investment. The second did the same. But the man with the single thousand dug a hole and carefully buried his master's money.

After a long absence, the master of those three servants came back and settled up with them. The one given five thousand dollars showed him how he had doubled his investment. His master commended him: "Good work! You did your job well. From now on be my partner."

The servant with the two thousand showed how he also had doubled his master's investment. His master commended him: "Good work! You did your job well. From now on be my partner."

The servant given one thousand said, "Master, I know you have high standards and hate careless ways, that you demand the best and make no allowances for error. I was afraid I might disappoint you, so I found a good hiding place and secured your money. Here it is, safe and sound down to the last cent."

The master was furious. "That's a terrible way to live! It's criminal to live cautiously like that! If you knew I was after the best, why did you do less than the least? The least you could have done would have been to invest the sum with the bankers, where at least I would have gotten a little interest.

"Take the thousand and give it to the one who risked the
most. And get rid of this 'play-it-safe' who won't go out on
a limb. Throw him out into utter darkness."

If you review this parable in an NIV or an ESV translation, you will
notice a significant difference in the word usage but little difference in
its meaning. This parable is traditionally called the parable of the talents
because the master who gave his servants $5,000, $2,000, and $1,000
in *The Message* gave each five talents, two talents, and one talent in the
traditional translations, thus the name the parable of the talents. As a
clarification, talent was a currency denomination in first-century Jerusalem
that amounted to seventy-five pounds of gold or approximately $1.2 million
in today's market (yes, it is appropriate to say "Wow, trust a servant with a
million bucks?").

Hopefully you see this parable is not about investing money. It is about
utilizing our abilities and resources for the Kingdom of God. This parable,
however, has some interesting advice that can be applied to the management
of our money. First, the two servants who received a return on the master's
money did something to get that return—in this case they invested the
money in something that was profitable. They researched investments,
found a trustworthy partner, and kept an eye on the progress of their
investment. They also made sure their investment choices were earning a
return. The third servant exerted no effort except to barely break a sweat
finding a hiding place. The point is investments require some level of diligent
effort to pay off.

Second, regardless of whether or not you like *The Message* translation
where the servants are given money in units of $1,000, or the traditional
translations where the servants are given money in bags of gold, the amount
of money each servant receives is more than pocket change. The one given
the least still had a substantial amount to invest. No amount is too small
to invest, especially considering it is in the Kingdom of God. The master
expected a return on a little amount just as he expected a return on the
larger amount.

Third, the servants were given money "depending on their abilities."
The effort required by the first two servants to make their investment was
the same. They both had to go through the same steps to get a return even

though they had different amounts and different abilities. Since they each had to work the same to get a good return, they were both made partners as their reward. Based on this correlation, if the one-talent servant (the $1,000 investor) had doubled his money as the other two did, in all likelihood he also would have been made a partner. We know he had fewer abilities, so he would have had more to overcome to get his comparable return. But because of that, he needed less total return to receive the same reward as the other two. Unfortunately, he could not overcome his lack of ability and lost everything. The lesson we can take away is by not making any investment, this servant had zero chance at success.

Last, each servant worked for the master, or in our case the Master (God). Do you suppose the servant with the smallest amount considered skipping town? Even this servant made some, albeit poor, attempt to do as the master asked. In no circumstance did the selfish desires of the servants overcome their obligations to the master. They all recognized that the money given was not theirs, nor was the interest they earned. All three servants understood they were but stewards and their performance reflected the quality of their stewardship. As shown in this parable, as a steward your first duty is to use your gifts to please the master.

Investment Advice

Following up on the general advice for investing money from the parable of the talents, we need to examine any concrete advice the Bible has about money management and investment strategies. Starting with recognizable verses about investing, Proverbs 13:11 says:

> Wealth gained hastily will dwindle,
> but whoever gathers little by little will increase it.

The generally accepted commentary on this verse is that the simple possession of riches is as nothing; they come and go, but the power to gain by skill of hand is everything. The lesson here is not investing in the traditional sense by looking for a grand-slam home run, but in working with diligence for a good return.

A second known verse about investing is Proverbs 28:8 (KJV), which says:

> He that by usury and unjust gain increaseth his substance,
> he shall gather it for him that will pity the poor.

This verse adds some complexity to the discussion of investing and is a warning to those who plan to profit by usury. I selected the King James Version of this verse because it uses the word *usury* instead of *interest*, even though the Hebrew word being interpreted means both interest and usury.[24] By definition, usury is interest collected on loans that is charged at a higher than normal interest rate. Every state in the United States has a legal usury rate, which is the maximum that can be charged on any loan in that state. This verse shows God considers any unfair interest to be usury because, as a practical matter, it is charged to the people who least can afford it.

Also included in this verse is the issue of an "unjust gain." Unjust gain is any economic increase a person gets unfairly. We all understand some things are legal but not moral. God will not bless those who take advantage of others, and in the long run, they will lose everything. In the providence and justice of God, such wealth will be forfeited by someone who treats the poor unfairly. God blesses those who help others—"give and it shall be given unto you" (Luke 6:38).

A third verse used as investment advice is found in Proverbs 13:22:

> A good person leaves an inheritance for their children's children, but a sinner's wealth is stored up for the righteous.

To understand this verse, we need to address the background behind it. There are many verses about being good in the Old and New Testaments, and leaving an inheritance is just one attribute of that good person. In the history of the Old Testament, the children of Israel were to inherit the land of Canaan, but their fathers would not follow God's ways by being faithful to His covenants. For every blessing God promises to the just, there is a corresponding curse to those who will not follow His ways. In this verse, it is about investing, but the investing is part of being good and not part of a financial investment strategy. A good Israelite father would focus on leaving a devotion to God as an inheritance to his children and grandchildren.

So far our scriptural advice regarding investing money from the Old Testament is, as suspected, not about money or financial investing. Another New Testament verse used as good investment advice is found in 2 Corinthians 9:6:

> The point is this: whoever sows sparingly will also reap sparingly, and whoever sows bountifully will also reap bountifully.

This sounds like great investment advice; if you invest just a little, you will get just a little return, and if you invest more, your return will be more. The problem is this verse is not about investing. The first verse in 1 Corinthians is about thanking the believers in Corinth for a generous gift that they had already promised. Verse 6 is not about investing money or even about getting believers to donate more money (as this verse is also misused). It is about the willing nature of giving. No gift is welcome if it is given grudgingly, with sorrow, or under duress. God does not want gifts that have to be taken or extorted. He wants gifts that are given voluntarily from the heart.

Biblically Investing Money

For the most part, Bible verses used to traditionally support investing money are not about money or financial investing. So what is the wisdom from the Bible about investing money? To answer this question, we need to look beyond individual verses and think about the overall message of scripture. It is not about traditional investment advice. It's not about various markets, investment vehicles, timing the market, brokers, or anything related to the physical act of what you do with money. It's about what God has entrusted you with and how to be a good steward. I believe the Bible addresses investing money through four basic principles that if followed will put you on the path of being a good financial steward.

The first investing principle is *ethical investing*. Ecclesiastes 12:13 says:

> The end of the matter; all has been heard. Fear God and
> keep his commandments, for this is the whole duty of man.
> For God will bring every deed into judgment, with every
> secret thing, whether good or evil.

The investment question is what are you doing with God's gifts of money and will it be pleasing to the Lord? By the end of 2013 there were over seventy-nine thousand mutual funds worldwide, not counting the number of individual stocks, exchange-traded funds (ETFs), and other trading vehicles. With the massive number of investment options, it seems impossible to select stocks, mutual funds, or ETFs that are ethically acceptable—assuming of course we have determined a definition for ethical investments. Throwing up our hands and claiming that ethical investing is impossible is not an option. We are still tasked with being good stewards and serving the Lord. Ignorance is not an option, and we need to be concerned about what our money is used for. Regardless of the difficulty perceived in placing God's money in ethically appropriate investments, we must try. There are investment options in the marketplace that are socially and ethically sound, and that is where we are called to place our money.

The second investing principle from the Bible is *find good counsel*. For most of us, investing as a sideline or hobby is nearly impossible. The time required to sift through the ocean of information available before any decisions can be made is too daunting for a casual investor. Proverbs 15:22 advises:

> Without counsel plans fail,
> but with many advisers they succeed.

Get good recommendations on financial advisers and planners. Find more than one source for advice, and do not forget to include your spouse. Talk to other believers and businesspeople, join discussion groups, and subscribe to publications that are known for good advice. Above all, make sure those who are giving you advice know your tolerances for investing. Tolerances need to include your desire for an ethical portfolio, as well as other risk tolerances allowing you to sleep at night.

In line with getting multiple sources of advice, the third investment principle is *diversification*. King Solomon wrote:

> Invest in seven ventures, yes, in eight;
> you do not know what disaster may come upon the land.
> (Ecclesiastes 11:2)

That's an impressive statement made three thousand years ago by a man who had multiples of everything—a king who was at that time the richest man in the world. Even the Queen of Sheba was amazed by his wealth and wisdom (1 Kings 10:7). The phrase "seven ventures, yes, eight ..." is Old Testament-speak for do everything you can and then one more. As investors, we hear and read all the time to divide your wealth into several parts and not to risk it all in one place. Diversify also in your advisors, and as your investments grow, diversify them also. Diversification does not increase your return or even guarantee success, but it does reduce your risk.

A deeper biblical view of diversification makes the concept even more interesting. God alone knows the future. We, on the other hand, are only given choices. To make the most of those choices we need to make the best plans possible, use our brains, examine all our options, seek wise counsel, do the best we can, and then leave the results to God. Do not be reckless; it will only lead to disaster. Invest your money in diversified investments, accept those limited risks, and let God take care of the future.

Last, a fourth investment principle is *manage your debt*. The Bible does speak to debt and its effects on the borrower. Proverbs 22:7 says:

> The rich rule over the poor,
> and the borrower is slave to the lender.

However, Matthew 5:42 says:

> Give to the one who asks you, and do not turn away from
> the one who wants to borrow from you.

Well, should we lend money or not; should we borrow money or not? The clear teaching of the Bible is God expects His children to act righteously when lending money. Remember, our ability to produce wealth comes from God. There is nothing wrong with legitimately lending money and expecting to be repaid at a fair interest rate. Yet we need to remember the Bible's teaching on money also includes borrowing money and indebtedness. Although the Bible does not forbid borrowing money, it doesn't encourage it either. Borrowing is not God's best for His people, as debt makes one a slave to the lender. God would rather have us look to Him for our needs than rely on lenders. When we loan money to someone, we increase that person's debt load, which makes it easier for him or her to fall prey to other worldly temptations, leading the person away from God. The answer to lend or borrow is between you and God.

Spouse and Children

For me the concept of investing in your spouse and children is more important than investing with money. And for business leaders, your investment in your family may be the only sanctuary you find during the workweek. Despite how hard we try, life at the office can be trying, hectic, full of uncertainty, and represent the "world" that Jesus calls us to be wary of. Despite what our work life throws at us, we must never forget to invest in our family.

Children

One of the definitions of *investment* is to "devote (one's time, effort, or energy) to a particular undertaking with the expectation of a worthwhile result." This is an epiphany for me—think of investing not in terms of money but in terms of everything else I do. I get stacks of investment newsletters, but none of them talk about anything but money. I cannot think of a better, more enjoyable, and more self-satisfying "undertaking with the expectation of a worthwhile result" than investing in my family and my wife.

I recently read an article that started with the comment that parenting is a *high calling*. In my experience a high calling is an act or service that is noble or of the greater good for everyone.[25] I'm sure many of you have been in an airplane, at a concert, or at a family reunion where someone brings his or her children, whose behavior makes you question the call to be fruitful and multiply. It seems at the time that the parents of these imps do not have the same appreciation for a higher calling than most parents. What we need to remember during these times is all children are born with a completely self-centered outlook on life. Everything revolves around them—for a while. At some point it is the parents' job to begin to instruct them about values other than being self-centered. My guess is there are more books on how to raise children than how to run a business. Although I have not read any of these books on raising children, I have read the one manual that helps us invest in children, and that is the Bible. As with what I have been demonstrating in business advice, the Bible is complete in its advice on investing in children.

Let's start with 2 Timothy 3:15–16:

> … and how from infancy you have known the Holy Scriptures, which are able to make you wise for salvation through faith in Christ Jesus. All Scripture is God-breathed and is useful for teaching, rebuking, correcting and training in righteousness, so that the servant of God may be thoroughly equipped for every good work.

The background for this verse is Paul writing to his young friend Timothy from prison (of all places). Timothy's mother was Jewish and had taught Timothy from the Old Testament since he was a very young boy. Consequently, Timothy had a good background in the Jewish church before Paul met him and he became Paul's protégé. The primary commentary on these verses focuses on the line "All Scripture is God-breathed," which is one of the foundational verses on the inerrancy of scripture. For our purpose here, however, we are examining the part where scripture is used to teach, correct, and train. It was the scriptures that were used to teach Timothy and on which he was to remember, rely on, and live by for the rest of his life. There is no single book that has so much power as the Bible and none so efficient in moving the hearts, consciences, and intellects of humankind.

The Bible was written to teach us how to relate to God and how to relate to one another. What could be a more important tool to use in investing in a child than that? Proverbs 22:6 says:

Start children off on the way they should go,
and even when they are old they will not turn from it.

Remember that Proverbs are not promises. They are general bits of wisdom that King Solomon collected and are to be used in conjunction with other biblical sources to confirm their use and meaning. This verse is about an adolescent child's entrance into the adult world. It has been used for years to comfort parents in their anxiety, guilt, fear, and hope concerning the complexities of child-rearing. It is also encouraging to parents, who are striving to balance work, family-life issues, relationships, and schooling, that their labors to raise this child are not in vain. Children rebel, go astray, and wander off into other social worlds, yet the parents' efforts to ground the child with the Word of God will always give hope that he or she will return to what they were taught.

Another verse about investing in children is Ephesians 5:1–2:

Follow God's example, therefore, as dearly loved children
and walk in the way of love, just as Christ loved us and gave
himself up for us as a fragrant offering and sacrifice to God.

Our investment in children is not just the children we produced in union with our spouse; it is all the children we daily encounter. We, on a moment-by-moment basis, are setting examples for all the children who are continually and critically watching us. We are a living example. How we talk, what words we use, how we respond when provoked, how we listen, what our body language is, and what we put into our bodies are all recorded by the eyes of children and will be used by those children to develop their own personality. If we show love and affection for our spouse, that action will be reflected by watching children. If we display respect to disadvantaged people or those of other cultures and races, those attitudes will be reflected back. How we conduct our business dealings, work hard, honor authority, and respect money and possessions as gifts from God will all be reflected back.

The question then is what are the consistent criteria, a yardstick if you will, that we use to establish what our actions are? Deuteronomy 6:6–9 says this:

> These commandments that I give you today are to be on your hearts. Impress them on your children. Talk about them when you sit at home and when you walk along the road, when you lie down and when you get up. Tie them as symbols on your hands and bind them on your foreheads. Write them on the doorframes of your houses and on your gates.

The Bible is the true source of our knowledge of how to invest in children. Its lessons and stories are a great source of the messages we convey to children and should be used to govern all our actions.

Spouses

Although this may sound contradictory, the idea of investing in my spouse is, on one hand, completely self-serving, yet on the other hand, being completely obedient to scripture. It is self-serving to want to live a long, healthy, happy life. Being a small business owner, I gamble every day I open the doors to my business; my days are spent managing risks. These risks include making sure drivers of my vehicles have proper training and are suited for the responsibility of handling a loaded vehicle on busy streets and highways. It also includes enforcing strict quality-control measures in our design process, which limits our liability exposure. I do everything I can to limit my risks and do not need to take on new chances. So, when I learn that happily married people are healthier and live longer than unmarried or unhappily married people, my nature is to keep the odds in my favor.

For the past three to four decades, family sociologists have been contributing to the ongoing body of research that points to the physical and mental health benefits of a happy marriage. This phenomenon is generally known as the "marriage effect." Research shows marriage is the best bet for both men and women living a long and healthy life. Studies of mortality and marital status of both sexes show the unmarried have higher death rates, whether it's by accident, disease, or self-inflicted wounds. One reason married people live longer is they are more likely to enjoy better physical health. Married people are more likely to recognize symptoms, seek medical treatment, avoid risky behavior, recover quicker, and eat a healthier diet.

Contemporary studies have shown married people are less likely to get pneumonia, have surgery, develop cancer, or have heart disease. Spouses are intimately aware of each other's choices and have a vested interest in watching out for each other.

The choice is clear; investing in a marriage to make it a happy marriage is synonymous with investing in a long, happy, and healthy life. The key to how to make that investment is found in the Bible. Per scripture, marriage is ordained by God as an intimate and permanent partnership between a man and a woman in which the two become one in the whole of life. Men and women are discussed differently in scripture, and God gives them different gifts and roles. Before going into detail about what scripture says about having a happy marriage, it is important we understand what the Bible says about those gifts and roles. Although the Bible has many appropriate and beautiful scriptures about marriage and the relationship between a man and a woman, I have elected to use one that is misunderstood and because of that becomes a point of controversy. Ephesians 5:22–33 says:

> Wives, submit yourselves to your own husbands as you do to the Lord. For the husband is the head of the wife as Christ is the head of the church, his body, of which he is the Savior. Now as the church submits to Christ, so also wives should submit to their husbands in everything.

> Husbands, love your wives, just as Christ loved the church and gave himself up for her to make her holy, cleansing her by the washing with water through the word, and to present her to himself as a radiant church, without stain or wrinkle or any other blemish, but holy and blameless. In this same way, husbands ought to love their wives as their own bodies. He who loves his wife loves himself. After all, no one ever hated their own body, but they feed and care for their body, just as Christ does the church—for we are members of his body. "For this reason a man will leave his father and mother and be united to his wife, and the two will become one flesh." This is a profound mystery—but I am talking about Christ and the church. However, each

one of you also must love his wife as he loves himself, and
the wife must respect her husband.

I know this is a lot of scripture to read and focus on, but that is the point of the controversy. Many read the first seven words and stop. Men presume this to be an argument to dominate and be in charge. Women see this as a command that they be subservient to and dominated by a man. Books have been written on these few lines so I do not intend to analyze these verses, but what I do want to point out is where the misinterpretation lies and how we need to think going forward to better invest in our spouse.

For women, a marriage can only thrive when the wife defers to the husband. This deferral is between the wife and God ("as you do to the Lord" [Ephesians 5:22]). The husband is not given any responsibility to make the wife obey or defer; she must do it willingly and out of love. As the years of marriage go by, the role of who defers to whom may change, so it is imperative the relationship between the man and woman be open so they can discuss these changes. Proverbs 19:13 points out:

and a quarrelsome wife is like
the constant dripping of a leaky roof.

My defense in using this verse is also in its misunderstanding. Is the wife quarrelsome because she needs another means to communicate with her husband, or is she quarrelsome because her husband refuses to acknowledge a needed change? Quarrelsome is not a derogatory description; it is a communication mechanism to get her husband to recognize the need for change.

For men, they need to remember that they are to love their wife with an unconditional, selfless kind of love and doing so will make it easier for her to defer to his leadership. Men need to understand what it means by "just as Christ loved the church and gave himself up for her" (Ephesians 5:25). This is sacrificial love and is the perfect example of how men are to love their wives. It's not dying for your wife (although it might be); it means sacrificing things daily and doing things that are in her best interest. Just because you love your wife does not guarantee she will love you in return. Scripture uses the analogy of the church and Jesus. Jesus always loves the church (us), but sometimes those that He loves do not love Him in return. We all sin daily, and the extent of that sinning is a reflection of the depth (or lack of depth) of our love for Christ. Regardless, He just keeps loving us and we men are to keep loving our wives.

Others

I saved the most important investing topic for last: investing in others. Investing money is about how we are stewards of God's gifts and how we juggle the physical things of this world with our need to be devoted to the eternal. Investing in our children and spouses should be a "no-brainer." Our intimacy with them should allow us to mature in the faith together, just like a family should. But investing in others is quite different. The others may be employees, subconsultants, the girl at the coffee shop, a client, the man at the DMV, etc. You may not even like that person. To invest in others is the real work of the Kingdom of God, and we are called to be a participant not a spectator. Think of it this way: who is going to heaven with you? The old adage "you can't take it with you" relates to our wealth. What you can take with you are others, people you have helped along your life's journey who have become believers in Christ. Because of your actions, those others will live for eternity.

Although I could have chosen dozens of verses, for purposes here I have selected only three verses from the Bible that exemplify how we should think about investing in others. While this discussion is limited to three verses, the Bible has no shortage of appropriate verses with applications to our business world.

Deuteronomy 15:11 states:

> For there will never cease to be poor in the land. Therefore I command you, "You shall open wide your hand to your brother, to the needy and to the poor, in your land."

Moses, writing in Deuteronomy, was not the only one who said the poor will always be with us. Jesus, as he was being ministered to by Mary, also said the poor will always be with us (John 12:1–11). It is so easy for us to view the poor (if we notice them at all) as being lazy, incompetent, addicts, and outcasts. What an unfair assumption. Poor is not necessarily in terms of wealth but also of spirit. Moses said that ideally there should be no poor people in God's land, but in reality there always will be poor people. Dawn will not rise on a day that we do not have the opportunity to help someone, and it is a gift to us who have some level of material possessions and spiritual maturity to always have someone with whom to share those gifts. In fact, it should be our joy to know that there will always be an "other" who we will encounter and be able to help in some way.

For small business owners with limited resources, we need to remember that the poor will always be with us. The danger we face is to think the need is so great and our resources so small that we cannot help. We need to budget a reasonable amount to help and make sure those monies are entrusted with a group that reflects our faith and is known to be effective, efficient, and caring. When looking for new employees, we need to avoid stereotyping and look for ways we can hire the disadvantaged and give them a chance for a better life.

My second verse is in 1 John 3:17:

> But if anyone has the world's goods and sees his brother
> in need, yet closes his heart against him, how does God's
> love abide in him?

Up to this point, chapter 3 of 1 John is about contrasting the righteous with the wicked and how it is the righteous who set their hopes on God, love one another, and do not sin. The wicked, on the other hand, engage in sinful acts, and are lawless and full of hate. In verse 17, the writer of 1 John calls on believers to help other Christians back up the claim of being believers. Our work environment does not place all employees on an equal status where everyone has the same education, pay, company title, or responsibility. Verse 17 implores those with more to be compassionate with those who have less. In a work environment, it is important that we enable those with more material wealth to fraternize with those who have less. The material things we have are all gifts from God, which he owns and has only loaned to us for our stewardship. In God's eyes, we are all equal and are in the position of material wealth and power to be a servant. This allows us to invest in others around us so they too can enjoy the benefits of eternal life.

My final verse is Philippians 2:4 and contains an interesting play on words as we finish our focus on investing and getting interest from our investments.

> Do nothing from selfish ambition or conceit, but in humility count others more significant than yourselves. Let each of you look not only to his own interests, but also to the interests of others.

The apostle Paul is writing to the believers in Philippi from a Roman prison cell as he is awaiting his trial before Caesar. Paul has a strong sense of attachment to the Philippian believers since he was the one who first came to Philippi with the Gospel, and he and Silas suffered a cruel beating and a night in prison before leaving the city (Acts 16:16–40). When Paul left Philippi, these believers continued to stand with him in the defense and proclamation of the Gospel. His letter encourages his friends and urges them to stand fast.

For business owners, these verses have two significant messages. The first is humility. The opposite of humility is selfish ambition, which I think of as working for personal gain and attention at the expense of others. Most of us did not get to where we are in the business world without a fair amount of ambition. However, there were those who through their own humility and grace allowed us to succeed. Pride and ambition are part of our fallen nature that we must contend with daily in our walk with Christ. What is significant here is the included definition of humility that we "count others more significant than yourselves." This does not mean that others are better than we are and that being humble means we are the lowest of the low, a doormat, and worthless. No, it means when considering others, our act of humility is to think of them first before we consider our own situation. We are to treat them as more important, but that does not mean we are to demean our own thinking of our self-worth.

The second message is a play on the word *interest*. We are to invest in others so they may receive the grace and salvation we hope to receive one day. That investment is to grow into an increase in faith for those with whom we come in contact. That increase in faith in our investment is the return on investment (ROI), which is the salvation of those in whom we invest time and prayers. That is exactly what Paul is saying, urging us to not look "only to his own interests, but also to the interests of others." We should put our material wealth aside and focus on investing in others so we earn interest in them through their salvation. That way we will see them again in the eternal world.

Zebedee

Zebedee knew more about investing than most financial planners. He practiced every principle of investing to perfection. He invested in a good boat and reinvested some of the profits, making sure the revenue-producing assets were always in operating condition. He invested in his family. Yes, two of his sons walked off with Jesus, but isn't that the sign of a great return on his investments? His wife, Salome, was also a follower of Jesus, so his investment in her was paying off. He invested in others; he took on two young men, gave them a chance, taught them character-building lessons, and they too went with Jesus. Zebedee was alone on the bow of one of his boats, but his chest was full of pride in how well his investments were paying off.

Summary

1. It is interesting to observe that Bible verses that have specific references to money are not about money. Pardon the pun, but money referred to in the Bible is simply a common currency; it is a similar point of reference that everyone understands. Think of the parable of the talents to remain grounded in understanding that the use of money in scripture is always about something significantly important but has little to with money.

2. Biblical investment advice about money is found in ethical investing (Ecclesiastes 12:13), good counsel (Proverbs 15:22), diversification (Ecclesiastes 11:2), and managed debt (Matthew 5:42).

3. Invest in children, including your own and all those around you. You are always an example to the young, inquiring eyes that are watching you.

4. Investing in your spouse will save your life. Happy marriages yield longer, happier, and healthier lives. More importantly, however, is Ephesians 5:22–33, which says men should love their wives as Christ loved the church and women should submit to their husbands as they do the Lord.

5. Your greatest investment is in others. They are the only things you can take with you to heaven. Lean on Deuteronomy 15:11 and 1 John 3:17 to remember the importance of all the other people with whom you are in contact.

Notes

CHAPTER 8
Bureaucracy for Zebedee

Maybe it's time to just quit, thought Zebedee. He realized that, with the loss of his four helpers, it might be a good time to get out of the business and not have to hassle with government bureaucracy anymore. "I could go to work for someone else," he countered, "but even that would not eliminate all the taxes I have to pay."

Zebedee's business world was not devoid of bureaucracy. Clearly, he did not have to stick government-mandated identifying numbers on the bow of his boats, wait in line for a business license, or have the health department inspector show up at his facilities. But Zebedee did have plenty of taxes to pay. The Roman Empire was an expensive venture to run, and it transferred as much of that cost as possible to its outlying providences. The Romans used an appropriate term I hope does not show up in the twenty-first century: *tax farmers.* Harvesting taxes is an accurate picture of the prevailing attitude Zebedee encountered on a regular basis. Zebedee's business paid income tax, import/export tax, crop tax, sales tax, and property tax. He also had to pay a poll tax collected as he carried his fish from the Sea of Galilee to market. And while there was a set tax rate, the process of collecting taxes was outsourced so he paid the rate the collector extorted. Zebedee really disliked bureaucracy; some things haven't changed in two thousand years.

I delayed diving into writing this chapter because I could not imagine where it would lead. My business world is built around bureaucracy.

Everything we do in my small engineering company involves some type of government entity. Our request to zone land for development goes before a nonelected planning and zoning commission. Our public infrastructure is designed to meet government-dictated guidelines. Much of our work is reviewed and approved by groups of somewhat nameless governmental employees. Property surveys that originated one hundred years ago must now meet twenty-first-century accuracy. We deal with floodplains that seem to have little to do with the contours of the ground. And we find ourselves involved in projects that include higher education, and federal, state, county, and city governments—all at one time. To say I'm cautious of bureaucracy is an understatement. But my caution is based on experience and not what the Bible instructs.

So my question to examine here is what does the Bible say about bureaucracy, and how should we react to our existing bureaucracy if we want to be true to the teachings of the Gospel? What is a Christian response to the edicts imposed by our government?

To accomplish this task, we will start with the Old Testament to see what the history of the Israelite nation can teach us. We will look at the history of the judges and a parable found in the book of Judges that explains why God chose to use judges and not kings. We will shift to the story of how the Israelites were given a king through a judge named Samuel and about their greatest king ever, King David. From the New Testament, we will look at Jesus's attitude toward bureaucracy and the apostles' attitude toward bureaucracy. Finally, we will read what the Bible says about civil disobedience.

History of the Judges

My journey to see what the Bible offers about bureaucracy began with a pleasant surprise in the form of some specific advice. I started researching all the way back in time to Moses, when he rescued the Israelites from the oppressive Egyptians. While the Israelites wandered in the wilderness for forty years, Moses maintained contact with God, who gave him the first five books of the Bible as a permanent Word of God for His people, the Israelites, to live by. Found in one of these books was a forewarning about creating a government:

When you enter the land the Lord your God is giving you and have taken possession of it and settled in it, and you say, "Let us set a king over us like all the nations around us," be sure to appoint over you a king the Lord your God chooses. He must be from among your fellow Israelites. Do not place a foreigner over you, one who is not an Israelite. The king, moreover, must not acquire great numbers of horses for himself or make the people return to Egypt to get more of them, for the Lord has told you, "You are not to go back that way again." He must not take many wives, or his heart will be led astray. He must not accumulate large amounts of silver and gold.

When he takes the throne of his kingdom, he is to write for himself on a scroll a copy of this law, taken from that of the Levitical priests. It is to be with him, and he is to read it all the days of his life so that he may learn to revere the Lord his God and follow carefully all the words of this law and these decrees and not consider himself better than his fellow Israelites and turn from the law to the right or to the left. Then he and his descendants will reign a long time over his kingdom in Israel. (Deuteronomy 17:14–20)

This prophetic advice from God proves to be the perfect instruction on how to avoid the destructive tendencies of government, and it is applicable even today if we had the courage to follow it.

Unfortunately, the Israelites did not follow this advice. Once the Israelites completed their punishment of wandering in the wilderness and conquered Canaan (as found in the book of Joshua), they settled down in individual tribal groups to inhabit the land promised by God. Joshua, their first leader, was a strong, God-fearing man. After his passing, God instituted a government for the Israelites whereby they would consider God their King and have a series of God-appointed *judges* to lead them. Each tribe had a smaller system of community and government, but God governed all of Israel. This is a theocratic form of government. Judges were men and women appointed by God to deliver and maintain order among the Israelites. These judges were spiritual leaders, military leaders, priests, prophets, law judges, and governors who interpreted God's law as it applied to individual situations. They were also people with their own characteristics and defects. Perhaps you are familiar with the story of Samson, who, with superhuman strength, fought the Philistines, but he was defeated when a seductress named Delilah cut off his long hair, which happened to be the source of his strength. Sampson was a judge as found in Judges chapters 13–16.

The Israelites' government was the least obtrusive, least costly method possible. If a neighboring nation wanted a war, the judge would go to each tribe and generate an army to fight the war. As recorded in Judges 21:25, "In those days Israel had no king; everyone did as they saw fit." That is both the beauty and problem with this form of government. When the Israelites relied on God for answers, they were blessed—they won battles, prospered in the land, and life was good.

> Yet they would not listen to their judges but prostituted themselves to other gods and worshipped them. They quickly turned from the ways of their ancestors, who had been obedient to the Lord's commands. (Judges 2:17)

The Israelites had a hard time adhering to the commands of God, even though they had the Ten Commandments, which were not all that strenuous to live by. The four-hundred-year period found throughout the book of Judges was a period of blunders, failure, sin, and forgetfulness. God's people would drift away from His commands; God would send a neighboring nation to punish His people; He would deliver a judge, and the judge would save them; the people would be faithful for a short time until they resorted back to their old ways; and the cycle would start over again. Each generation would forget the lessons learned from the previous generation. Even though God gave His people advice about the dangers of government and instructed them in the best form of government, they rebelled and continuously attempted to follow their own ways.

The Parable of the Trees

In the middle of the period of the Judges, there was a judge named Gideon, who was raised by God. Gideon was from a pagan home, from the weakest clan, of the smallest family, of the weakest tribe in all Israel. Despite that, he was a great and popular judge for the Israelites (chapters 6–9). An angel of the Lord came to Gideon and brought him up to lead the Israelites to defeat the mighty Midianites. After the victory, the Israelites wanted to make him king regardless of the commands from God. Gideon voiced his objections by saying, "I will not rule over you, nor will my son rule over you. The Lord will rule over you" (Judges 8:23). Technically, Gideon followed what he said; he did not accept being king. He did, however, command everyone to give him a portion of the plunder from the war as if he were king. So instead of being king, he became rich enough to live like a king without the worries of a king.

Unlike most other judges and servants of God, Gideon failed to give any credit for his success as a judge to God, so the Israelites were again in trouble. First, the Israelites stepped outside of the directions from God and attempted to make Gideon king. Second, Gideon failed to give proper credit. Finally, Gideon became a self-serving idolater spiraling down into rebellion against God. Despite God's commands, Gideon took on many wives who bore seventy sons. Although Near Eastern kings took on many wives to demonstrate their power and success, God forbade it for the Israelites. To compound the problem, one of his wives was a Canaanite woman and not an Israelite, which was also forbidden.

So our lesson begins after Gideon's death. One of Gideon's sons is a man named Abimelech, which ironically means "my father is a king." He is the son of the controversial Canaanite wife. Instead of Abimelech's father being a king (which he was not), Abimelech aspires to be the first Israelite king. To make this happen, he goes to his mother's Canaanite family and asks, "Which is better for you: to have all seventy of Jerub-Baal's [Gideon's] sons rule over you, or just one man? Remember, I am your flesh and blood" (Judges 9:2). With his mother's family's consent, Abimelech and his thug friends attempt to kill the other sixty-nine sons of Gideon. But one son, Jotham, escapes.

Shortly after Abimelech's bogus coronation, Jotham, who is running for his life, gets an opportunity to speak to the Israelites. From a secure hiding place, he relates a parable:

> He climbed up on the top of Mount Gerizim and shouted to them, "Listen to me, citizens of Shechem, so that God may listen to you. One day the trees went out to anoint a king for themselves. They said to the olive tree, 'Be our king.'
>
> "But the olive tree answered, 'Should I give up my oil, by which both gods and humans are honored, to hold sway over the trees?'
>
> "Next, the trees said to the fig tree, 'Come and be our king.'
>
> "But the fig tree replied, 'Should I give up my fruit, so good and sweet, to hold sway over the trees?'
>
> "Then the trees said to the vine, 'Come and be our king.'
>
> "But the vine answered, 'Should I give up my wine, which cheers both gods and humans, to hold sway over the trees?'
>
> "Finally all the trees said to the thornbush, 'Come and be our king.'
>
> "The thornbush said to the trees, 'If you really want to anoint me king over you, come and take refuge in my shade; but if not, then let fire come out of the thornbush and consume the cedars of Lebanon!'" (Judges 9:7–15)

This parable is powerful and enlightening from three perspectives. The first is in managing a private business. My own experience in the design world has revealed numerous occasions where a star designer, for example, is promoted to a management position as an act of respect and admiration for the designer's skill and commitment to the profession. This star designer represents the *fig tree* and is taken from what he or she does best and enjoys, and placed in a role that industry says is a career-growth move. But the company needs to consider that it may be losing this designer's (*fig tree's*) valuable skill and gaining an executive who is not trained for the new job. Neither result is beneficial for the company. On the other hand, you could have a designer who is mediocre at his or her job. In this example, the designer represents the *thornbush*. When the *thornbush* is promoted to make room for more competent designers, the company gets an executive who is not only a mediocre designer but also not trained for the new position. The result is frequently an inept manager who micromanages and mismanages at every opportunity.

The second perspective is the governmental bureaucratic world. My personal experience reveals such a world full of employees who worry more about the nuances of their job than the intent of the position they hold. Profits drive many, if not all, decisions made in the private business world. They allow for great places to work, competitive salaries, quality yet cost-conscious products, investment opportunities in future ventures, and the needed drive to risk going into business in the first place. Marketplace competition keeps profits at a reasonable level. When profits are not part of the business's decision process, there is no single element that substitutes for the results caused by profits. Government agencies do not have to contend with profits so they frequently lose the drive to worry about customer service, product quality, future investments, etc. Hence, government bureaucracy seems to be an occupation that accumulates more than its fair share of thornbushes.

The third and final perspective is politics. Although I follow politics closely, I'm most familiar with local politics from the perspective of attempting to get good people to run for local offices. Men and women who understand financial management, have great communication skills, use wit and wisdom to lead people, and have empathy for their community are more like the *olive tree, fig tree,* and *vine*. People of this caliber are always busy with their own lives and engaged in their own enterprises, whether it is a business, family, a community organization, or other passions. They understand getting involved in politics will detract from their main interests and will weigh that detraction before becoming involved in any political endeavor. As for the thornbush, I believe in the advice to be wary of a person whose main interest is only to get into politics.

From a business perspective, consider who and why employees are being promoted. Are they olive trees, fig trees, and vines? And if so, is the promotion good for the overall business? Or are they thornbushes? If so, should they be promoted or replaced?

Samuel

The Israelites narrowly avoided having Abimelech become their king—a woman dropped a millstone on his head and killed him (Judges 9:53), ending his political career. Unfortunately, the issue of a king arose once again several hundred years later. All Gentile nations surrounding the Israelites had kings, and the temptation to be like their neighbors was too great. Regardless that God had foretold this would happen, as we saw with the text from Deuteronomy, it broke His heart. What His people were saying was "we do not want to rely on a godly king anymore; we want an earthly, human king on whom we can place our hearts and trust."

At this time came the greatest judge delivered by God. His name was Samuel, and he was more than a judge; he was also a priest and a prophet. But that did not stop two things from happening. First, he grew old, not infirm by any stretch, but old enough that one starts to think of a succession plan and retirement. Second, despite Samuel being a man of God with integrity, righteousness, faith, and love, his sons did not inherit those qualities. Samuel appointed his sons judges, but they failed to earn the respect of the people. In fact, they were known to have taken bribes and pervert justice. We see in 1 Samuel 8:4–5:

> So all the elders of Israel gathered together and came to Samuel at Ramah. They said to him, "You are old, and your sons do not follow your ways; now appoint a king to lead us, such as all the other nations have."

From reading the entire story we know Samuel was not that old or his sons that bad. The elders were just looking for an excuse to demand their one God-appointed judge to appoint them a king. Although Samuel was not pleased with the actions of the elders (1 Samuel 8:6), he took the request to God in prayer. God was also none too pleased, but He instructed Samuel to acquiesce and gave Samuel the following directions to convey to the Israelites:

> So Samuel told all the words of the Lord to the people who were asking for a king from him. He said, "These will be the ways of the king who will reign over you: he will take your sons and appoint them to his chariots and to be his horsemen and to run before his chariots. And he will appoint for himself commanders of thousands and commanders of fifties, and some to plow his ground and to reap his harvest, and to make his implements of war and the equipment of his chariots. He will take your daughters to be perfumers and cooks and bakers. He will take the best of your fields and vineyards and olive orchards and give them to his servants. He will take the tenth of your grain and of your vineyards and give it to his officers and to his servants. He will take your male servants and female servants and the best of your young men and your donkeys, and put them to his work. He will take the tenth of your flocks, and you shall be his slaves. And in that day you will cry out because of your king, whom you have chosen for yourselves, but the Lord will not answer you in that day." (1 Samuel 8:10–18)

This sounds exactly like the kind of government we deal with today. Although they have not made chariots for a while, governments continue to take our money in the form of taxes and fees and use that money however they see fit. We are better off than many other government-led countries in that we have a representative form of government, but the news of what our tax dollars are spent on continues to be shocking.

What God spelled out in detail to the Israelites was the cost to have a *king* form of government versus a *judges* form of government. These costs were both monetary increases and losses of freedom. The tax increase from a judges form of government, which is inexpensive with no capitol building, standing army, or bureaucracy, to a king form of government was immense. Freedoms were lost by requiring family members to spend time in government service. The Israelites also lost their freedom to do "what is right in the eyes of God" (Judges 21:25).

> But the people refused to listen to Samuel. "No!" they said. "We want a king over us. Then we will be like all the other nations, with a king to lead us and to go out before us and fight our battles." When Samuel heard all that the people said, he repeated it before the Lord. The Lord answered, "Listen to them and give them a king." (1 Samuel 8:19–22)

One message here, which will become more obvious as we get deeper into Israelite history, is to be careful what you ask for. God told the elders exactly what they would get with a king, and that is exactly what they got. The Israelites were not thinking about the form of government they needed or wanted; they just wanted what all the surrounding godless nations had: a government whose authority is given by man and ruled by man.

King Saul, King David

God knew the Israelites would eventually demand a king. The temptation to be like the surrounding nations was too great to overcome. Don't we see that as well in both our personal and business lives? We want what our neighbors have, drive what our friends drive, and buy what our favorite celebrities sell on television. In business, we buy the technology our competitors have, employees demand the benefits our industry suggests, and we chase the products that trade magazines promote. But God had a plan for the Israelites. Neighboring nations were ruled by kings who were men driven by human desires. God would have Samuel anoint a king who would be driven by godly desires. God's laws would drive the principles on which the Israelite government was based.

Thus far we have seen that God is not particularly fond of bureaucracies. In the days of Samuel, all the Israelites' neighboring nations were pagan nations that worshipped many gods and practiced rather bizarre and disgusting rituals, such as infanticide. God's command for His people was to set them apart, that they might be different from the rest of the known world. He wanted to be the only God they worshipped (known as monotheism), and through Moses, He had given the Israelites a series of laws they were to follow. His method of governance was simple: rely and trust in Him and follow His simple and straightforward series of laws as summarized in the Ten Commandments. To ask for a king differed in many ways from God's plan as given to Moses. First, it made His people like the surrounding nations and not set apart. Second, His people wanted to rely on a human king and not on God. His people wanted a larger-than-life man who would sit on his throne and make all the day-to-day decisions required to run a small nation. With this kind of king, the Israelites would not have to worry about making any decisions. Life would be good, or so they thought. Still, this was not unanticipated by God. Remember the Deuteronomy verse that says:

> Be sure to appoint over you a king the Lord your God chooses. He must be from among your fellow Israelites. Do not place a foreigner over you, one who is not an Israelite. The king, moreover, must not acquire great numbers of horses for himself or make the people return to Egypt to get more of them, for the Lord has told you, "You are not to go back that way again." He must not take many wives, or his heart will be led astray. He must not accumulate large amounts of silver and gold. (17:15–17)

So God set the stage for Samuel to meet a man named Saul. In typical God fashion, He arranged for Saul to lose his donkeys, and while looking for them, Saul walked up to a stranger and asked if he had seen his donkeys (this is why you need to read the Bible; these stories are entertaining, educational, comical, true to life, and reflect the true nature of our God). That man, who happened to be the judge and prophet Samuel, replied, "Don't worry about your father's three donkeys, and oh, by the way, let me anoint you as king of Israel." Well, there was a little more to the story than that (see 1 Samuel 9). Saul was a big, strapping guy, good looking, bright, and articulate. He was also known as a moral and ethical man. As prophesied, God selected Saul, and Saul was to rule as God wanted him to rule. Saul was a good king for a while. He won battles, he won the affection of the Israelites, and he listened to Samuel, who told him what God wanted him to do. But after a time, the temptations of being king grew on Saul and he lost his humility. He began to think the Israelites' successes were his and that he no longer needed God's direction.

The breaking point came one day as he was waiting for Samuel to arrive to make the appropriate altar sacrifices to God before Saul could take his army into battle. Saul became impatient and proceeded to make the altar sacrifices himself (1 Samuel 14:8–14). Although this sounds innocent enough, to God it was a major faux pas. Saul's lack of humility continued to haunt him, and his neglect for doing exactly what the Lord asked of him continued to grow. Finally, Saul and his men took the livestock from the Amalekites as a prize for defeating them in battle, regardless of God's command to take no booty, and God had had enough. He said, "I regret that I have made Saul king, because he has turned away from me and has not carried out my instructions" (1 Samuel 15:11). From that day on, God was going to select a new king, and through Samuel, Saul knew of this decision.

Once again God sent Samuel out on a mission to find the new king whom God had preselected. Samuel was told to go to Bethlehem, to the house of Jesse. One of his sons was to be king. Saul met all Jesse's sons, but none of them caused God to tell Samuel that this was the one. Samuel was frustrated until he discovered the youngest son still in the fields tending to the sheep. David was this young man's name and ultimately became the greatest Israelite king ever. David's account in the Old Testament is a great story about historic events, wisdom, sacrifices, irony, leadership, and humility. Samuel anointed David as the new king while he was yet a boy. Anointing a person king only indicated that God said he would be king, but he was not king until the Israelites picked him as king. At this point, David was the anointed king and Saul was the ruling king, but Saul did not know of David's anointment. Through God's plan, King Saul employed David to play music, one of his many talents (1 Samuel 16:23). It was during this time that David had the opportunity to demonstrate his faith in God by being allowed to defeat the Philistine Goliath in battle (1 Samuel 17). As time went on, David became more important to Saul. 1 Samuel 18:5 says, "Whatever mission Saul sent him on, David was so successful that Saul gave him a high rank in the army. This pleased all the troops and Saul's officers as well."

At first David's successes were good for King Saul. But as time evolved, King Saul became jealous. Eventually David and Saul had a falling out, and David had to run and hide in fear of his life. King Saul became so jealous of David, he sent his armies out to find and kill David. After months of running, hiding, and fighting, David found an opportunity to quietly and quickly kill King Saul and end all his troubles. But instead …

> He said to his men, "May the Lord not let me put out my
> hand against my leader, for he is the Lord's chosen one" (1
> Samuel 18:5)

David did not kill Saul.

After all this narrative about David, Saul, and Samuel, let's discuss three lessons that are revealed for the first time in the Bible about government and bureaucracy. First, Saul was a great king until he distanced himself from what made him king and what gave him the ability to justly rule. He was humble in the beginning and relied on God and God's direction through Samuel. It was only when he began to consider himself above everyone else that he lost his ability to rule fairly. In our world today, this transition from humility to pride and conceit destroys our leaders' ability to govern fairly and efficiently. Many problems of governing begin when we lose sight of the real purpose given to us by the people.

Second, David knew he was to be king. He was in no hurry to assume that role and, in fact, spent time preparing himself in the service of the sitting king to be ready when his time came. Too many government officials, whether elected, appointed, or employed, are not prepared for all the aspects of their job. Many elected officials are not prepared for the time required to do a good job, do not possess the knowledge required to understand their job, or are unprepared for the public reaction from making hard decisions.

Third, David showed total respect for King Saul. It didn't matter that the king was trying to kill him; Saul was the king, and by virtue of that office, David was bound to display complete respect for Saul. God put Saul in that position, and the same is true for everyone in a position of governmental authority today.

In the beginning, God advised the Israelites to completely rely on Him for their governing. In the end, against God's recommendations, they developed a kingly form of government that, when ruled by a godly king like David, could work. But to work, the king needed to remain humble, the king-in-waiting needed to be educated in all aspects of the job, and the people needed to respect and honor that king regardless.

Jesus and Bureaucracy

What we have seen so far is not that God wants smaller governments and less bureaucracy; He wants us, as His people, to rely and trust in Him to provide. This is clear from this Deuteronomy text:

> When he takes the throne of his kingdom, he is to write for himself on a scroll a copy of this law, taken from that of the Levitical priests. It is to be with him, and he is to read it all the days of his life so that he may learn to revere the Lord his God and follow carefully all the words of this law and these decrees and not consider himself better than his fellow Israelites and turn from the law to the right or to the left. Then he and his descendants will reign a long time over his kingdom in Israel. (17:18–20)

The Gospels reveal Jesus had two distinct encounters with bureaucracy that we can learn from. One encounter (actually one three-year encounter) was with the Pharisees and the second was with Caesar.

For many Christians, the Old Testament ends with Nehemiah rebuilding the temple wall in Jerusalem. Several minor prophets, such as Haggai and Zechariah, were still communicating between God and the Jewish people, but for the most part the Bible was silent for about four hundred years until Christ was born and the story of the New Testament was written in real time. During this intervening four-hundred-year period, the Jewish people worked to recover their faith in God and to live according to the Bible. The Bible for the Jewish people is generally what we know as the Old Testament, which is the Torah (the law), the prophets, and the writings. To rule themselves, the Jewish people developed their own bureaucratic system. In first-century Jerusalem, the Jewish people were governed by the Sanhedrin, a body of seventy elected Jews. The Jews who participated in this governance were either a Sadducee or a Pharisee. The Sadducees were the wealthy elite who wanted and needed to maintain peaceful relations with the occupying Roman government. They were for the most part believers in the written word of God. The Pharisees were upper-working-class men who believed in strict interpretation of the written word and any oral traditions that may have been passed down over the centuries back to the time of Moses.

By Jesus's time, Jerusalem was completely ensconced in a bureaucracy typical of what we see today. You do not have to visit with many of your neighbors to hear stories of bureaucracy run amok. We have all read of $3,000 coffee makers in the Department of Defense, unanswered suicide hotlines in Veteran Affairs, and greenhouse-gas regulations that will have no measurable effect on our environment. In first-century Judea, the bureaucratic extravagance was similar, but they were about the laws God had given the Jewish people in the first five books of the Bible (Genesis, Exodus, Leviticus, Numbers, and Deuteronomy—the Torah). One of many examples is in Matthew 12:1–8.

> At that time Jesus went through the grainfields on the Sabbath. His disciples were hungry, and they began to pluck heads of grain and to eat. But when the Pharisees saw it, they said to him, "Look, your disciples are doing what is not lawful to do on the Sabbath." He said to them, "Have you not read what David did when he was hungry, and those who were with him: how he entered the house of God and ate the bread of the Presence, which it was not lawful for him to eat nor for those who were with him, but only for the priests? Or have you not read in the Law how on the Sabbath the priests in the temple profane the Sabbath and are guiltless? I tell you, something greater than the temple is here. And if you had known what this means, 'I desire mercy, and not sacrifice,' you would not have condemned the guiltless. For the Son of Man is lord of the Sabbath."

In referring to the comment, "Look, your disciples are doing what is not lawful to do on the Sabbath" (Matthew 12:2), the Pharisees thought they were referring to the fourth commandment of the Ten Commandments, which says:

> Remember the Sabbath day, to keep it holy. Six days you shall labor, and do all your work, but the seventh day is a Sabbath to the Lord your God. On it you shall not do any work, you, or your son, or your daughter, your male servant, or your female servant, or your livestock, or the sojourner who is within your gates. For in six days the Lord made heaven and earth, the sea, and all that is in them, and rested on the seventh day. Therefore the Lord blessed the Sabbath day and made it holy. (Exodus 20:8–11)

But give the Pharisees some credit; their intent was to help their fellow Jews keep the Sabbath holy. Nowhere, however, is there a reference that insinuates that plucking grain from the heads of wheat and eating it is a violation of the fourth commandment. Jesus's disciples were not breaking any other known laws. In early Judea it was permissible to go through a man's field, pick his produce, and eat it as long as you did not carry the produce away (Deuteronomy 23:24). Likewise, you could pluck heads of grain with your hands, but you could not bring in harvesting equipment (Deuteronomy 23:25). Additionally, farmers were prohibited from harvesting their entire fields so the needy could have access to their produce (see the story of Ruth).

What the Pharisees were referring to was their own extrapolation of God's laws. The Pharisees believed the oral traditions passed down over the centuries were equal to the written Bible. Some of these oral traditions bordered on ridiculous. For example, you could only eat an egg that was laid on the Sabbath if you killed the chicken for Sabbath-breaking (working by laying an egg on the Sabbath). You could spit on a rock, but you could not spit on the ground because that made mud and mud was mortar and making mortar was work, which could not be done on the Sabbath. It is amazing how this same ability to take well-intentioned laws and pervert them through intent or imagination into ridiculousness has existed for over two thousand years. We make the interpretation of the law more important than the law. As we move forward, we need to always be mindful of the difference between the laws of men, such as the Pharisees' interpretations, and the laws of God.

Jesus's response was perfect. He referred the Pharisees back to their own laws. The story Jesus was referring to was about the soon-to-be King David. While he was fleeing from King Saul, David entered the temple and ate the holy bread on the altar (1 Samuel 21:1–6). If violating that law by David was acceptable to God, why wasn't His disciples' eating handpicked grain because they were hungry also acceptable? Jesus put the Pharisees' own question back on them. Of course, from a theological standpoint, Jesus was pointing out the Pharisees' were justifying keeping the Sabbath holy as a means of earning righteousness instead of receiving it as a gift of grace from God. Consequently, Jesus said, "And if you had known what this means, 'I desire mercy, and not sacrifice,' you would not have condemned the guiltless" (Matthew 12:7).

It would be a mistake to assume all the Pharisees were like the ones recorded encountering Jesus, but those He did encounter he referred to as "fools" (Matthew 23:17), "hypocrites" (Matthew 23:23, 25, 27, 29), and "blind guides" (Matthew 23:16). For the most part, it was not the Pharisees whom Jesus became irritated with; it was their zeal to keep the law. Our application should be no different. We should not be angry with individual bureaucrats but be angry at their enthusiasm, which they apply to following their interpretation of the law and not the spirit of the law.

Jesus's second interaction with bureaucracy was with Caesar—well, not with Caesar himself but with his image on a coin. I suppose some countries today allow the man or woman in power to place his or her image on their currency, but for the most part, the developed world avoids this act of vanity. Two thousand years ago, however, it was commonplace. During Jesus's time, the ruler of the Roman Empire was Tiberius Caesar, who claimed to rule the entire world, politically and spiritually. Having his face on the coin was synonymous with being worshipped as an idol, and this violated the first and second commandments for the Jews. Since Tiberius Caesar was not popular with the Jewish citizenry—and neither was the idea of paying taxes (some things never change)—Jesus's interaction had multiple meanings.

Jesus's encounter with the image of Caesar is in Mark 12:13–17.

> And they sent to him some of the Pharisees and some of the Herodians, to trap him in his talk. And they came and said to him, "Teacher, we know that you are true and do

not care about anyone's opinion. For you are not swayed by appearances, but truly teach the way of God. Is it lawful to pay taxes to Caesar, or not? Should we pay them, or should we not?" But, knowing their hypocrisy, he said to them, "Why put me to the test? Bring me a denarius and let me look at it." And they brought one. And he said to them, "Whose likeness and inscription is this?" They said to him, "Caesar's." Jesus said to them, "Render to Caesar the things that are Caesar's, and to God the things that are God's." And they marveled at him.

Earlier I mentioned the need to be cognizant of the difference between the laws of God and man-instituted laws. In the previous section with the grains of wheat, the Pharisees were trying to trap Jesus in their own variations of God's laws. Jesus stuck with the laws of God and had no part in the man-made interpretations of those same laws. The circumstances in Mark 12:13–17 are also about man-instituted laws. Jerusalem had been under Roman occupation for about thirty years. Being under Roman occupation provided protection by the massive Roman armies, access to the excellent (at least in their day) road networks, and access to an extensive commercial network to buy and sell goods. Those benefits all required money, which was raised in the form of taxes—probably as much as 40 percent on the residences of Jerusalem.

A key word in the verse is *render* (Mark 12:17). It is the Greek verb *apodidomi*, which means to meet a contractual obligation, to pay out, or to fulfill.[26] The Roman government issued the denarius; it had Caesar's image on it, and so it belonged to Caesar. To "[r]ender to Caesar the things that are Caesar's" is to give him back his own money, which has his image stamped on it. Following the same logic, to render to God the things that are God's means everything. Literally everything. God owns it all; He is our Creator and our Provider. God provided everything we have—our health, our job or business, our family, our relationships, our happiness, and like it or not, our government. Jesus is saying that God put Caesar in the role of governing the Jews, and even if Caesar thinks the coin with his image on it belongs to him, it actually belongs to God. Giving to Caesar is giving to God because it's all God's to start with. God is asking us to understand that governments are all part of His plan. It is this same understanding that everything is part of God's plan that leads us into the apostles' interpretation of God's intent.

The Apostles and Bureaucracy

For me, this is the hard part of understanding what the Gospels say about bureaucracy. Let me paint what the setting was like in first-century Judea. The date was early AD 57, and Nero was on the throne of the Roman Empire. He had not gone off the deep end yet, so Christians and Jews had not yet experienced the depth of his ultimate depravity. Don't misunderstand, things were not good for Christians and Jews at that time, but they would get worse. The previous emperor was Claudius, and he had evicted all Christians and Jews from Rome in AD 49. The Christians, whom the apostle Paul was writing to in the book of Romans, were slowly making their way back into Rome. They were still part of the Jewish community, but not really since they were a mixture of Jews converted to Christianity (although it was not called that yet) and Gentiles. The local government was just beginning to persecute Christians by arresting some on fictitious charges and using them in the gladiator games as food for the lions or for entertainment by being burned at the stake. The apostle Peter penned his epistle 1 Peter about AD 62–64, which coincides with the emperor Nero's persecution of Christians. Both Peter and Paul suffered serious persecution (as if there is nonserious persecution) during this time, and they both died at the hands of the Roman government. The reason this background is significant is because both Peter and Paul wrote in their epistles about how to react to authorities, and as amazing as it seems, they did not make the kinds of recommendations you would assume coming from a persecuted person.

The apostle Paul's advice is in Romans 13:1–7:

> Let every person be subject to the governing authorities. For there is no authority except from God, and those that exist have been instituted by God. Therefore whoever resists the authorities resists what God has appointed, and those who resist will incur judgment. For rulers are not a terror to good conduct, but to bad. Would you have

no fear of the one who is in authority? Then do what is good, and you will receive his approval, for he is God's servant for your good. But if you do wrong, be afraid, for he does not bear the sword in vain. For he is the servant of God, an avenger who carries out God's wrath on the wrongdoer. Therefore one must be in subjection, not only to avoid God's wrath but also for the sake of conscience. For because of this you also pay taxes, for the authorities are ministers of God, attending to this very thing. Pay to all what is owed to them: taxes to whom taxes are owed, revenue to whom revenue is owed, respect to whom respect is owed, honor to whom honor is owed.

With no hesitation, the man who lived a life of persecution by the Roman government said, "Let every person be subject to the governing authorities" (Romans 13:1). Is Paul saying that resisting the government is synonymous with defying God, that Nero is not the terror we thought he was, and we must be subject to the government to avoid God's wrath? Wow! Here is a guy whose friends were mauled by lions to entertain the Romans. He knew people who were tiki torches for Nero's parties. Yet, we see throughout the Bible, the authors never just gave advice, they always lived and experienced the advice they were giving. We get irritated when we get hit with a 0.40 percent tax on a material we use in our business, or our water bill goes up two cents per thousand gallons, or our employment tax increases, and we are ready to go to the governor's mansion and protest. Yet, Paul, who was on the verge of being a lion's lunch, calmly advised us to be subject to our government.

To make sense of all this we must first go back to the beginning of the chapter and remember Deuteronomy and God's recommendation on how a king should rule and how God warned His people what the future ruling entity would take from His people (and from everyone else). Next we saw how Samuel listened to God in instituting a kingly form of government for the Israelites. Then we saw how King Saul failed and how soon-to-be King David continued to honor the sitting king despite being chased into hiding. Finally, Jesus said to give to Caesar what is Caesar's, and to God what is God's. The theme throughout the Bible is that all governance is given by God for His purpose and intent.

Our government's authority is given by God. Daniel 2:21 says, "He removes kings and sets up kings," and Daniel 4:32 says, "The Most High rules the kingdom of men and gives it to whom he will." In John 19:10, Jesus answers Pilate as he was threatening to crucify Him, "You would have no authority over me at all unless it had been given you from above." Paul writes in Romans 13:1, "For there is no authority except from God, and those that exist have been instituted by God." Once we come to grips with the concept that even our government and all its departments, agencies, levels, bureaus, prefects, commonwealths, etc. are authorized by God, the remainder of Romans 13:1–7 begins to make sense. God would understand, given the sinful nature of humans, that the alternative to no government would be anarchy, which would be worse than having a government full of imperfect, fail-able people.

Peter's variation on this theme is consistent:

> Be subject for the Lord's sake to every human institution, whether it be to the emperor as supreme, or to governors as sent by him to punish those who do evil and to praise those who do good. For this is the will of God, that by doing good you should put to silence the ignorance of foolish people. Live as people who are free, not using your freedom as a cover-up for evil, but living as servants of God. Honor everyone. Love the brotherhood. Fear God. Honor the emperor. (1 Peter 2:13–17)

Like Paul, Peter understands we are all under some form of authority. The takeaway from this chapter is for business leaders to fully understand that all our bureaucratic leaders are authorized by God, and knowing the long history behind this belief should make accepting this understanding easier. It is hard to think that a leader who promotes laws we see as unbiblical is put in place by God. But our response is given to us from the Word of God. David respected Saul, Jesus said to render to Caesar what is Caesar's, and Paul said to be subject to the governing authorities. The action step from this chapter is to manage your business in the best way possible and to follow the laws of the land as adopted by our elected government.

Civil Disobedience

Most of us have a boss, supervisor, foreman, superior, or commander. Even if you are president and CEO, you report to a board. If you are the chairman, you have the SEC, IRS, and Labor Commission, to name a few, that you must answer to. The president has Congress to work with and ultimately the voters to answer to. And we all answer to God.

But what if what we are asked to obey is not right? For all the stories of obeying our governing authority found in the Bible, there are just as many that show we are not to obey our governing authority. Moses survived because his mother disobeyed Pharaoh and hid him (Exodus 1). Daniel disobeyed the Babylonian king and was thrown into the lion's den, only to be saved by God as an example of His boundless power (Daniel 6). The same was true of Daniel's three friends, Shadrach, Meshach, and Abednego, who were thrown into the burning furnace because they would not bow to a golden idol but were saved by God (Daniel 3). Peter and John were commanded to stop preaching but continued after being imprisoned (Acts 4 and 5).

These acts of civil disobedience are consistent with the directives from the Bible about obeying our government authorities. Wherever and whenever possible, we should work nonviolently to change laws that are unbiblical and in contrast to our faith. However, we are to disobey laws that are clearly in violation of the laws of God and the teachings of Jesus. And in doing so, we should always be willing to accept the penalty as imposed by the laws of man. We should never forget we have the right as members of Christ's family and as citizens of our country to work to elect people who will help ensure that the actions of our government are consistent with the Bible.

Zebedee

Fishing was hard work. It payed well enough to make a living but not much more. Zebedee made enough income to be a leader in the synagogue, but he was still in the working class—and proud of it. He was thankful God placed in his heart the desire to work with his hands. He had good health and the self-respect of paying his own way. He payed plenty of taxes and was pleased about some of them. He had a good road to take the fish to market, he lived in a crime-free area, and others made enough money to buy his fish. Maybe if Jesus could get some changes made in his local government, life might be even better.

Summary

1. The parable of the trees teaches us about the olive tree, fig tree, vine, and thornbush. Are the people you place in a position of responsibility an olive tree, fig tree, and vine, or are they a thornbush? Be wary of those who want to be in politics.

2. Because all the neighbors had a king, God knew the Israelites would eventually demand a king. Are you doing what your competitors and your industry are doing, or are you working to set yourself apart? God's plan for His people was for them to be set apart from their neighbors by their actions and their faith.

3. Managing, governing, and ruling all require humility. Make sure you have people around you to remind you that you need to be more like King David and less like King Saul.

4. King David, Jesus, Peter, and Paul all demonstrated an unimaginable level of respect for those who were responsible for governing. They understood the people placed to govern us were placed there by God as part of His plan. Regardless of party affiliation, social outlook, business background, and personal preference, those in authoritative positions deserve our respect.

5. Civil disobedience is scriptural, Obey the Word of God first and foremost, but be prepared to accept the punishment set by man-made laws for your actions.

Notes

CHAPTER 9

The Sabbath for Zebedee

The question of observing the Sabbath was never an option for Zebedee. Sunset on Friday to sunset on Saturday was mandated by God to be set aside for worship. No questions asked, no excuses accepted. It was not a matter of worrying if the Pharisees or Sadducees would catch him. It was a matter of who Zebedee was and what the God he worshipped and believed in instructed him to do. Yes, the Pharisees had hundreds of rules they required everyone to follow. Sometimes late at night, sitting on his boat as it slowly rocked by the waves, Zebedee wondered where these rules came from since they were not in the scriptures he read in the synagogue. While he knew it was not his position to question them, this man Jesus was. "Maybe, if nothing else, Jesus will be able to convince the Pharisees not to have so many rules that Jews like me have to follow," Zebedee said. He laughed as he thought of life with fewer laws. "That would be a good thing."

Few other topics bring into focus the goal of this book better than this discussion of observing the Sabbath in the workplace. You may think this topic is irrelevant because you are closed on Sunday. Or, because of your profession, you must work on Sunday so others can take that day off. Possibly, to be competitive, you feel that you must be open on Sunday. Those are all great responses, but the issue is they are focused on you and what this world expects.

This chapter is not here to prove you need to be closed on Sunday. It is here to show you that it's possible to be consistent with the teachings of the Bible and still be competitive in today's world. The intent of *Zebedee and Sons Fishing Co.* is to demonstrate that all the business advice needed to successfully manage a small (or even a large) business is found in the pages of the Christian Bible. When we look at what the Bible says about the Sabbath, we are not only learning what is important about the Sabbath, but we also are setting a pattern by which we can look at other important business topics and see how we can, on our own, study the Bible and arrive at sound business practices that are also scriptural. Studying and learning from the Bible is not only for followers of Jesus. Unbelievers, new believers, and lifelong believers can all benefit from the stories and business lessons found in the sixty-six books that make up the Word of God.

Observing the Sabbath is a commitment believers are to follow, and that obligation seems to run contrary to how our secular world operates today. Without fully understanding this commitment, I suspect many nonbelievers and new believers find the biblical requirement of observing the Sabbath to be too onerous and one of their reasons to not rely on the Bible for business management advice, let alone life advice. I encourage you to not give in so quickly.

In this chapter, I will first provide some background on what the Bible says about the Sabbath and why many Christians feel compelled to make one day per week a time of rejoicing and glorifying in the Lord. Second, I will discuss how our weekends in the contemporary world started out as free time off. But these two free days per week evolved into a drive to get more work completed, which ended up ruining lives and families. Third, I will discuss some of the hurdles I've encountered in observing the strict letter of the Sabbath and include ideas on how to cope or avoid them. Finally, I will discuss how observing the Sabbath provides an incredible framework for thinking about where God is in your life and where you want Him to lead you.

Think about this: if all the other advice in the Bible is so foundational and true to leading and managing a great business environment, why would His advice about observing the Sabbath be any less great?

Background

Old Testament

Although there are many theories about the origin of the Sabbath as a special day of the week or month, the Hebrew Bible (basically the Old Testament) says God declared one day of the week to be special.

> By the seventh day God had finished the work he had been doing; so on the seventh day he rested from all his work. Then God blessed the seventh day and made it holy, because on it he rested from all the work of creating that he had done. (Genesis 2:2–3)

Beginning in Genesis chapter 1, the Bible tells one of the two creation stories of the earth. This chapter is about the first six days of creation during which God said let there be light, He separated the waters from the dry land, He commanded the land to produce vegetation, He divided the day into light and dark, and He commanded the earth to be filled with living creatures. Finally on the sixth day, he said, "Let us make mankind in our image" (Genesis 1:26), and He commanded "mankind" to be fruitful and multiply. Regardless of whether you think the work completed by God took six twenty-four-hour days, or each day is a figure of speech for multiple centuries of time, He identified as his final step (the seventh day) a period of rest. This sacred day of rest, following six days of productive and creative work, was not for Him because God, being God, needs no rest. It is for us. After all that work, He commanded there to be a full day of rest, which He called holy and which was intended as a period to reflect on what had just happened.

Now the word *Sabbath* (or actually *šabbāt*) is never used in Genesis. The first occurrence of *šabbāt* is in the book of Exodus, which is about God, through Moses, saving the Israelites from being slaves in Egypt. The story, as we have covered in earlier chapters, is about Moses, a former Egyptian prince by adoption, who is instructed by God through a burning bush to go to the Egyptian pharaoh and demand he set God's people (the Israelites) free. Through a series of amazing miracles, God convinces Pharaoh to acquiesce and allow his main source of labor to leave Egypt. To appreciate how big of a decision this was, think in terms of a building contractor who allows all his concrete suppliers, concrete trucks, and laborers to walk away before they finish the building. Or you are in software development and allow someone to take away all your computers. Whatever the line of business, imagine losing whatever it is that produces your main product or service. With that gone you are out of business. With the loss of the Israelites, Pharaoh could no longer build pyramids, shrines, and whatever else pharaohs build, which is why he resisted so hard to keep his slaves.

In fleeing from Pharaoh, Moses led his followers across the Red Sea and into the Desert of Sin. It was here when the Israelites were starving that God provided manna from heaven. This manna was provided once each day and twice as much on the sixth day of each week. The second portion was saved to be eaten on the Sabbath, the seventh day of the week. Exodus 16:25 says:

> Bear in mind that the Lord has given you the Sabbath; that is why on the sixth day he gives you bread for two days. Everyone is to stay where they are on the seventh day; no one is to go out. So the people rested on the seventh day.

About a month later Moses went to Mount Sinai to ask God for further instructions. It was here that God gave the Ten Commandments of which commandment four said this:

> Remember the Sabbath day by keeping it holy. Six days you shall labor and do all your work, but the seventh day is a sabbath to the Lord your God. On it you shall not do any work, neither you, nor your son or daughter, nor your male or female servant, nor your animals, nor any foreigner residing in your towns. For in six days the Lord made the heavens and the earth, the sea, and all that is in them, but he rested on the seventh day. Therefore the Lord blessed the Sabbath day and made it holy. (Exodus 20:8–11)

Of all the commandments, this was the one that was the most detailed. Most others were simple one-line commandments, e.g., "You shall not steal" (Exodus 20:15). For the Sabbath, however, God elected to be specific and spell out His exact intentions to keep it holy.

Moses later expanded the understanding by giving additional reasoning found in Deuteronomy 5:13–15:

> Observe the Sabbath day by keeping it holy, as the Lord your God has commanded you. Six days you shall labor and do all your work, but the seventh day is a sabbath to the Lord your God. On it you shall not do any work, neither you, nor your son or daughter, nor your male or female servant, nor your ox, your donkey or any of your animals, nor any foreigner residing in your towns, so that your male and female servants may rest, as you do. Remember that you were slaves in Egypt and that the Lord your God brought you out of there with a mighty hand and an outstretched arm. Therefore the Lord your God has commanded you to observe the Sabbath day.

Notice the difference between Exodus and Deuteronomy. Moses expanded this commandment to reflect it was a gift from God to leave time and space for rest. The Sabbath was to be a moment of re-creation. Just as God rested when he created the world, the former Egyptian slaves (the Israelites) needed to rest one day a week to symbolically give thanks to God for delivering them from their bondage. Just as importantly, the commandment stipulated that the time and space for rest and re-creation should be made available to those who did *not* know God (e.g., animals and servants) as well as those who did.

Old Testament references to Sabbath are scattered throughout its pages. The King James Version contains over one hundred passages about the Sabbath in the Old Testament alone. Unfortunately, most of them are about the Israelites' inability to honor the Sabbath and warnings from God's prophets about the impending punishment because of their disobedience. What is interesting though is that the scriptures on Sabbath are about rest, not about worship.

Before we get to the observance of the Sabbath in the New Testament, we need to cover some of the frequently misunderstood semantics about the Sabbath. Specifically, we need to understand the concept of the first day of the week and the seventh, and the difference between Saturday and Sunday. How Sunday became the first day of the week is unknown. Babylonian calendars dating back hundreds of years before the birthing of the Hebrew people have been found that show a day seven identified as a name akin to Sabbath. The Hebrew people did not invent the name Sabbath or single it out as the seventh day. Remember, the Genesis story did not name the seventh day but identified the seventh day as a day of rest. Further research into the oldest known languages also shows that the seventh day,[27] regardless of its name, was as decreed in Genesis as a special day. The Sabbath, as described in the Old Testament, is on Saturday. Therefore, Sunday, the day that most twenty-first-century Christian churches celebrate their worship, is the first day of the week. Furthermore, as described in the Bible, days begin at sundown and end at the following sundown. So the Sabbath is sundown Friday night to sundown Saturday night. Think of the creation story in Genesis. Here "the earth was formless and empty, darkness was over the surface of the deep" (Genesis 1:2). Then in Genesis 1:3, "God said, 'Let there be light,' and there was light." Darkness came first, then light; so a day is made up of darkness first and then light.

New Testament

I promise all this history about the Sabbath will be important soon, but we now need to look at the New Testament. Without question, Jesus and the apostles celebrated the Sabbath just as decreed in the Old Testament. They were all Jews so they followed the customs of their fathers and attended the synagogue on the Sabbath to study the writing of the Pentateuch, the wisdom literature, and the writings of the prophets. Jesus said in Mark 2:27, "The Sabbath was made for man, not man for the Sabbath." Jesus was a Sabbath keeper, "He went to Nazareth, where he had been brought up, and on the Sabbath day he went into the synagogue, as was his custom" (Luke 4:16).

Even after Jesus's death and resurrection, the apostles continued this tradition. Acts 13:14 says of Paul and his companions, "On the Sabbath they entered the synagogue and sat down." Furthermore, Acts 18:4 says of Paul, "Every Sabbath he reasoned in the synagogue, trying to persuade Jews and Greeks." If the Bible is built around the worship of God on Saturday—the Sabbath—why are we holding church on Sunday?

Sunday, or the first day of the week, is mentioned only eight times in the Bible. The transition away from the Sabbath is shown in Romans 14:5–6, which says:

> One person considers one day more sacred than another; another considers every day alike. Each of them should be fully convinced in their own mind. Whoever regards one day as special does so to the Lord.

Colossians 2:16–17 says not to judge anyone if they worship on the Sabbath or not:

> Therefore do not let anyone judge you by what you eat or drink, or with regard to a religious festival, a New Moon celebration or a Sabbath day. These are a shadow of the things that were to come; the reality, however, is found in Christ.

And finally, Galatians 4:9–10 asks if the Galatians are to again be enslaved by the Old Testament laws that were forms of bondage, such as the observance of the Sabbath:

> But now that you know God—or rather are known by God—how is it that you are turning back to those weak and miserable forces? Do you wish to be enslaved by them all over again?

Many feel Sunday (the first day of the week) was selected because Acts 20:7 reads: "On the first day of the week we came together to break bread."

The Old Testament identifies the Sabbath as a day of worship, yet the New Testament leads us to believe it is acceptable to worship on Sunday. To keep from being caught up in the Saturday versus Sunday argument, we need to remember several things. First, observing the Sabbath is an agreement between God and the children of Israel forever. God made the earth in six days, rested on the seventh, and was refreshed. Second, it is the engagement in Sabbath rest that represents the promise of eternal rest in the place God is preparing for us. Finally, Jesus said in Matthew 11:28–29:

> Come to me, all you who are weary and burdened, and I will give you rest. Take my yoke upon you and learn from me, for I am gentle and humble in heart, and you will find rest for your souls. For my yoke is easy and my burden is light.

Jesus is inviting us to rest and God has provided a day to accomplish that.

For the first three hundred years or so of the church, Saturday (or the Sabbath) was a day of rest, and Sunday was the day of worship. After the death and resurrection of Jesus Christ, the Christians and Jews were dispersed throughout the Middle East and persecuted. For the Christians, worship took place in homes and was done in hiding and in secret. From a rather elusive line of thinking, Sunday became known as the Lord's Day (Revelations 1:10, 1 Corinthians 16:1–4, Mark 16:2). In short, Jesus was resurrected on a Sunday, and therefore, it is the Lord's Day and consequently became the day of Christian Sabbath. In the fourth century, Constantine finally enacted legislation making it possible for Christians to observe Sunday as a day of rest and worship.

Permissible Sabbath Activities

Before moving on to the business application of the Sabbath, we need to think for a moment about what is permissible when observing the Sabbath. Recall its origin in Deuteronomy 5:13–15. It says for six days you shall work, and on the seventh, you and everyone, including animals, slaves, and foreigners, will do no work. Isaiah 58:13–14 is generally regarded as the key verse in understanding acceptable activity on the Sabbath:

If you turn back your foot from the Sabbath,
from doing your *pleasure* on my holy day,
and call the Sabbath a delight
and the holy day of the Lord honorable;
if you honor it, not going your own ways,
or seeking your own *pleasure*, or talking idly;
then you shall take delight in the Lord,
and I will make you ride on the heights of the earth;
I will feed you with the heritage of Jacob your father,
for the mouth of the Lord has spoken.

The key word is *pleasure*, found twice in these verses (emphasis added in the scripture above). It is easy to see why many interpret this verse to mean we cannot enjoy any recreational activities on the Sabbath. In reading these verses in context, however, the distinction made is between doing what is pleasing to God versus what is pleasing to ourselves but is in opposition to God.[28] With this interpretation in mind, Isaiah is telling us God's judgment against the Israelites for violating the Sabbath was because of their involvement in commerce on the Sabbath. There is nothing about a prohibition of recreation on the Sabbath.

Another prophet, Amos, confirmed Sabbath commerce was a problem in the following passage:

Hear this, you who trample on the needy
and bring the poor of the land to an end,
saying, "When will the new moon be over,
that we may sell grain?
And the Sabbath,
that we may offer wheat for sale,
that we may make the ephah small and the shekel great
and deal deceitfully with false balances,
that we may buy the poor for silver
and the needy for a pair of sandals
and sell the chaff of the wheat?" (Amos 8:4–6)

During the time of Amos, the Israelites were not only selling produce on the Sabbath, which was a violation of the commandments, but they were also cheating people on the Sabbath. And God knew it. The point is the Israelites were seeking their own pleasure on the Sabbath rather than doing what was pleasing to God.

There are many who feel strongly about worshipping on the Sabbath, as well as many who feel strongly about worshipping on Sunday. Those who are Sabbath worshippers have commandment four of the Ten Commandments to rely on when defending the traditional Friday night-Saturday night worship practice. The downside for this group is they must reconcile the command "to death" for anyone caught violating the Sabbath (Exodus 31:14). On the other hand, those who believe in the Sunday practice of the Lord's Day can rely on the New Testament's identification of Sunday (first day) as the day Christ was resurrected. Unfortunately, this group must deal with the cultural loss of God's intent to have a mandatory day (Sabbath) of rest that includes significant time spent with Him.

The Contemporary Weekend

Regardless of whether you are a believer or not, you may ask why all the introduction and detail about the Sabbath and the Day of the Lord (the two days that comprise the weekend)? Let me ask a parallel question: if you purchased an expensive, high-maintenance piece of equipment or software that was critical to your business, wouldn't you want to know everything you could about it? Wouldn't you want to know its history, where it was manufactured or developed, who else uses it, its track record, what was included in the latest round of updates, and what its limitations are? What I find overlooked are those same considerations for employees. The better I know my employees and their limitations, the better I'm able to productively and profitably manage them. The conversation about observing the Sabbath offers an incredible insight for supporting each of my employees better.

Let's consider the weekend for a moment. The term *weekend* is appropriately named in that it is comprised of the first day of the week, Sunday, and the last day of the week, Saturday. They are the week's bookends. The establishment of the weekend has been traced to a New England cotton mill in 1908. Although it had mainly Jewish workers, the owners realized they'd risk offending the Christian townsfolk by closing on Saturday in honor of the Sabbath instead of Sunday. The solution to this problem was to close both days.

Henry Ford adopted the practice of closing on Saturday and Sunday for a different reason. If people had these two days off work, the enthusiasm for recreational activities would increase, which meant more people would want to buy a car so they could enjoy these newfound hobbies. From this time on, there was no stopping the drive to buy things designed to enhance our weekends. Weekends were free time to be enjoyed. Just look at any advertisement. Advertising is designed to show how to have more fun, eat better (not necessarily healthier), get homework done quicker, and allow you to experience something never considered before. All this is tailored for a freer weekend.

The weekend is portrayed in North American culture as a time of respite and revitalization. Songs are written about weekends (Grateful Dead's "One More Saturday Night," Tom Waits's "The Heart of Saturday Night," Of Montreal's "Everyday Feels Like Sunday"), popular shows are named for the weekend ("Saturday Night Live," "Saturday Light Brigade"), and activities like farmers' markets, art shows, health fairs, beer and barbecue festivals, and employment fairs are all staged around the weekend. It is presumed this free time away from work is beneficial.

Contemporary psychological research concludes that the introduction of the weekend has had two main psychological influences. One is the "blue Monday[29] phenomenon," in which Monday is worse than any other day of the week. The second is the "weekend effect,"[30] where the mood is more positive and less negative on the weekend than during the rest of the week. For many people, weekdays are a time of assigned work, fixed schedules, and a significant amount of time with colleagues, classmates, and coworkers rather than with family and friends. The weekend, however, is identified as a time of self-direction, leisure, and recreation. The results of many of these studies reveal this is true even for those lucky enough to have interesting, prestigious, high-status jobs. All work groups, including lawyers, secretaries, construction crews, and physicians, are affected. The weekend effect reveals just how important free time on weekends is to an individual's well-being.

Unfortunately, many employees, voluntarily or not, use the weekend as an extension of the workweek. One study in London reveals that those who work more than fifty-five hours per week have a 33 percent increased risk of stroke when compared to those who work a thirty-five- to forty-hour week. Researchers cannot connect the hours worked to the cause of a stroke but suspect it's the result of a repetitive triggering of the stress response. One study in Canada shows workers who increase their hours from less than forty hours per week to over forty hours per week experience an increase in tobacco and alcohol consumption, an unhealthy weight gain in men, and an increase in depression in women. A Cornell University study shows approximately 10 percent of employees who work fifty to sixty hours per week report severe work-family conflicts. This number jumps to 30 percent for those who work over sixty hours per week. Divorce rates also increase as weekly hours increase.

In addition to physical and mental health issues, working long hours increases the chances of accidents and results in a decline in productivity. In white-collar jobs, performance decreases by as much as 25 percent when sixty or more hours are worked in each week.

Two other impacts of extreme work hours are the increase in absenteeism and the increase in turnover. Tasha Eurich, PhD, author of *Bankable Leadership*, feels we get "stupider" the more overworking we do. A study published in the *American Journal of Epidemiology*[31] had participants complete a variety of tests to evaluate intelligence, verbal recall, and vocabulary. When compared to the participants who only worked forty hours per week, those who worked fifty-five hours per week showed poorer vocabulary and reasoning.

What we do not know is if these kinds of statistics are true for everyone. There are those who are so passionate about their jobs they focus on them even in their free time. Startup CEOs and entrepreneurs in many job sectors, but especially the tech sector, feel disconnected from their work. This loss of connectedness to the pulse of their business and industry causes severe anxiety. While there are success stories of CEOs and entrepreneurs who have survived the initial stages of their business venture, without question there are many whose drive to stay connected and nurse their fledgling business to life has caused physical health problems and serious family issues, and taken its toll on the mental health of many involved.

What Do We Know So Far?

1. We have been given a gift to rest one day each week from our Creator. That day is to be devoted to our physical and mental health.

2. Excessive work hours, whether during the week or extended over the weekend, will, without question, have a negative impact at some point in time. I know many who think they can slip on their Superman shirt and crank out work at the rate of sixty or seventy hours per week. And they may be fine for now. But at some point, their work-life balance will erupt; health issues will become minor problems that grow to become substance abuse problems, which escalate into absenteeism, and finally their world crashes around them.

3. Those reading this book, whether employer, manager, or employee, are doing so because they want to create a better business environment, care about their employees, and have an interest in a Christ-centered business practice.

Incentives to Violate the Sabbath

Before moving on to why honoring the Sabbath is beneficial to secular employers/managers/employees, as well as those of faith in Christ, we need to address the incentives of violating the Sabbath. Earlier in my management career, I loved overtime and the people who worked ridiculous hours like I did. My rational was if my base budget covered all my regular hour costs, any extra hours during the week were a bonus to the project because all overhead costs were already accounted for. Sure, I had to pay time and a half for hourly employees, but the salary employees were all free. Nice bonuses and cash distributions were made to compensate them, but I ultimately came out ahead financially. I personally hit a wall, and it was the insane hours and stress that brought me to understand there was a better way to run a business. When I considered my management style (or lack of it), I realized I not only had myself to be concerned about, but I had the well-being of all my employees and their families to consider. For me that was an epiphany.

I concede the Sunday sale of products is a major component of the United States economy. Not only are weekend sales important for a company's bottom line, but weekend jobs are also the source of income, primary or supplemental, for many people. In many industries, employees who work long and stressful hours are considered ambitious, loyal, and climbing the corporate ladder. They're seen as acquiring additional skills for the benefit of the company and are thought of as highly productive employees. Corporate life is competitive. Unfortunately, the costs of forgoing leisure activities or rest are too great. We seldom hear about the overstressed employee who fell off the corporate ladder, got divorced, and is living with life-threatening mental and physical health problems. Gratefully, we are now seeing many successful companies who have broken from the mold and are controlling workers' hours, closing on Sundays, and caring for their employee's well-being.

Solution: Honor the Sabbath

From a secular standpoint, keeping overtime hours to a minimum is a must. Let's revisit the idea that your employees are your production, your inventory, and your source of income. Wouldn't you want to keep them in perfect operating condition? Working excessive overtime and weekends destroys your production machinery; it wears it out and you lose all your production capacity. Paychecks and decent benefits cannot keep this machine running efficiently. This machinery needs care, and that care comes from company ownership, management, and co-employees.

But the company's responsibility to care for its production capacity (employees) does not stop at forty hours. The time away from work needs to be quality time—weekends free, evenings off, and blocks of time for the employee to recharge. Despite the controversy about the Saturday Sabbath versus the Lord's Day, for me observing the Sabbath in the workplace is about providing a time for the employees to accomplish the things God gave the Israelites (which is the reason for the extensive history lesson). They need time to rest, time away from commerce so free time is truly free, and time to contemplate their existence. We do not need the extensive rules the

Pharisees developed to observe the Sabbath. God commanded a day to allow our production machinery to recharge and reenergize for a reason. Our God always cares for us, and we need to incorporate that care into our workplace.

At its core the Sabbath is less about a specific day of the week and more about the sacred, special, one-on-one time spent with God. We are called to intentionally set apart time to restore the mind, body, and spirit. The Sabbath is a decisive, concrete, and visible way of aligning with God so He can fulfill our need for rest. Consider again Isaiah 58:13–14:

> If you turn back your foot from the Sabbath,
> from doing your pleasure on my holy day,
> and call the Sabbath a delight
> and the holy day of the Lord honorable;
> if you honor it, not going your own ways,
> or seeking your own pleasure, or talking idly;
> then you shall take delight in the Lord,
> and I will make you ride on the heights of the earth;
> I will feed you with the heritage of Jacob your father,
> for the mouth of the Lord has spoken.

God gave us the Sabbath for a reason. We have been hardwired to work from the beginning of Genesis. But we are also to enjoy our labor as well as our time away from labor.

To honor the Sabbath does not necessarily mean we must choose to be closed either on a Saturday or Sunday. What it does mean is we need to proactively schedule our employees so they get quality time to worship, recharge, and reenergize. Time off needs to coincide with times when others are worshipping so our employees can receive the benefit of congregational worship. And most importantly, honoring the Sabbath needs to reflect a genuine commitment and concern for the well-being of those who work for us as well as those whose work is associated with our business.

Zebedee

Life in Capernaum on the shores of the Sea of Galilee is pretty good. Everyone here is a Jew, and we all worship together. We know if one of us sneaks out on a Saturday to repair some fishing nets, put a coat of paint on the boat, or collect some eggs. Yes, we've got the Pharisees and their rules to be concerned with, but not really. They have their own world and their own problems. We have our neighbors and peer pressure to keep us from breaking the Sabbath, but not really. Life is too full to have to worry about keeping track of our neighbor's activities. What we all have is God. We know everything He says and does is for our own good. We need no other reason to keep the Sabbath other than to know it's a gift from God.

Summary

1. Genesis 2:2 says, "So on the seventh day he rested from all his work." God gave us as a gift a day to rest and rejuvenate. Exodus 20:11 tells us, "Therefore the Lord blessed the Sabbath day and made it holy." Not only are we to rest one day each week but to worship our God and Creator on that day.

2. Acts 20:7 says, "On the first day of the week we came together to break bread." Early Christians celebrated God on the first day of the week, which is Sunday.

3. The prophets Isaiah and Amos confirmed the Israelites were violating the Sabbath laws and were engaging in commerce on the Sabbath. Conforming to scriptural adherence to the Sabbath laws means whatever we do on our day of rest and worship must be pleasing to God and not only to ourselves.

4. Studies from the secular work world agree that allowing or forcing our labor force to work excessive hours is detrimental to the employee and to the company. We spend time and money maintaining our expensive production machinery; we should be willing to spend as much or more effort in maintaining our human staff by showing concern for their mental and physical health.

5. As employers, we need to seriously consider God's commands to observe the Sabbath. Our concern for the physical, mental, and

spiritual well-being of our employees should result in a strategy where we can be competitive yet allow time for everyone to rejuvenate, reenergize, and connect with God. Maybe we do have to be open on weekends, but that should not preclude anyone access to a place and time for worship.

Notes

CHAPTER 10

Did Zebedee Fail?

As the morning sun continued to rise on Zebedee, he thought about whether the loss of his two sons and his two prize employees was somehow a sign of his own failure. "What could I have done differently?" sighed Zebedee. Was it an unconscious act, an unintended slight, or a thoughtless comment that caused these young men to leave? Was he too overbearing or too demanding, or had he expected too much from these men a generation removed from his own work ethic? Maybe he was too protective and did not show how a career in fishing could be a great life. Being a Jew, Zebedee knew failure. He had heard all the stories and had read the prophets so he understood his people's propensity for failure to meet the commands of the God he worshipped. He knew all these extra rules placed by the Pharisees on the laws were a hedge against failing to meet what God had decreed. Given the circumstances, all Zebedee needed to focus on now, since he was starting over, was to understand if any mistakes were made and to not make them this second time.

Failure is an interesting topic for me to write about. Based on what my ego has defined as failure, I have never failed so I have no real experience to share. I was always a straight-A student, never went bankrupt, never was in a failed marriage, never did anything for which I could conceivably be indicted and convicted. I'm just a boring engineer who thinks in a linear fashion and is not prone to compulsive actions. Yet God has pushed me to discuss failure for a reason, and I believe by having to think through and research this topic, I have discovered why.

What I have learned is my understanding of failure is not as it should be. To explain, I have divided failure into three individual topics and will examine each as they relate to the Gospel. The first topic is the fear of failure, the second is failure itself, and the third is the troubling issue of discouragement or discontent that is often the companion of the first two topics.

Fear of Failure

The topic of *fear* is an industry by itself. What would movies, books, theatrical plays, and works of art be without the element of fear? A search on Amazon for books about fear produces over forty thousand possibilities. Many consultants make their living dealing with people's (and animals') fear of something. Fears can range from death, flying, spiders, public speaking, and social encounters to losing a job, going broke in the stock market, and having a loan recalled; and the list goes on forever. Focusing on fear has negative implications for both our health and our ability to make sound decisions.

My topic, which is only a small slice of the world of fear, is the fear of failure and what the Bible shares that will help us cope. But, before moving on to the Bible, I want to mention the two sides of fear. On one side, fear can be good. It's what keeps an inexperienced sailor from attempting to sail across the Atlantic in January in a sixteen-foot dingy. Fear stops you from driving a 1980 sedan with worn-out tires and bad shock absorbers through the back roads of the Colorado Rockies at record speeds, or reaching across a stout fence to pet a barking dog who is baring his teeth and crouched ready to attack. Fear causes us to pause one second and evaluate the chances of success and the implications of our actions.

On the flip side, fear adds to the fabric of our lives. Sailing with experienced sailors in a stiff wind with the spinnaker up is more than a little exhilarating. Driving off road in a four-wheel drive vehicle to see vistas not experienced by most people is worth the effort, time, and anxiety. Spotting a business opportunity and then transferring that enthusiasm to investors, which allows a dream to come true, is without question worth the risks. Life is to be lived, not observed, and to live life, risks need to be accepted and chances taken. And that happens with a little fear and uncertainty.

As expected, the Bible is littered with stories of fear, the effects of fear, and overcoming fear. But we need to remember that fear is not of God. Isaiah 41:10 says:

> Fear not, for I am with you;
> be not dismayed, for I am your God;
> I will strengthen you, I will help you,
> I will uphold you with my righteous right hand.

Isaiah was a prophet during a turbulent period that marked the expansion of the Assyrian empire and the decline of the Israelite nation—roughly the years 745 BC to 700 BC. Isaiah was writing to the Israelites who were stubbornly resisting the advice of God. Due to their sinful nature, the Israelites were destined to be punished, and God decided to punish them (specifically the northern kingdom) by having the Assyrians capture them and place them in exile. Other prophets, such as Micah, Hosea, and Amos, were also tasked by God to counsel and warn the Jewish people to repent. God and the prophets knew they were fighting a losing battle. Yet they continued to deliver the message that God loved them and they were not to fear.

For a Bible reference explaining the concept of fear, I have opted to not use familiar stories, such as David and Goliath (1 Samuel 17:1–58), Moses at the Red Sea (Exodus 14:6–31) or Daniel in the lion's den (Daniel 6:1–28), but to visit two other Old Testament heroes who each overcame fear, enabling them to honor and glorify God.

Elijah

The first story selected about fear of failure is about the prophet Elijah. The irony of selecting Elijah is that he is known for many great attributes, but fear is not one of them. Elijah is the Old Testament version of Michael Jordan or Tiger Woods. His stories are worth reading again and again because his relationship with God and his acts of prophesying are beyond legendary (read 1 Kings 17–19, and 2 Kings 1–2).

Elijah became a prophet during the time when the northern kingdom of Israel had a wicked king named Ahab, who married a wicked woman named Jezebel. God gave Elijah the task of telling this wicked pair to repent, and if not, there would be a famine in the land. They did not repent so the famine came to pass. At one point in the story, Ahab and Elijah meet:

> When Ahab saw Elijah, Ahab said to him, "Is it you, you troubler of Israel?" And he answered, "I have not troubled Israel, but you have, and your father's house, because you have abandoned the commandments of the Lord and followed the Baals." (1 Kings 18:17–18)

As the king and queen had their pagan gods try to free the kingdom from the grips of famine, Elijah went through the land showing acts of kindness and miracles, demonstrating God's goodness and righteousness. Elijah saved a widow woman from starvation (1 Kings 17:8–16) and brought a young boy back to life (1 Kings 17:17–24). My favorite story is when Elijah challenged the priests of the pagan gods to a duel (1 Kings 18:16–40). If you think the Old Testament lacks humor, this chapter is a must read. Elijah challenged the 850 priests of Baal and Asherah to have their gods roast a slaughtered bull. After praying, dancing, singing, and pleading all day, they were unsuccessful. Elijah, alone at the sacrificial altar with his bull soaked in water, called on God who sent down a fire so powerful it consumed the meat and firewood as well as the altar stones. Elijah was a rock star; he was at the top of his game and seemed all powerful. He could call on God to help him anytime he wanted. He was invincible.

In a business world, Elijah is like the executive or project manager who is on a roll in picking up new clients, winning new contracts, and making inroads into new, profitable ventures. He is like the lady who designs exactly what the next wave of fashion wants or the guy who develops the next got-to-have app. These are the businesspeople whose names are listed in magazines and newspapers under the heading of "Most Dynamic," "Under Forty Up-and-Comers," "Next Generation," and "Rising Stars." They are in touch with their business and market, just like Elijah.

Elijah, however, was courting danger and he knew it. Jezebel had a hobby of having prophets of God killed, and Elijah was just about the only one left (one hundred prophets of God were hiding in caves out of fear of Ahab and Jezebel). Following Elijah's duel with the priests of Baal, the Israelites killed all 850 priests. To say Jezebel was furious would be an understatement. She was out to kill Elijah. At this point we learn something new: Elijah was human and maybe wasn't perfect. He became afraid. The man who had gone face-to-face with the evil king Ahab, who could command a jar to produce an unending supply of flour, bring a boy back to life, call down a lightning bolt from heaven, and call for the end of a nationwide famine became afraid. How could a man so seemingly powerful become afraid? To start, Elijah was threatened personally by Jezebel. 1 Kings 19:2 says:

> Then Jezebel sent a messenger to Elijah, saying, "So may the gods do to me and more also, if I do not make your life as the life of one of them by this time tomorrow."

Elijah had killed all her priests, and now she was out to kill Elijah. The next verse says:

> "Then he was afraid, and he arose and ran for his life" (1 Kings 19:3)

Something else must have been bothering Elijah. Ahab and Jezebel had been looking for him for over three years, and he had not been afraid. He had met with Ahab face-to-face, and he had stood on Mount Carmel in public where he called on God to defeat the pagan priests. Yet none of those times did he fear being killed. So why be afraid now? Let's think back to Elijah's career as a prophet. All his actions were big events: he delivered a famine, caused a jar to provide an unending supply of flour, and brought a boy back to life. But 1 Kings 18:1 says:

> After many days the word of the Lord came to Elijah, in the third year, saying, "Go, show yourself to Ahab, and I will send rain upon the earth.

But that is not what Elijah did. Instead he picked a fight between himself and 850 priests to see who could incinerate a bull on the sacrificial altar the quickest. God obliged and delivered a lightning bolt, making Elijah the victor, but the point was Elijah won, not God. Fortunately, the Israelites recognized who was deserving of their worship, and they responded by shouting, "The Lord, he is God; the Lord, he is God" (1 Kings 18:39)—and then they immediately killed all 850 prophets of Baal and Asherah. Elijah's next actions were critical. He called on God to send a mighty thunderstorm ending the drought and then drew on the strength of the Lord to race sixteen miles to King Ahab's palace to confront him. It was here where he faltered. Up to this point Elijah had been a man in control—he was fearless, zealous for God, and loathed idolatry. God had used him to display the mighty strength of the Lord. The kingdom was now praising the God of history, and Jezebel knew there was one man to blame. She had nothing to lose, and Elijah knew he had an opponent who was different from any other he had faced. He was lost on how to proceed in fighting her. The moment he should have turned to God for help, fear took over.

Let's consider again the up-and-coming account manager or the next-generation designer who is experiencing success beyond expectation. Or consider the entrepreneur who is receiving praise for outstanding innovation and creativity. At this pinnacle of success, they enter a new phase of their career. Maybe it is running a business instead of innovating, or managing a team instead of working alone, or signing up for an operating loan multiple times larger than they have ever experienced. Fear creeps in and they begin to question what they are doing. Is it right, will they be successful, can they keep up the innovation, how will all this work out in the end, or where did the simple days of just me and my cell phone go?

Chapter 19 of 1 Kings tells the second half of Elijah's story. Elijah ran and tried to hide. He wandered for forty days and ended up hiding, curled up in a cave on Horeb, also known as Sinai, the mount of God. Here is one of the greatest exchanges ever with God:

> And the word of the Lord came to him: "What are you doing here, Elijah?"

> He replied, "I have been very zealous for the Lord God Almighty. The Israelites have rejected your covenant, torn down your altars, and put your prophets to death with the

sword. I am the only one left, and now they are trying to kill me too."

The Lord said, "Go out and stand on the mountain in the presence of the Lord, for the Lord is about to pass by."

Then a great and powerful wind tore the mountains apart and shattered the rocks before the Lord, but the Lord was not in the wind. After the wind there was an earthquake, but the Lord was not in the earthquake. After the earthquake came a fire, but the Lord was not in the fire. And after the fire came a gentle whisper. When Elijah heard it, he pulled his cloak over his face and went out and stood at the mouth of the cave.

Then a voice said to him, "What are you doing here, Elijah?" (1 Kings 19:9–13 NIV)

God asked Elijah what he was doing, and Elijah gave a list of excuses. God knew what had happened and did not need Elijah to tell Him. It was a rhetorical question, and God's response was to demonstrate four ways He could communicate. The first three were the loud, magnificent, and majestic examples of God's power. The forth communication was a whisper, which was the one Elijah responded to; it was also one Elijah had never attempted in prophesying. God then asked a second time, "What are you doing here, Elijah?"

Doing big projects, receiving notoriety and praise, and being recognized for our efforts are all highlights of our careers that need and deserve attention. Although we receive accolades for our efforts, we must realize they are not ours. Others brought us to the point where we had the opportunity to succeed, and recognition needs to be given to that support group and to our God-given talents. God is responsible for our perceived successes and failures. Recognition for our successes is also elected by God; He may or may not choose to make a big deal out of the actions He planned for us. We cannot let our fear of failure hinge on receiving notoriety and attention since God is in control of the plan. Just remember:

> Every good gift and every perfect gift is from above, coming down from the Father of lights with whom there is no variation or shadow due to change. (James 1:17)

Caleb

One of the most powerful Old Testament stories about fear of failure is the story of Caleb. This interesting, yet mostly unknown story is about the Israelites' faith in God and God's plan of redeeming His people. The fear of failure in this story could be a setback, but as with all God's plans, great things happen.

The background to this story begins when Moses rescued the Israelites from bondage in Egypt. God, through Moses, caused plagues, pestilence, and death in Pharaoh's family and fellow Egyptians to force the release of the Israelites. Pharaoh changed his mind, but the Israelites escaped Egypt when Moses (actually God) parted the Red Sea, which then closed in on their Egyptian pursuers. The Israelites were finally free and on their way to the promised land. Canaan was the land God had promised to Abraham many, many years earlier and was "a land flowing with milk and honey" (Exodus 3:8). The route to the promised land was circuitous because of persistent unbelief and disobedience among the Israelites, but they finally arrived at the Jordan River with Canaan on the other side. The problem was the Israelites were not the first people to discover Canaan. Being a land of milk and honey, other people had found this land and claimed it as their own. God decreed, however, that the Israelites were to take this land from these other people by force if necessary.

The beginning of chapter 13 in Numbers finds Moses across the Jordan River from Canaan speaking to God. There was to be a military operation, and God instructed Moses to send spies into Canaan. The instructions were specific. They were to see what the terrain was like, to determine if the people who lived there were strong or weak, and to find out if they were few or many in number, if they lived in cities or camps, if the ground was fertile, and if there were trees. Of course, God knew all this, but He wanted the Israelites to find out for themselves. Finally, if possible, they were to bring back "some of the fruit of the land" (Numbers 13:20).

After spying in Canaan for forty days, the spies returned. The good news was they confirmed this land was indeed a land of milk and honey, and to prove it, they brought back one cluster of grapes so large it took two men to carry it. The bad news was the land was not only populated by the Canaanites but also the Hittites, Jebusites, Amalekites, and Amorites. The worst news of all was the Nephilim also dwelled there. The Nephilim were giant people who were known to be fierce fighters in combat.

> The land, through which we have gone to spy it out, is a land that devours its inhabitants, and all the people that we saw in it are of great height. And there we saw the Nephilim (the sons of Anak, who come from the Nephilim), and we seemed to ourselves like grasshoppers, and so we seemed to them. (Numbers 13:32)

With this news, the Israelites panicked as fear and discouragement set in. The Israelites had escaped a life of slavery in Egypt, been chased by Pharaoh's armies who were intent on killing them, and endured hardship in the wilderness for years, only to find themselves across the Jordan River from what they conceived as their largest challenge yet. "Then all the congregation raised a loud cry, and the people wept that night" (Numbers 14:1). They were not only afraid but they also were terrified. Instead of success, they thought they were staring failure in the face. Inexplicably, the immediate reaction was to call for new leaders to replace Moses and go back to Egypt to again be slaves.

In thinking through this story in detail, the Israelites only knew what the spies had told them. They sent twelve spies, and all but two had messages that produced extreme fear in all the people. The reports of ten of the twelve spies convinced the Israelites to throw out all their dreams of living in the promised land and become slaves to the Egyptians once again. These ten spies did not return to deliver the detail of their mission; they returned to deliver fear, and the people heard only fear. They said, "We are not able to go up against the people, for they are stronger than we are" (Numbers 13:31). Two spies, however, did not return to deliver fear. Joshua and Caleb returned with a different perspective on the land and the possibility of conquering it.

> The land, which we passed through to spy it out, is an exceedingly good land. If the Lord delights in us, he will bring us into this land and give it to us, a land that flows with milk and honey. Only do not rebel against the Lord. And do not fear the people of the land, for they are bread for us. Their protection is removed from them, and the Lord is with us; do not fear them. (Numbers 14:7–9)

They understood that the information they were sent to collect was already known to God; He was not sending them to a land they could not conquer. Unfortunately, this nice speech did not alter the people's fears, so God intervened and sent the Israelites to spend the next forty years wandering in the desert before He would again allow them to see the promised land.

There are two significant messages in this story. First, it is a story of how the fear of failure turned into a failure of massive proportion. Moses rescued the Israelites and led them to the riverbank of the promised land only to have a small group of misunderstanding people instill fear in everyone else, which resulted in their unbelief of God's promises. Ten of the spies were afraid to tackle a difficult task, so instead of evaluating their strengths (God on their side) and planning accordingly, they only conveyed emotions that influenced the masses and resulted in total failure. Fear of failure guaranteed total failure. The fear of failure was a manifestation of the Israelite's unbelief in the God who had been merciful, loving, and gracious. This fear of failure caused God to render a judgment against them and sent them wandering in the wilderness until an entire generation passed away. Spying on Canaan was a military operation with God as the commander, yet it was not successful because not everyone was committed to the operation. In business, even with the best plans, financing, and procedures, success is not always guaranteed, and not even possible, until everyone involved is committed.

Only two of the spies understood the task at hand and knew how to be successful in conquering Canaan. They were not, however, successful at dissuading God's anger toward the Israelite's unbelief. Joshua and Caleb spoke honestly and were ready to act decisively. God promised them a land of milk and honey and allowed the spies to return with one bunch of grapes as proof. But conquering Canaan was not going to be an easy task. If a land were that fruitful, everyone would want it and everyone would try to take it from whoever possessed it. God showed the Israelites what they were going to be fighting for, yet they could not see the value in the tasks needed to win the land.

Second, remember who got you where you are. God saved and protected the Israelites up to the Jordan River. He promised to do the same once they invaded Canaan. Fear caused the Israelites to forget about God's limitless protection and to focus only on their humanly limited resources. As a lesson, God sent the Israelites back to the desert only to return to the Jordan forty years later when they relied on God to give them Canaan by delivering them victories in battles.

One characteristic of company rock stars and up-and-comers is they are not willing to listen to the crowd but will try what everyone else is afraid of. The crowd always has excuses. "Our competition has that market sewed up." "That's outside of our wheelhouse." "What if it doesn't work?" But dynamic companies are full of Calebs and Joshuas, and management lets them conquer their fears and try new ideas. They see the big picture, are willing to plan accordingly, and want to be assertive and aggressive. Regardless of whether their idea works or not, they are still in the game ready to try yet another idea that everyone else is afraid to try.

Failure

Most people don't grasp that the Bible is about real people. The people portrayed in the Bible are not faultless or perfect; they are far from it. A study of biblical characters shows most are men and women who have faults and have failed at some point in their journey with God. And in this journey, they have picked themselves up and gone on to accomplish the task our Lord has given them. They may not have become successful by worldly standards, but they were successful in what mattered the most, which was to represent God. The list is long from which to select an example for our purposes here. Abraham, the father of Christianity, was old and childless when God called him, and even then he was plagued by doubts and poor decisions. Moses, who led the Israelites out of slavery in Egypt, stuttered and questioned God's decision to use him. King David, the man who as a boy slew Goliath and wrote many of the Psalms, had an affair and had the woman's husband killed as part of the cover-up scheme. Jacob, the grandson of Abraham, was a serial liar and a deceiver. The apostle Paul was known as Saul early in his career when he zealously persecuted Jews. I have chosen, however, to look at failure through one of my favorite characters of the New Testament: the apostle Peter.

Peter, also known as Simon Peter and as Cephas (John 1:42), was born in a small village named Bethsaida in Galilee, Israel. Peter was one of Zebedee's partners in Zebedee and Sons Fishing Co. His father was also a fisherman, so fishing ran in his blood. It has been said that Peter was a tall, thin man with a short, curly black beard. We can assume he was Jewish, but as a fisherman he had little formal education, and the only leadership training he had probably came from Zebedee.

Simon Peter first met Jesus through his brother Andrew (John 1:35–36), and when they met, Jesus gave him the name Cephas, which means "rock" in Aramaic and "Peter" in Greek. The story of Jesus calling Simon Peter to follow him is found in Luke 5:1–11. He and his four business partners had been fishing all night with no luck. As they were stowing their gear, Jesus called them to go back out to sea and told them exactly where to drop their nets. They caught so many fish their nets were breaking and they needed help to haul them to shore. Simon Peter, only a simple fisherman, immediately recognized Jesus was special and said, "Depart from me, for I am a sinful man, O Lord" (Luke 5:8). Jesus responded, "'Do not be afraid; from now on you will be catching men.' And when they had brought their boats to land, they left everything and followed him" (Luke 5:10–11).

For the next three years, Peter lived as a disciple of Jesus Christ. He was a natural leader but prone to impulsive and even impetuous actions. In many places in the New Testament, Peter was the de facto spokesperson for the twelve disciples. It was Peter who was the first to confess that Jesus was the Son of the Living God:

> He said to them, "But who do you say that I am?" Simon Peter replied, "You are the Christ, the Son of the living God." And Jesus answered him, "Blessed are you, Simon Bar-Jonah! For flesh and blood has not revealed this to you, but my Father who is in heaven. And I tell you, you

are Peter, and on this rock I will build my church, and the
gates of hell shall not prevail against it. I will give you the
keys of the kingdom of heaven, and whatever you bind
on earth shall be bound in heaven, and whatever you
loose on earth shall be loosed in heaven." Then he strictly
charged the disciples to tell no one that he was the Christ.
(Matthew16:16–20)

What a prodigy. What expectations. How could a man, a simple
fisherman at that, with only the education of spending three years next to
Jesus be called on for such greatness?

Before continuing with Peter's story, let's think of the business
application of what we have learned so far. Have you selected an heir
apparent to succeed you? Have you identified a business prodigy, rock star,
up-and-comer, or genius on which you have placed a significant amount
of dependence? Is that dependence warranted and appropriate based on
this person's skill and training? Have I described you? Are you the future
of the business you're in? All successful businesses have employees who
are exceptional at designing, reading the market, understanding buying
patterns, or managing fast-paced design teams. But we need to remember
they are human and fallible (even if they will not admit it). As business
leaders, we need to consider the expectations we place on our next generation
of leaders and ensure they are prepared emotionally and spiritually for the
task. Let's see how Peter responded.

Unfortunately, Peter's impetuous nature kept getting in his way. One
great story was as Jesus was foretelling of His death, Peter took Him aside
to rebuke Him (rebuke Jesus?). He was swiftly and firmly corrected by Jesus,
"Get behind me, Satan! You are a stumbling block to me; you do not have in
mind the concerns of God, but merely human concerns" (Matthew 16:23).

Peter's lack of understanding was apparent during the transfiguration
where Jesus met Moses and Elijah. Here he was in the presence of three of
the greatest figures in the Bible and the best idea he could come up with
was to build three apartments for them to stay in (Matthew 17:4–6). Peter
was the one who drew his sword to protect Jesus from the servants of the
Jewish high priest and cut off an attacker's ear, only to be told to resheath
his sword as Jesus miraculously reattached the ear (John 18:10–11). And

finally, it was Peter who boasted he would never forsake the Lord, even if everyone else did, and he failed miserably.

It is this particular failure that is of interest. We pick up the story in Matthew 26:30–35:

> And when they had sung a hymn, they went out to the Mount of Olives. Then Jesus said to them, "You will all fall away because of me this night. For it is written, 'I will strike the shepherd, and the sheep of the flock will be scattered.' But after I am raised up, I will go before you to Galilee." Peter answered him, "Though they all fall away because of you, I will never fall away." Jesus said to him, "Truly, I tell you, this very night, before the rooster crows, you will deny me three times." Peter said to him, "Even if I must die with you, I will not deny you!" And all the disciples said the same.

Peter's boasting became a failure several hours later:

> Now Peter was sitting outside in the courtyard. And a servant girl came up to him and said, "You also were with Jesus the Galilean." But he denied it before them all, saying, "I do not know what you mean." And when he went out to the entrance, another servant girl saw him, and she said to the bystanders, "This man was with Jesus of Nazareth." And again he denied it with an oath: "I do not know the man." After a little while, the bystanders came up and said to Peter, "Certainly you too are one of them, for your accent betrays you." Then he began to invoke a curse on himself and to swear, "I do not know the man." And immediately the rooster crowed. And Peter remembered the saying of Jesus, "Before the rooster crows, you will deny me three times." And he went out and wept bitterly. (Matthew 26:69–75)

Peter was human and his fears led him to deny Jesus. He was afraid, but to his credit, he was the only disciple to follow Jesus after His arrest. He was able to watch from the courtyard as Jesus was being falsely accused, beaten, and insulted. Peter was afraid for Jesus, and he was afraid for his own life. Despite Jesus warning his followers what the end would be like, Peter was not prepared for the hate the world had for Jesus. Peter also loathed the fact that Jesus foretold of Peter's failure and that he was not as bold and fearless as he thought. Why did Jesus allow Peter to fail so miserably and completely?

The answer is found in Luke 22:31–32:

> Simon, Simon, behold, Satan demanded to have you, that he might sift you like wheat, but I have prayed for you that your faith may not fail. And when you have turned again, strengthen your brothers.

Satan had asked to sift Peter like wheat, to test and tempt him to see his true loyalty. Jesus could have protected him, but Jesus had a higher goal. He was equipping Peter to strengthen his brothers. "And when you have turned again" (Luke 22:32) is about Peter's failure and his recovery. Not only did Peter strengthen the other disciples, but he also became the pillar of the early church in Jerusalem. He exhorted and trained others to follow the Lord Jesus (Acts 2), and he continues today to strengthen believers through his epistles, 1 and 2 Peter. Going through the experience of failure made Peter the great apostle and leader he was. He was crucified years later in Rome for his unwavering faith that was built on his earlier failures.

This story has two takeaways. First is the business aspect. The twenty-first-century critique of failure stresses that failure is only a disaster if we do not learn and grow from it. This lesson is found in Peter's story; he had plenty of failures to learn from. Yet despite all Peter's failures, Jesus continued to see the good that Peter brought to His group of apostles. Let's consider Peter's good attributes. First, he was committed; he was a devout follower of Jesus Christ. Second, although he was not educated or trained in the Torah or other rabbinic materials, he was teachable. He was the product of classical on-the-job training. Third, he was passionate to a fault about what he and the other disciples were doing. Although they did not understand how, they nevertheless were out to change the world. Finally, Peter was true to the calling. He did not divert from, compromise, or modify his mission. Along with Jesus, they had a single mission, and whenever anyone attempted to convince Jesus that they should follow a different path, be it easier or safer, Jesus rebuked them to stay true to the job at hand.

In today's world, businesses fail for several reasons. First, businesses fail because the reason for the business is not sound in the first place. Maybe the entrepreneur wanted to make a lot of money, travel, or have a lot of time off. These reasons have nothing to do with the actual business, which is to satisfy a need in the marketplace. Second, businesses fail because of poor management. Management gets sidetracked and forgets to "keep their eye on the ball." Most new small businesses lack management expertise in every area of their business. No single small business owner is an expert in production, shipping, financing, and human resources. Not having this expertise is exacerbated when the businessperson is unwilling (prideful) to ask for advice and help. Third, businesses fail because of lack of capital. Incoming revenue is not sufficient to cover the outgoing expenses required by the mission of the business. Some businesses can survive on a low level of revenue because they manage with a low level of expenses. For most businesses, though, revenue must always match or exceed expenses (dot-coms seem to be different, but that's outside my expertise). Finally, businesses fail because they lack proper planning. They did not forecast ahead with sufficient detail to anticipate the rocky road the business was liable to encounter. All these reasons for failure are also learning lessons for the businessperson.

Businesses fail just like Peter failed. Yet just like Peter, each successful business has strong and pervasive attributes that remain despite the occasional failures. Small businesses are predominantly dependent on one person (or a small group) that is responsible for the business's success. That single entrepreneur must have the right vision, have a perpetual handle on cash flows, be humble enough to seek advice, and be properly funded to succeed. That person also must be committed to the business—like Peter and the small group of disciples. They exemplify the characteristics needed to be successful—they have a mission to fill a known need, and they stay true to the mission. And, although they all have minor personal failures, those failures don't detract from completing the mission.

The second takeaway is that God is in control, always. Jesus Christ was in constant contact with God the Father through his consistent use of prayer. Sometimes we celebrate our own personal success, and sometimes we cry over our own failures. Yet, if you understand that God is involved in both the success and failure, you will be better able to capitalize on the successes and learn from the failures. Success given to God gives credit where credit is due. Failure given to God is found in the humility to ask him not "why" but "what's next."

Discouragement from Failure

As we have learned in the story of Caleb, fear of failure is as debilitating and disastrous as the actual failure. Failure is mostly predictable, and by employing a certain set of character traits, such as those of Peter, and following good business-management practices, the chances of failure are somewhat ameliorated. Of course, if you do not want to ever fail, just do nothing. Never make a decision, take a chance, risk anything, or position yourself to receive any criticism. To make a difference, create something, help people live better lives, accomplish dreams, and make the world better, we must take risks. It's that drive to make a difference that causes us to dream of being successful; nobody dreams of being a failure. But the simple reality is we all fail and will all fail again. James 3:2 says:

> For we all stumble in many ways. And if anyone does not
> stumble in what he says, he is a perfect man, able also to
> bridle his whole body.

We know there has only been one perfect man: Jesus Christ. As odd as it may seem, it is comforting that the Bible has shown us over and over even the most successful and God-loving people fail. They failed before God used them, and they failed after they accomplished God's purpose for them. King David committed adultery after he solidified the Israel nation. Noah got drunk after he rode out the flood in a boat full of animals. Some of the failures were large and impactful; some were small and insignificant. But they were failures nonetheless.

Acknowledging that we all fail, as leaders we need to manage those failures and the resulting discouragement. First, we need to consider the way a leader handles his own failures. And secondly, we need to consider how a leader handles the failures of those around him and how the potential for discouragement is deflected.

A Leader and Failure

Remember Jeremiah, the Old Testament prophet whose task from God was to convey the meaning and understanding of His actions to the Israelites for their disregard of His commands? Even though God was angry with His people and was in the process of punishing them, Jeremiah 8:4–5 conveys a God who understands human nature:

> You shall say to them, Thus says the Lord:
> When men fall, do they not rise again?
> If one turns away, does he not return?
> Why then has this people turned away
> in perpetual backsliding?
> They hold fast to deceit;
> they refuse to return.

God's people, as well as all humans, will fail and, unfortunately, without help and guidance will get back up, try again, and fail again. Many chapters later Jeremiah writes on behalf of God:

> "Know the Lord, for they shall all know me, from the least of them to the greatest," declares the Lord. "For I will forgive their iniquity, and I will remember their sin no more." (Jeremiah 31:34)

God's people failed, and he punished them by sending them into exile, but he forgave them, erased all their sins, and allowed them to start again.

Understanding the amazing grace of God and his incredible forgiveness and acceptance is our primary defense against being discouraged in our failings. Our failures, no matter how large or small, are not the end of our effective ministry with God. As business leaders who want to be good leaders and follow the teachings of Christ, we need to understand everything begins and ends with God's purpose for us. Our failures are rungs on the ladder of growth. Our failures teach us about who we are, who God is, and more importantly, what God has in store for us. Proverbs 24:16 says, "For the righteous falls seven times and rises again."

Leaders in the Bible fail and through God's grace rise and eventually succeed. The great apostle Paul started a successful church in Corinth on his second missionary trip. This church endured significant opposition and was proud of its accomplishments and of its newly found faith. It did, however, develop some theological fundamentals that were not from Paul. To correct them, he wrote two letters to the church (1 and 2 Corinthians) in which he gently and lovingly rebuked it and set it on a proper theological course. Regardless of whether Paul failed to teach the Corinthians appropriately or if they failed to understand, in his corrective action he wrote:

> We are hard pressed on every side, but not crushed; perplexed, but not in despair; persecuted, but not abandoned; struck down, but not destroyed. (2 Corinthians 4:8–9)

Paul, who included himself in his criticism with the use of *we*, was encouraging the Corinthians to know they would receive opposition and criticism and fail, but they should not despair. Through the death of Jesus on the cross, we are assured of God's love and forgiveness, and He will always be with us in our times of trouble.

Having God with you in your business enterprises is your foundation to overcome small and large failures. King David wrote many of the Psalms in the Bible, and they represent him in his darkest times. In these Psalms he conveys the wisdom he learned through a life with God. Psalm 37:23–24 says:

> The steps of a man are established by the Lord,
>   when he delights in his way;
>   though he fall, he shall not be cast headlong,
>   for the Lord upholds his hand.

This psalm uses "though he fall" as if it is inevitable. Equally as inevitable is "for the Lord upholds his hand." We will fail and God will catch us. As disquieting as it is that we are incapable of not failing, it is assuring that God is always there to catch us. As business leaders, we need to understand and appreciate the inevitable failures that will come our way. We cannot let these failures detract from our primary mission and what God has planned for us.

Leaders and Failures of Others

To effectively comprehend how we are to respond to the failure of others, we need to think through how failure is defined. Defining failure in our culture is more difficult that one would initially think. First, traditional definitions of failure mostly include "lack of success" and "nonperformance" somewhere in their descriptions. Most articles about failure include countless stories of famous people who experienced some level of failure before becoming an outrageous success. Following this concept that failure is a precursor to success, it is always interesting to see what is considered a failure in our culture, as well as what is considered a success. An example is a famous basketball player who missed an X number of shots (failure) on his way to being a dominant professional basketball player (success). Or better yet, a famous media personality was cut from a TV show or record label (failure) on the way to becoming famous in his or her craft (success). Or an entrepreneur had numerous startups that did not reach critical mass (failure) before uncovering the right combination of ingredients to produce the next popular nutritional drink (success). I think these examples of failure are hardly fair. If missing a basket is a failure, then there are many failures on front driveways, school gymnasiums, and backyards across the country. Being cut by a record label or a TV show is more of a failure of the record label and the TV show than it is of the performer. And how is anything ever invented or created without the trial-and-error process that has been used for centuries? I see none of these as failures.

For a business example of success and failure in our culture, let's think of bankruptcy. Bankruptcies have historically been the predominate label of a business failure. But since the turn of the century, this has changed, and many reports suggest that one third of bankruptcies today are from unexpected medical costs. Those bankruptcies are not failures. Also since the turn of the century, we have seen one of the most significant market adjustments, which caused regulatory adjustments and shifted how business risks are assumed and executed. Many people found themselves in bankruptcy because their bank called in their loan, the regulating agencies changed the rules, or their investors got cold feet. It's hard to put those circumstances in a fixed definition of failure.

As for the examples of successes, they are successes in terms of individuals achieving a goal they may have established in their career. But is that single accomplishment a success, or is the success about the person? Many studies have suggested that success does not lead to happiness, but happiness leads to success. Does the accomplishment make the person happy for life, or does a happy life lead to an attainable success? Did the success of the basketball player, the television star, and the entrepreneur make them happy for life?

Secondly, I do not think of win/lose situations as failures; that's competition. When one team wins the basketball game, the reality is the other team loses. When I focus on failure, I think of it in terms of performance. Were the actions of the person up to or above industry standards, and did they perform to the level of their God-given abilities to complete the assignment for the advantage of the business? Did the engineer adequately and professionally design the bridge so it would not fall down? If the engineer erred in his or her calculations, he or she failed. If it fell down because of unforeseen circumstances, such as a semi running into it, that was not a failure of the structural engineer. If someone designed an app that connected doctors to patients based on significant research of both the doctors and patients, yet it still was not popular, the designer did not fail. If someone designed the same app in his or her corner office without ever consulting anyone else and it was not popular, that designer failed. The point is the failure is connected to the process used to make the decisions arriving at the final product, not to the final product itself. Think of the *who* in success/failure as if going to the clinic to get well and the doctor gives you a bottle of pills. Is the final success/failure based on the doctor or the pills? The process in determining which pills to prescribe led to the success and not the pills themselves.

It's important to contemplate this elusive definition of failure so we can understand how a leader handles the failure of a peer or subordinate. We need to learn how to handle a situation in which a leader entrusts a decision to one of his peers or subordinates and the result is a disaster. In all circumstances, knowing all the facts is a prerequisite before taking any action or making any decisions. If the facts show the subordinate was derelict in his or her responsibilities, my practice has always been that the individual should get to enjoy the employment of another business as soon as possible—meaning he or she is quickly fired. Those situations are infrequent. More than likely several extenuating circumstances were involved that clouded the facts, which led to the resulting disaster. A clear decision path is seldom available for a business leader.

At this point, our thought process should turn to the story of the apostle Peter as earlier described. Part of the time Peter was the team leader, biggest advocate, energetic disciple, and voice of the followers of Jesus. But for an equal amount of time, he was putting his foot in his mouth, boasting when he should have been praying, and trying to figure out how to understand Jesus's teachings while Jesus kept talking in parables. One moment Jesus was praising Peter, and the next he said, "Get behind me, Satan! You are a hindrance to me" (Matthew 16:23). As a leader, we need to focus on Jesus and his actions and responses in these situations. His compassion and grace is overwhelming—of course he is God and we are not. But if we can reflect even a small amount of that in our response to a failing by an assistant or direct report, we will become better leaders, and our followers will become better followers.

Zebedee

Zebedee had the Old Testament to fall back on for advice, so he knew the story of Elijah and his fears. But being a first-century, working-class Jew, I doubt he had any notion of being a failure in either business or life. One of the benefits of being in a business like fishing was an understanding of the circumstances of nature. He did not think of the days when he caught fish as being successful and the days he did not catch fish as a failure. They were both part of his business life. He could, however, honestly look back on the nights in the middle of the Sea of Galilee fishing with his four partners and reflect that they were all successful nights, whether they caught fish or not.

Summary

1. Isaiah 41:10 says, "Fear not, for I am with you; be not dismayed, for I am your God." We get to choose the level of risk we add to our lives. Too much risk places us at unreasonable levels of fear that will impact our health and future. But a healthy dose of risk allows

us to connect with the fear so eloquently conveyed in the Bible and understand we have a God who loves and protects us.

2. Even great men like Elijah experienced moments of fear. Those moments are coincidental with times where they find themselves far from God. They stop placing their reliance on God and start thinking they can do what they want. God will go along with us when we are on our own, but He only goes so far. We need to remember God's purpose for us is to rely on Him and Him alone.

3. Remember Caleb (Numbers 13). Are you conveying a message of fear and failure? Or are you looking through the lens that God has given you and understand He is in charge and your job is to follow His will? The crowd around you might be panicking and planning for failure. As a follower of Christ, you are to look to Him for guidance and believe that His hand is in all circumstances. We are to trust in His plan and His judgment.

4. Our New Testament role model is Simon Peter. Peter had the uncanny ability to vacillate between borderline brilliance and abject stupidity. He was simultaneously a success and a failure. But he believed in the mission he was working for and did not let his setbacks deter him from being one of the greatest apostles for Christ.

5. Leaders make mistakes. True leaders know this and know how to learn and teach from them. Leaders understand and know God, for He said, "For I will forgive their iniquity, and I will remember their sin no more" (Jeremiah 31:34).

6. Peter is a great example of how all the disciples were not the perfect followers. They perpetually bickered and misunderstood Jesus's teachings. Yet Jesus could lead the disciples through their failures to greatness beyond expectations. As business leaders, we know our teammates will fail; it is through the example of Jesus's leadership we are able to overcome those disappointing times and keep focused on our business's mission.

Notes

CHAPTER 11
Zebedee's Leadership

Being the leader of a two-boat fishing company can't be that tough, thought Zebedee as he finished cleaning his boat while the terns noisily screeched along the shore looking for breakfast. "Of course it will be easier now that it's just me," he said in resignation.

Leadership is never easy. It may be rewarding, it may be our calling, it may be in our nature, and it may be fun, but it's seldom easy. Zebedee knew this from years of fishing, hiring workers, adjusting to competition, buying equipment, fighting the weather, and working nights when the rest of the world worked days; the list of responsibilities just never ended. The question was who did Zebedee have to go to for leadership advice? Zebedee did have Salome, his wife, to confide in. She was smart, strong, savvy, and also a follower of Jesus. But for a guy running a business in first-century Galilee, the most important thing to do was fall back on the teaching of his ancestors. "Maybe I should talk to the rabbi and get his advice," murmured Zebedee as he finally found the strength to crawl out of the boat and start planning for the future.

Using the Bible as a reference for leadership is not as easy as I thought. For personal situations, we can turn to pastors and friends who believe for help with good scriptural advice. Business advice found in the Bible often seems elusive because we do not think stories from two thousand years ago have anything to do with twenty-first-century commerce. I've attempted to demonstrate in this book, however, that the Bible is a resource for running an efficient, ethical, moral, and profitable business. The challenge is knowing where in the Bible to find that advice and then correctly interpreting it for each situation. Leadership advice in the Bible is similar to biblical business advice in that we perceive few similarities exist between being a leader today and being a leader two thousand years ago. Leaders in the Bible did not turn around a Fortune 500 company. They did not take on a governmental bureaucracy and prevail. They did not run for public office, fighting for the rights of the disenfranchised, and upset an incumbent. They did not sell a million books on leadership and spend all their time on a speaking tour. Leadership advice from the Bible is completely counterintuitive to our culture of today. But that's what makes it so special.

Most leaders found in the Bible are examples of humanity rather than leadership. Moses is listed as one of the greatest leaders in the Bible, but he was a reluctant leader who failed to reach the goal of seeing the Israelites settle in Canaan. King David, the greatest Israelite king ever, committed adultery and then had the husband killed to cover up his own sin. David's son, King Solomon, received the gift of wisdom and, using this gift, became the wealthiest man ever. Yet by the end of his reign he had hundreds of wives and even more concubines, which violated the commands of God. Further, neither King David nor King Solomon established a monarchy that lasted more than one generation after their time in power. So who are we to draw on for leadership advice?

One of the best examples of biblical leadership is the apostle Paul. His style of leadership was based on serving people. He traveled thousands of miles on foot, was beaten numerous times, was jailed and scorned, and is still considered one of the greatest leaders of all time. Paul's example, as found in the Bible, stresses a counterintuitive servant leadership style that is impossible for human nature to sustain on its own. Servant leadership is established in Matthew 20:25–28:

> But Jesus called them to him and said, "You know that the rulers of the Gentiles lord it over them, and their great ones exercise authority over them. It shall not be so among you. But whoever would be great among you must be your servant, and whoever would be first among you must be

your slave, even as the Son of Man came not to be served
but to serve, and to give his life as a ransom for many."

To be a true leader is to become a servant among those we lead. Even leaders in the Bible, called by God and counseled by prophets, had a hard time continuing to be a servant leader. How hard is it for us today to be that type of leader when we have no direct communication from God and no reliable prophets to advise us? The Bible is full of stories of men and women who tried and failed to be consistent godly leaders, and it is for us to learn from those stories and use them to support our own attempts to be better business leaders.

To help us develop a style of servant leadership, the Bible stresses the importance of being wise, but wisdom does not automatically create leadership and lead to good decisions. Ezekiel told the king of Tyre:

> By your great wisdom in your trade you have increased your
> wealth, and your heart has become proud in your wealth—
> therefore thus says the Lord God: "Because you make your
> heart like the heart of a god, therefore, behold, I will bring
> foreigners upon you, the most ruthless of the nations; and
> they shall draw their swords against the beauty of your
> wisdom and defile your splendor." (Ezekiel 20:5–7)

The wisdom needed for good leadership comes from prayer, which is our pathway to God's guidance. All Bible stories demonstrate that success in leadership comes while the leaders are engaged with God. Their failure always occurs when the leaders begin to feel self-sufficient and think they no longer need God. Proverbs 1:7 says, "The fear of the Lord is the beginning of knowledge; fools despise wisdom and instruction."

I've selected four examples from the Bible to display biblical leadership. The first three leaders were selected because they were, well, more like you and me. They don't have large roles in the scheme of the Bible. They were not driven by ostentatious plans that took them across continents; they did not lead millions of people, nor did they face death daily. They were not placed in life-choice situations that caused them to cry out to God. They were people doing the simple things God calls each of us to do every day, just leading a good and godly life. My fourth leader is Jesus, of course, because he is Jesus and there is so much to learn from the perfect example.

Deborah

Although I've lightly touched on the background of biblical judges in earlier chapters, let's recap. Moses delivered the Israelites out of bondage from Egypt. He led them through the desert to the Jordan River where everyone could see the land God had promised them. Here they faltered and Moses was not allowed to enter Canaan, so a man named Joshua led God's people into Canaan to claim it for God. In this part of the world, Canaan was a fertile land, which all the surrounding nations desired. Joshua was a great Israelite leader, but like many of the biblical leaders, he also failed in the end to obey God. God had commanded him to rid Canaan of all other nations so the land of Canaan would be occupied by only the Israelites—and he chose not to obey.

Following Joshua's death, the Israelites had no human leader and that was by God's design. After all, the Israelites had a God who had shown them that He would always provide. The Israelites won in battle when they trusted in God and they lost when they did not—it was that simple. Joshua's failure to follow God's command left scatterings of other nations living with the Israelites throughout Canaan. Once the Israelites conquered Canaan, they began to assimilate with these other people and with the surrounding nations. The Israelites began to take on the culture of their neighbors, live the way they lived, marry into these other nations, and soon began to worship their gods. They ceased to rely on God and began to rely on themselves and these foreign gods. The book of Judges says, "In those days there was no king in Israel. Everyone did what was right in his own eyes" (21:25). This meant when the Israelites relied on God, they were able to do right. When they did not rely on God for guidance and instruction, they were only able to do wrong. This attitude of every man for himself allowed the Israelites to do a lot of wrong.

The Israelites began to find themselves in a cycle that started with oppression by a neighboring nation. They then remembered God, repented, and cried out for mercy. God responded by sending a leader who saved His people, and they enjoyed a short period of peace until the cycle started over again by ignoring God. The leaders sent by God in these cycles were the judges. The book of Judges identifies twelve judges who fulfilled different types of roles depending on the Israelites' circumstances. The Hebrew word from which we get judges is *shopetim*, which is interpreted as both a judicial role and a leading, defending, and avenging role.[32] The leadership style of many of these judges was more charismatic, as they were often called to rally the tribes, go to battle, and provide positive advice and support.

Our story is about a woman named Deborah, who was the fourth judge after the death of Joshua. She was one of only two judges who were both a judge and a prophet (prophetess). Before going into her story, one of the first remarkable observations is that scripture lacks any special indication or reference that she is a woman. That she is a woman is simply a fact, and there seems to be nothing special or surprising about a woman judge, as if it was expected and accepted.

Deborah's story begins with the Israelite cycle beginning once again:

> And the people of Israel again did what was evil in the sight of the Lord after Ehud died. And the Lord sold them into the hand of Jabin king of Canaan, who reigned in Hazor. The commander of his army was Sisera, who lived in Harosheth-hagoyim. Then the people of Israel cried out to the LORD for help, for he had 900 chariots of iron and he oppressed the people of Israel cruelly for twenty years. (Judges 4:1–3)

And all we learn about Deborah is this:

> Now Deborah, a prophetess, the wife of Lappidoth, was judging Israel at that time. She used to sit under the palm of Deborah between Ramah and Bethel in the hill country of Ephraim, and the people of Israel came up to her for judgment. (Judges 4:4–5)

Deborah, a wife, a mother, and a respected judge was given an established place where all could receive her judgment and advice. The respect for her was so high, she had her own palm tree. We will soon see she was a prophetess and a singer/poet and was referred to as the "the mother of Israel" (Judges 5:7). In our story, God heard once again His people crying and called on Deborah to save them. Without hesitation, she called on an influential Israelite named Barak and instructed him to gather an army of ten thousand soldiers. Barak, knowing the Israelites would be outmanned and have only ancient weapons and farming tools to fight with, responded, "If you will go with me, I will go, but if you will not go with me, I will not go" (Judges 4:8).

Deborah agreed to go and laid out a plan where she would take one group of Israelites to lure out the evil enemy leader Sisera and his chariots, and then Barak with the remainder of the army could surprise him. God ensured an Israelite victory by causing a massive rainstorm, which made the enemy chariots unusable and caused complete disruption in the Canaanite army. The Israelites prevailed and slew all the army of Sisera by the "edge of the sword." Sisera, however, escaped, or thought he did. He ran for his life and happened upon the tent of Heber the Kenite (Judges 4:18), who at that moment was at peace with the king of Canaan, Sisera's boss. Exhausted as he was, Sisera fell asleep whereby Jael, wife of Heber the Kenite, drove a tent stake through his temple, just as Deborah prophesized before the battle began, when she said, "For the Lord will sell Sisera into the hand of a woman" (Judges 4:9). Chapter 5 of Judges is devoted to the Song of Deborah where she gives credit to God, Barak, and the Israelite tribes who fought with her, and concludes by criticizing the tribes of Israel who failed to help when called upon.

Although the entire story of Deborah in the Bible consumes only two short chapters in the book of Judges, it contains many leadership lessons for today.

1. First is the idea of Deborah having her own palm tree. All the rest of the Israelites had fallen to the customs and culture of the surrounding nations. Not Deborah. The palm tree was representative of Deborah remaining true to her original beliefs and true to God. She was willing to stand alone if necessary. Others could come to her for advice, but under her palm tree she represented a rock, a touchstone, the one constant in an ever-changing world. How easy is it for us to fall into the trap of doing what everyone

else is doing, even though it may be questionable? It is easy for us to act on an insider stock tip or believe an interpretation of the employment laws or tax code we know is not accurate. We tend to follow the crowd. We need to set our beliefs and know we will stand on them regardless of what our culture is doing. Being a biblical leader in today's world means we need to become a touchstone for our business and industry. We need to be the one constant in an ever-changing world—and that constant comes from the Bible.

2. Second is the relationship between Deborah and Barak and how they responded to what needed to be done. Deborah asked, Barak responded positively, and they acted. No lengthy negotiations, no egos to massage, no discussion of who is in charge and who gets the credit, and no hesitation when it was time for action. I think back to an experience I had during a local community crisis. It was during this time that several competitors—fierce competitors who seldom talked to each other—banded together to present a united front for the community good. There are times when egos and our competitive nature need to be put aside.

3. Deborah participated. She did not get the message from God and pass it on and then recline under her palm tree. She did not lead from the rear. When Barak said he would go to battle if Deborah went as well, she went. Leadership means participation, especially in the small business world. If your team needs to work late hours to meet a deadline, as a leader you need to be there as well if for nothing else than to keep the coffee pot full and pass out pizza at midnight.

4. Once the battle was over, Deborah passed out ample praise to those who deserved it and scolded those who needed to perform better. Then she went back to passing out judgment under her palm tree. The battle was over, and there was no need to continue to fight. You ran for public office and lost; it's time to move on. Your company finished a major advertising campaign and it is over; it's time to move on to the next project and not dwell on old projects. You

worked hard to get a major design project and you won; now turn it over to the designers and start looking for the next project. Or maybe you lost; it's time to move on and look for the next project.

5. Finally, Deborah and her war with the Canaanites is one of the few stories in the Bible where the hero does not become a failure in the end. By trusting in God completely and relying on Him to give direction, Deborah did not succumb to the temptation of power and the lures of the flesh in this world. She did not try to become a king, take on any new non-God-given responsibility, or expand her consulting business out from her palm tree. She accomplished God's assignment and returned to her previous calling. Our culture today is full of managers who are looking for a springboard to the next opportunity. Our focus becomes what this one success will do for me as opposed to what this one success will do for others. As business leaders, we need to keep the focus on the good we are doing for God.

King Asa

Let's jump now to the next period of Israelite history, which is the period of the kings. Remember, God did not want His people to have kings as was the custom in the surrounding nations. He wanted to be the King of His people and have them rely on Him solely. But like all good fathers, He knew His children well and foresaw the day when they would demand an earthly king. In fact, He described that happening in Deuteronomy:

> When you come to the land that the Lord your God is giving you, and you possess it and dwell in it and then say, "I will set a king over me, like all the nations that are around me." (17:14)

As we saw earlier, the judge and prophet Samuel led the transition from judges to kings. God directed Samuel to anoint Saul as their king. Saul succumbed to his human nature and relied on his own wisdom and conceit, which caused God to anoint a new king named David. King David was a great king but had his own issues, namely a love affair and murder. King Solomon, one of David's sons, was the next king. He received the gift of wisdom, which he imparted in the books of Proverbs and Ecclesiastes, and the Songs of Solomon, but over time he bought into worldly temptations. Shortly after the reign of King Solomon, the Israelite nation divided with the northern portion becoming the House of Israel and the southern portion becoming the House of Judah. Each of these newly established kingdoms selected their own king.

The House of Israel (or the Northern Tribes) was a disaster. Each king failed in honoring and glorifying God. After nineteen kings (sprinkled throughout 1 Kings and 2 Kings), God finally had had enough, and He allowed the Assyrian nation to conquer the House of Israel, take the inhabitants into captivity, and repopulate the land with outsiders.

As for the House of Judah (the Southern Tribes), its people tried to obey God. They would have a few bad kings, and then a new king would see they were falling away from God and would work hard to return to the faith. That would work for a few kings, and then they would backslide with a few bad kings. Early in this progression of bad kings and good kings was King Asa. Ironically the name Asa means *healer* in Hebrew,[33] which was the task given to King Asa, a task he was up to—at least in his early years.

The story of Asa is found in 2 Kings 15 and 2 Chronicles 14.

> Abijah slept with his fathers, and they buried him in the city of David. And Asa his son reigned in his place. In his days the land had rest for ten years. And Asa did what was good and right in the eyes of the Lord his God. He took away the foreign altars and the high places and broke down the pillars and cut down the Asherim and commanded Judah to seek the Lord, the God of their fathers, and to keep the law and the commandment. (2 Chronicles 14:1–4)

King Asa did right in the eyes of God. He placed his faith in God and began to rebuild the kingdom. Never does the story say he followed the teachings of Moses, or the Ten Commandments, or the Torah (which is the book of laws). He followed God. Furthermore, in addition to removing all the foreign idols and pagan worship symbols, he built walls around his cities and enlisted and trained an army to defend Judah. King Asa went to war on idols and prepared for a war against his kingdom. And after about ten peaceful years, King Asa got the war he knew was coming.

> Zerah the Ethiopian came out against them with an army of a million men and 300 chariots, and came as far as Mareshah. And Asa went out to meet him, and they drew up their lines of battle in the Valley of Zephathah at Mareshah. And Asa cried to the Lord his God, "O Lord, there is none like you to help, between the mighty and the weak. Help us, O Lord our God, for we rely on you, and in your name we have come against this multitude. O Lord, you are our God; let not man prevail against you." So the Lord defeated the Ethiopians before Asa and before Judah, and the Ethiopians fled. (2 Chronicles 14:9–12)

God gave King Asa and his people victory and, true to King Asa at this point in his career, he gave all credit to God. Giving credit to God reinforced his efforts to keep his people from slipping back into the practices of the surrounding nations. Yes, his men were required to fight and kill, but the victory went to God. The peace that followed this victory, however, had a strange quality to it. No specific details are given in scripture, but God commanded a prophet named Azariah to speak to King Asa. The prophet Azariah said to King Asa:

> The Lord is with you while you are with him. If you seek him, he will be found by you, but if you forsake him, he will forsake you. (2 Chronicles 15:2)

I'm sure King Asa was thinking, "What did I do?" Up to this point in the story King Asa was a staunch follower of the Word of God. The prophet, however, went on to point out that times were good, but he warned King Asa about the dangers of contentment and that other kings had failed. He needed to be vigilant. The message was received; King Asa redoubled his efforts to remove all idols from the kingdom. In fact, he was so zealous in his efforts, he even deposed his grandmother because she had one of the detestable idol images in her garden. He made all people swear a covenant to God and cleansed his kingdom of all idol worship.

But King Asa was again tested. This time it was twenty-six years after God defeated the Ethiopians (2 Chronicles 14:9–12), and the test came from the House of Israel immediately to the north. The king of Israel built a blockade to stop all commerce from entering Judah from the north, which in ancient days was a prelude to an invasion. Instead of taking this problem to God, King Asa decided to tackle the problem alone. He paid the Syrians to attack Israel from the north, causing the king of Israel to remove the blockade from Judah and focus on fighting the Syrians. This strategy was sound and successful with one exception: God was not part of the plan. King Asa allowed his ego to get in the way of his relationship with God, and God was not pleased. God had Hanani the seer meet with King Asa to inform him:

> For the eyes of the Lord run to and fro throughout the whole earth, to give strong support to those whose heart is blameless toward him. You have done foolishly in this, for from now on you will have wars." (2 Chronicles 16:9)

Asa completely lost his humble attitude and raged against Hanani and his own people. Asa died a broken man with diseased feet because "he did not seek the Lord, but sought help from physicians" (2 Chronicles 16:12).

Despite his sad ending, King Asa is still regarded in the history of Judah as a good king—a testament to his efforts to rid the kingdom of idols and to how bad the bad kings were. King Asa is a great study in leadership skills for us to consider today.

1. One of the greatest leadership lessons from King Asa is how he approached ridding the kingdom of idols. Asa knew what God wanted of His people, and he zealously went after the forbidden idols of worship. Let's say, for example, you are taking over a company, an operational division, or a small business that needs a change. This operation may have been inflicted with a poor work ethic, have developed a culture that is not conducive to innovations, or have convinced itself that it is never going to be able to compete.

When you, as the organization's new leader, realize the right thing to do, the only thing left is to proceed and get it done. Asa did not ask for other opinions or worry about hurting the feelings of those who lost the pagan altars they had crafted in their backyards (including his grandmother). As leaders, it is our responsibility to learn what action is needed and then act. Learning what is needed is found through good business practices, observation, sound advice, and an understanding of doing what is right in the eyes of the Lord.

2. Second, develop your relationship with God and put your trust in Him. King Asa's army of three hundred thousand was up against one million soldiers plus chariots—he had no chance without God. And remember his prayer. "O Lord, there is none like you to help, between the mighty and the weak" (2 Chronicles 14:11). It was nothing fancy with complex theological-sounding words and long, drawn-out praises and petitions. It was straight to the point: God, I need your help now. He had done all the work beforehand by building a relationship with God so he knew God would answer and would help. Our business application is for each one of us to build a relationship with God and then trust in Him.

3. A famous saying that has been credited to many is "Pray to God, but row away from the rocks." That's what King Asa did. He put his entire trust in God but built walls around his cities and trained a small army to defend his kingdom. Granted, deciding when to trust God and when to act on your own is a decision you need to take up with God. But it seems to me that getting an operating line of credit with a bank before you need the line of credit is a good hedge. Knowing several talented designers you would like to work with before you need any additional designers is a good idea. Owning key-man insurance, backing up computer files, not relying on one source for raw materials, having a backup IT plan, and developing new markets while you are swamped with work all sound like self-driven ideas but are more likely God teaching you to be ready for His next set of instructions.

4. King Asa died alone in pain and separated from God, yet he is
    considered a good king. Despite King Asa falling away from God
    in the end, God's grace allows us to respect and honor the good
    work he did for his kingdom. Competitors, business associates,
    and peers who have not made the best decisions and have fallen on
    hard times deserve our grace. Lending a hand, offering advice, and
    showing compassion are the least we can do. Even in markets where
    the competition is fierce and tempers run hot, in victory as well as
    defeat, we need to continue to display the love and compassion of
    God who gave us everything in the first place. Asa was buried as a
    king should be buried:

    They laid him on a bier that had been filled with various
    kinds of spices prepared by the perfumer's art, and they
    made a very great fire in his honor. (2 Chronicles 16:14)

Despite how we finish, we should hope for as much respect.

Luke

Luke is such a great name. I think of Luke Skywalker of *Star Wars* fame,
Paul Newman's Cool Hand Luke, golfer Luke Donald, basketball player
Luke Walton, and country-western singer/songwriter Luke Bryan. But
most of all I think of a mysterious man named Luke, who wrote two of the
most influential books of the Bible. Luke was not an apostle, not a disciple,
and not a Galilean; he was not even Jewish. So how could a man so different
from all other authors and main characters in the Bible be able to make such
a world-affecting impact? That alone is why he deserves our attention when
thinking about biblical leaders.

In a nutshell, we know very little about Luke. It is presumed his name
is an abbreviation for the Greek name *Louknaos*, as this shows up several
times as the title of the third Gospel.[34] This name, however, only shows up
three times in scripture as references in three of the apostle Paul's letters
(Colossians 4, 2 Timothy 4, and Philemon 1). Most biblical scholars support
Luke as the author of the Gospel of Luke and the book of Acts since both
books have similar writing styles and vocabulary usage. Also, the author

of Acts uses the word *we* several times as he describes his travels with Paul throughout the book. We know Luke was a Gentile because Paul differentiates him from "those men of the circumcision among my fellow workers for the kingdom of God" (Colossians 4:11). Jews were one of the few nationalities who performed circumcision on male infants as a covenant sign of their faithfulness to God.

Luke first shows up with Paul while Paul is in Troas on his second missionary trip. It is presumed Luke came from a Gentile life to become a Christian after Jesus had been crucified, buried, and resurrected. Most likely Luke never met Jesus personally, and he only encountered a few of the original disciples. His birthplace and home are undetermined, but his upbringing and education was without doubt highly cultured. That he was a physician is without question, as Paul referred to him as "the beloved physician" (Colossians 4:14), and his use of medical terms permeates his writings. With the number of beatings Paul endured as he delivered the message of Jesus throughout the Roman Empire, having a doctor along probably saved his life a number of times. Although there were a few short periods of missionary trips that Paul took alone, Luke was Paul's inseparable companion up to the time of Paul's death. Remember, Paul died in Rome during Nero's persecution of Jews and Christians. Luke may have been the only follower able to stay with Paul and be at less risk since he was a physician and a Gentile by birth.

Although he may have kept a written record over the years, it is presumed that Luke wrote the Gospel of Luke and the book of Acts in AD 63, which was around the time Paul was beheaded. The question is why would a Gentile convert to Christianity, forego his medical training and a comfortable life, follow the apostle Paul throughout the Roman Empire, and then sit down and produce fifty-two chapters covering the life of a man he never met and document the rise of Christianity through the activities of several devout disciples? That is a great question and one with no indisputable answer.

Luke begins his Gospel with this:

> Inasmuch as many have undertaken to compile a narrative of the things that have been accomplished among us, just as those who from the beginning were eyewitnesses

and ministers of the word have delivered them to us, it seemed good to me also, having followed all things closely for some time past, to write an orderly account for you, most excellent Theophilus, that you may have certainty concerning the things you have been taught. (Luke 1:1–4)

To start looking at Luke and his writings, it is important we remember that while Luke was the human author, all works in the Bible were authored by God. It was God who superintended Luke as he labored over his two books of the New Testament. Luke felt as if he were writing to an unknown man named Theophilus, who was a Gentile struggling to understand all he had heard and seen about his new faith. The unknown Theophilus is not important because in God's plan Luke was writing to us all who, like Theophilus, struggle to understand the Christian faith. Luke, being a man of education and respect, wanted his account to add to the other Gospels written about Jesus; he wanted it to be from reliable sources and be thorough, orderly, and accurate. On top of that, Luke's Gospel is beautifully written. He is the consummate storyteller. Through his research, he found and told stories that are not found anywhere else in the Bible. He brought the people who were important to Jesus to life and made them important to the reader. We get to know Mary, Zechariah, Elizabeth, Simon the Pharisee, and Zacchaeus. Jesus's compassion to foreigners and social outcasts is revealed to depths not seen in the other Gospels. Women who ministered with Jesus and who Jesus ministered to are brought out by Luke in his presentation of Jesus's life. His writing covered the most amazing sixty-year period in world history.

As we focus on leadership, I cannot but help think Luke's role in this historical period contains many important lessons for us today.

1. The most important lesson from Luke is the role of number two. By number two I mean the second in command, the vice-chair/president/chancellor/commander, the number one assistant, and the indispensable person who is just off the screen and out of the limelight. Every success story has one of these characters. Famous basketball players always have someone to throw them the ball, world-famous singers have an unnamed piano player, and

every politician has a speechwriter who keeps him or her from saying the thing he or she wants to say. Every medical recovery has someone supporting it, and every startup business has an investor, a purchaser, a broker, or a fan who helps drive the owners to kick off their business.

But no one grows up planning to be the number two person. Early on, no one intentionally plans on being out of the limelight and not being famous or receiving the awards, accolades, and press. As we mature, however, we begin to understand the importance of the number two. We see how we can fill that role and be happy in watching someone else achieve a level we know we cannot achieve on our own. Luke had to be that kind of guy. He was satisfied letting Paul run the show, make the speeches, start churches, and handle the difficult arguments with the orthodox Jews. I'm sure Luke did his share of the work, and as many of us know, starting a church may be the easy part, but keeping it functioning is the bulk of the work. For Luke, an educated physician, to be able to be the number two man to the apostle Paul is a testament to his clear understanding of leadership.

2. Once Paul was beheaded, it would have been easy for Luke to return to one of the towns where he helped start a church, open a small medical clinic, and live out the sunset years of his life. The opposite became true. He turned his energy toward writing how Jesus Christ's life on earth was part of God's plan. This God who loves us, but who is hard to comprehend, wishes for us salvation that is found in everyone who comes to Jesus in faith. God's grace is ours in this fallen world. For Luke to accurately tell this story required him to travel and spend time with those who heard and saw the story firsthand. He had to check stories not included in other accounts to ensure he was true to his task. And once he had all the facts, he had to turn these facts into a compelling account that reflected the life and cause of Jesus and his disciples. For me in the twenty-first century, the commitment required to write a book in first-century Judea is mind-boggling—no office supply store, no computer, no Google, no spell-check, no printer, not even a

typewriter to be found. Yet he had a mission, and it proved to be one that found its way into the Bible and is changing millions of lives. Are you committed to your business and its cause to the same level Luke was committed to writing his Gospel?

3.   For Luke it was not about Luke. It was about the Gospel of Jesus Christ. It was about a gospel that was not popular; it was about a Messiah who did not physically come to rescue the Jews but saved them for something bigger and better. It was about expanding the message to everyone who wanted a better life, something to live for, something to live by, and eternal life. He did not populate his works with stories of his own efforts and trials. Only reluctantly did he refer to himself and that was as "we." All the glory went to God who was exemplified through the apostle Paul. In reading about Luke and Paul's travels, even though the stories are about Paul, you come to appreciate that Luke was more than an innocent bystander. When Paul was shipwrecked, so was Luke. When Paul was run out of a village for preaching the Gospel, Luke was not far behind trying to collect their personal items and catch up with him. But Luke is not going to tell that tale. His God-given role was to glorify God. He was not thinking of future book-signing events, a television interview, or maybe a reality show. His singleness of purpose is a leadership trait that would help many businesses prosper. We need to keep focused and not let all the side attractions get in the way of the mission of our work.

Luke was the consummate second man. His leadership as the second man is equally as important as the role the apostle Paul played. He understood his role in the success of God's work and did not let his ego interfere with being able to fulfill the objectives of spreading the work and love of Christ.

Jesus

As promised earlier, I would include Jesus as part of our leadership discussion. There is no better leadership example than Jesus. He is perfect—have you noticed there are never adjectives attached to Jesus? Our efforts to be a good leader are imperfect because we suffer from the fall of Adam and Eve and the depravity of human nature. Jesus is perfect, so anything he does also will be perfect and therefore be a good example. The other part of me feels this is not fair. Jesus is God. Imagine yourself playing a game of cards with God. He knows what's in your hand, what you're going to do before you do it, and that He will win before the game starts. That's not much fun, but it would be a good learning lesson.

As we've done throughout this book, let's look at one story of Jesus and then examine how He uses his leadership skills. The story I'm compelled to use is one that includes two of Jesus's most famous acts. Many think of the act of Jesus feeding the five thousand and walking on water as two distinct stories, but I prefer to see them as one continuous act. This story is found in three of the four Gospels: Matthew 14:13–33, Mark 6: 30–52, and John 6:1–21. Luke includes only the story of feeding the five thousand (Luke 9:10–17).

To summarize the story, the apostles have just returned from a ministry trip where they all experienced the power of healing and preaching. Jesus just received the news His cousin John the Baptist had been beheaded, so He decided it was time for Him and His apostles to get away to rest and reflect. He directed his apostles to go to a remote, desolate place. But unfortunately, their fame would not let them enjoy any peace. Five thousand men plus women and children followed them, so it became a working vacation, and Jesus began to preach and teach.

At the end of the day, the crowd still wanted more from Jesus, but everyone was getting hungry. Desolate places are sort of defined by being, well, desolate—no grocery stores, restaurants, markets, or anything else for that matter. Jesus took command, had the disciples collect the available food—five loaves of bread and two fish— blessed it and fed all the people with twelve baskets of food left over. Still concerned for his apostles' well-being, Jesus immediately instructed them to get into a boat (perhaps one of Zebedee's boats) and cross the Sea of Galilee. He would follow after them later (no instruction when or how). A storm developed while the disciples were crossing, and it not only impeded their progress, but they also found themselves in danger of capsizing and drowning. Keep in mind, more than half of these men had made their living on a boat on this lake before choosing to follow Jesus. Considering their expertise and experience, it had to be an unusual and perilous situation for them to be in danger. Meanwhile, Jesus remained behind to pray before following the apostles. He was simply going to walk across the lake in the same direction the boat had gone. When Jesus caught up to the apostles, they called out to him for help. Peter, seeing Jesus walking on the water, tried for a short time to also walk on water. Jesus rescued Peter, got into the boat, and calmed the storm, and they continued to the other side of the lake. It was just another typical day of being with Jesus.

Of course, there is much more to the story when reading it from Matthew, Mark, and John, but our focus here is on Jesus's leadership. As we will see, His leadership differs from the secular leadership style found in our current business environment.

1. Compassion and love are the hallmark of Jesus's leadership, traits that are missing from most corporate boardrooms. At the beginning of the story Jesus instructed:

> And he said to them, "Come away by yourselves to a desolate place and rest a while." For many were coming and going, and they had no leisure even to eat. And they went away in the boat to a desolate place by themselves. (Mark 6:31–32)

They were so busy that none of Jesus's disciples had time to eat. Jesus was concerned for them and wanted them to rest and rejuvenate so they could continue their ministry. He recognized what they were all doing was hard work. Yes, Jesus was on a timeline that only he knew, and there was a lot to accomplish and only a few workers who could minister, preach, and teach (Matthew 9:37). But the people and their needs would not go away, so they followed Jesus and his disciples to the desolate place:

> But when the crowds heard it, they followed him on foot from the towns. When he went ashore he saw a great crowd, and he had compassion on them and healed their sick. (Matthew 14:13–14)

Even though Jesus and his disciples needed rest, Jesus's compassion for the crowd trumped his own needs, and He continued to teach and heal. He could have said go away, I'm on vacation, I'm off the clock, call me tomorrow at the office. Not with Jesus. Compassion for these people had Jesus even feeding them when he did not invite them in the first place. He put their needs ahead of His.

How can this kind of compassion manifest in our current workplace? Legitimate and genuine concern for our employees, partners, and helpers must become a priority over written regulations and political correctness. A commitment to our job and to make right our obligation to our clients and customers, regardless of the inconvenience, must become commonplace. Finally, we must have compassion for the community we live in, not just for publicity, but a real concern for those we call neighbors.

2.   In reading the story of Jesus and how He fed the five thousand and then later that evening walked on water and stilled the violent storm, I'm guessing you were either impressed or cynical. Regardless of your reaction to Jesus's acts, what is significant about these miracles is how they were used. If I could turn five loaves of bread and two fish into a picnic for five thousand men and their families, I would be so impressed with myself that it would be difficult to keep this power and authority under control. "Hey, look what I can do." "Watch this." "Bet you can't do this, ha-ha." Think what you could do if you could walk on water and still violent storms.

> Now the day began to wear away, and the twelve came and said to him [Jesus], "Send the crowd away to go into the surrounding villages and countryside to find lodging and get provisions, for we are here in a desolate place." But he said to them, "You give them something to eat." (Luke 9:12–13)

His disciples conceded they had no ability to feed these people. Jesus instructed everyone to sit in groups of fifty. He gave thanks and blessed the food, and fed everyone with plenty left over.

The same is true for walking on water. It appears Jesus's intent was to walk on water later in the evening when no one was watching. Unfortunately, the violent storm impeded the progress of the apostles and Jesus happened upon them just in time. The miracles of walking on water and stilling the storm were of no importance to Jesus. They were all for the benefit of others and the glory of God.

Leadership is not displaying the power at your fingertips. Maybe you can command many people to do your bidding, or spend large amounts of money on a whim, or have an impressive-sounding address, or arrive at a meeting in a fancy car or plane. None of this mattered to Jesus. In His style of leadership, he went out of his way to make those abilities inconspicuous unless they could be used for others and for God's glory.

3. Although there are thousands of resources on leadership, my sense is today's typical leader defaults to a charismatic type of leadership. As portrayed on television, charismatic leaders should have this big, bold personality and are the figureheads both figuratively and literally for their business. They are the face, the word, and the embodiment for which the business stands. Charismatic leaders like grand entrances, sitting at the head table, parking in the front row, and being the person everyone wants to talk with and listen to.

But the Bible shows us a different style of leadership. In servant leadership, the leader understands he or she is there to serve the mission of the business and those who serve the same mission. These leaders give selfless service and are more concerned with the idea of service than with the benefits from the position of leadership. Humility is the attribute of this type of leader.

In Jesus's action of feeding the five thousand, he demonstrated these two styles are not incompatible. It was Jesus's charisma that drew the crowds to him. It was His magnetism that caused them to walk for miles to see Him, sit for hours to listen to Him, go hungry just to be in His presence, and forsake their friends and relatives just to understand His message. His miracles glorified the One whom He was talking about, not Himself. Although somewhat different from many leaders of today, Jesus was bigger than life; he had this special way about Him that drew people to Him and made Him stand out. People wanted to listen to Him, and they wanted Him to acknowledge them.

This powerful, charismatic presence was completely offset by his humble service. Yes, He was tired and so were His disciples, but He needed to be of service so He taught and fed the five thousand. While his persona drew people to Him, nothing He did or said was directed at Himself, but to the One whom He called Father. He used His charisma to draw people and His humility and service to make people believe and understand. Think of the amazing impact that could occur if our charismatic leaders today would step away from the perks of being leaders and focus on the service they could add.

4. The four accounts of feeding the five thousand and the three accounts of walking on water/stilling the storm are all different. They come from four individuals who each had their own appreciation for what transpired or were told happened. In feeding the five thousand, all four accounts include Jesus giving the disciples the opportunity to feed the people, and upon hearing they could not, Jesus fed them. There was no rebuke or chastising, just a simple miracle demonstrating His power from God, and in all likelihood, only the disciples immediately in His presence knew what was happening. Scripture makes no big deal about what transpired. When Jesus walked out to the boat, saved Peter from drowning, climbed into the boat, and calmed the storm, "those in the boat worshipped him, saying, 'Truly you are the Son of God'" (Matthew 14:33). These miracles were designed to build His team and assure the disciples that Jesus was the Son of God and the Messiah, despite the common misconception that the Messiah would be a warrior-type leader who would overthrow the Roman oppression. In retrospect, Matthew's account of the disciples worshipping Him is probably not an exact understanding of what happened. If it were, Jesus would not have had to continue demonstrating His divine nature to them on a regular basis. It was not until after His resurrection that

they believed Jesus was the Messiah. The leadership style of Jesus, however, was to build and support His team despite their failings and their questions. Jesus had selected them, and they were going to be His management team even if they ran away once He was imprisoned and crucified. Jesus was committed to them.

How about our teams, our staff, our organizational structure? Are we committed to them? Are we giving them undying support and backing? Maybe they are not totally committed yet, but they are your team and will be your team until you replace them. It's black and white. Your employees, especially your management team, are 100 percent your team and deserve your full commitment—or change your team. Without question, just like Jesus, you need to commit to your team members while they are still your team.

Zebedee

Guys like Zebedee have the best leadership style of all. They know who they are. Zebedee doesn't have to think about how to handle certain situations, what is politically correct, the exact interpretation of any laws, or if certain decisions will upset someone. Zebedee has a heart for God. It was the way he was brought up, and it is ingrained in who he is. Zebedee knows honesty is the only way; he speaks plainly and openly. He also listens intently because he wants to understand. He is charismatic because he is friendly and open to people. Best of all, he has a servant heart because he works every night, shoulder to shoulder, with his team.

Summary

1. Deborah teaches us to stay true to our calling. She was a judge with her own palm tree when God called her to save the Israelites for the Canaanites. Without hesitation, she went into action, put a plan together, elicited help to organize an army, and won the war. She then went back to her palm tree and continued dispensing judgments and advice. God did not call her to use winning the war as a springboard to something bigger and greater. She knew being a judge under the palm tree was already something bigger and greater.

2. King Asa teaches us to bring zeal to our work. In removing the foreign idol from the kingdom of Judah, King Asa proceeded with a gusto seldom seen in today's workplace. Once he knew what course of action was needed, he proceeded without any favoritism or exceptions. Some actions must be black or white to be effective. Too often we make solid decisions followed by pages of exceptions and excuses that render the original decision worthless.

3. Luke represents the perfect number two. Look around your business, competing businesses, businesses you admire and respect, and highly successful businesses in your community. I'd wager the most successful ones have one or more behind-the-scenes employees you know are invaluable to that business. You'll not be able to hire them away because their bosses also know their employees' value. Likewise, if you find an employee who wants to be a number two and will let you lead them, do everything you can to keep him or her as part of your team.

4. Jesus led a ragtag team of disciples whom He had to retrain and reteach. They quarreled, asked stupid questions, and could not figure out His parables. But they worked hard and with passion. He loved them. They were His team through the good times and bad. Do you treat your management team that way?

Notes

_____

_____

_____

_____

_____

_____

_____

_____

_____

_____

_____

_____

_____

_____

_____

CHAPTER 12
Zebedee's Prayer

Zebedee slowly got out of the boat he was sitting in and, after some effort, was able to make his tired old body stand erect. He lifted his eyes skyward and began to say in Hebrew, "Exalted and hallowed be His great name in the world, which He created to His will. May He establish His kingdom in your lifetime and in your days, and in the lifetime of the whole household of Israel, speedily and at a near time." Being a devout Jew, Zebedee was acquainted with prayer through his time in the synagogue and the Siddur, the Jewish prayer book. The Old Testament fathers commanded the faithful to pray and to pray earnestly and sincerely.

"Father, I ask you to watch over James and John and Peter and Andrew as they travel and learn from Jesus. And I ask for your guidance about the next steps I am to take in preparing Zebedee and Sons Fishing Co. for the next phase of its life," prayed Zebedee.

Up to this point, my intent has been to demonstrate how a background in knowing the Bible, historically and theologically, can benefit any business enterprise. Stories included here only represent a small fraction of the business knowledge that can be gained from reading and knowing the Bible. Knowing certain stories from the Bible enables us as business leaders to tap into the lessons from those stories. And through those stories we will arrive at the same or better solutions and outcomes as found in many of the trendy how-to business advice books. Knowing how King Solomon treated both his

Israelite laborers and pagan workers tasked with building the magnificent temple to God three thousand years ago tells us how to treat our employees in today's world. The story from Ezekiel about the watchman on the wall is a great metaphor for how we should demonstrate accountability. We should remind ourselves of Abraham's negotiating ability each time a contract crosses our desk, a lease is renewed, or new equipment is purchased. And as hard as it may first appear, lessons from the Bible about dealing with bureaucracy are designed to help us avoid losing our focus.

This chapter on prayer, however, is going to be different. So far I have given biblical examples in the form of stories found in all scriptures and then related those stories to a handful of typical business issues prevalent in the corporate world. Whether you are a believer or not, those stories contain real solutions to real workplace problems, and they can be applied to business issues, whether they are found in large multinational corporations or in small, Main Street mom-and-pop stores. You may have noticed that I have not always provided a direct application tying the Bible to the problem being discussed. Part of the education this book provides is how to address business problems through the Bible on your own. The answer to applying the Bible to any business situation is between you and God; the stories are just an example of how God and His people responded two thousand years ago to very similar problems. The key, which is consistent in every story, is the relationship between the person with the problem and God.

Statistically, nearly every household has at least one Bible, so the stories, their lessons, and the solutions are available to everyone. There is no need to buy new books, keep track of the latest business guru's blog, or find time to keep up with the accumulating business podcasts. All you need to remember is a key part of any one story and you will be able to find the rest of the story through the cross-references found in most Bibles. You may have noticed that, since this is a book about the Bible, most stories have someone at some time praying to God. The connections I developed between the story and how it relates to a specific business activity intentionally never included the need for you, the businessperson, to pray. However, to get the most out of what the Bible has to offer, learning the prayer part of each story is important.

Amos

Amos, one of the prophets from the Old Testament, provides a great example of living in a difficult time yet relying on prayer to accomplish the task God has given him. Amos lived in the northern kingdom of Israel during the reign of King Jeroboam II, and life was good. King Jeroboam II had increased the kingdom's reach and made peace with Israel's twin kingdom, the southern kingdom of Judah. With this political alliance came much prosperity. The wealthy got wealthier and the poor became poorer. Government leaders credited this "prosperity" to God, yet they continued to build altars to the Canaanite gods Baal and Astarte. Golden calves were worshipped, and the laws that Moses gave to the Israelites were held in contempt. Alliances were made with other neighboring nations, and the Israelites continued to adopt the ways and beliefs of these pagans despite the many warnings from their true God.

Amos was a single employee, a small business owner; he was a shepherd and a dresser of sycamore trees (you don't see that on many résumés today). Through Amos's travels, he became aware of the disparity between the wealthy's life of luxury and the despairing circumstances of the poor. The kingdom of Israel's leaders insisted it was their faithful performance of observing the required ritual obligations that provided the wealthy with prosperity. To them, the obvious reason the poor were poor was they failed in these ritualistic obligations. These leaders were too oblivious to their own personal failure to actually follow the true commands of God.

One day, the Spirit of God came over Amos, and he began to have dreams and visions. Several of these dreams are recorded in the book of Amos. In one dream he saw a man with a plumb line measuring a wall that was about to fall. The man was told the bulging wall was the house of Israel, and it was about to fall; the interpretation was the house of Israel would soon go into captivity. A second dream was about a basket of fruit representing the people of Israel. Their material prosperity was just like the fruit when perfectly ripe, but just like the fruit, ripeness only lasts a short while and then the fruit rots and decays. So, just like fruit rotting, the peaceful days of prosperity were soon going to end. A third vision was of a swarm of locusts just about to devour the produce of the land. The locusts represented the evil days ahead for the kingdom of Israel. With these dreams in his head, Amos could not idly stand by. Although he had no training to be a prophet or a public speaker, and his audience was certain to be hostile to any message of repentance, he had to speak out.

> And he said:
> The Lord roars from Zion
> and utters his voice from Jerusalem;
> the pastures of the shepherds mourn,
> and the top of Carmel withers. (Amos 1:2)

Amos became the quintessential Old Testament prophet using powerful and forceful declarations, such as:

> "So I will send a fire upon the house of Hazael,
> and it shall devour the strongholds of Ben-hadad.
> I will break the gate-bar of Damascus,
> and cut off the inhabitants from the Valley of Aven,
> and him who holds the scepter from Beth-eden;
> and the people of Syria shall go into exile to Kir,"
> says the Lord. (Amos 1:4–5)

And:

> "So I will send a fire upon the wall of Gaza,
> and it shall devour her strongholds.
> I will cut off the inhabitants from Ashdod,
> and him who holds the scepter from Ashkelon;
> I will turn my hand against Ekron,
> and the remnant of the Philistines shall perish,"
> says the Lord God. (Amos 1:7–8)

These images of destruction and ruin were directed toward Israel's neighbors. For the kingdom of Israel, Amos had words like these:

For three transgressions of Israel,
and for four, I will not revoke the punishment,
because they sell the righteous for silver,
and the needy for a pair of sandals—
those who trample the head of the poor into the dust of
the earth
and turn aside the way of the afflicted;
a man and his father go in to the same girl,
so that my holy name is profaned." (Amos 2:6–7)

These declarations did not make Amos a popular man; his audience thought they were righteous toward God. For six chapters, he declared God's wrath on the people of the northern kingdom of Israel. At one point, one of the pagan priests incited a riot against Amos, and Amos was saved only by the mercy of the king who, despite being the object of much of Amos's message, was smart enough to realize the hand of God at work. Amos became tormented by the plight of the kingdom of Israel and the forthcoming wrath of God as described in the dreams. While Amos was working overtime to get the people to see the error of their ways, he became aware that these same people, his people, could not withstand the devastating actions intended by God. For the vision of the locusts, Amos prayed:

This is what the Lord God showed me: behold, he was forming locusts when the latter growth was just beginning to sprout, and behold, it was the latter growth after the king's mowings. When they had finished eating the grass of the land, I said,

"O Lord God, please forgive!
How can Jacob stand?
He is so small!"
The Lord relented concerning this:
"It shall not be," said the Lord. (Amos 7:1–3)

For the vision of the fire and drought:

This is what the Lord God showed me: behold, the Lord God was calling for a judgment by fire, and it devoured the great deep and was eating up the land. Then I said,

"O Lord God, please cease!
How can Jacob stand?
He is so small!"
The Lord relented concerning this:
"This also shall not be," said the Lord God. (Amos 7:4–6)

Despite the fierce and angry prophecy Amos directed at the kingdom of Israel, he could not stand to think of the destruction God had in mind for the Israelites. In his prayers Amos asked, probably begged, God to relent and not go through with His plans. And through the first two prayers, God relented. As for the third vision with the plumb line, the prayer between God and Amos went like this:

This is what he showed me: behold, the Lord was standing beside a wall built with a plumb line, with a plumb line in his hand. And the Lord said to me, "Amos, what do you see?" And I said, "A plumb line." Then the Lord said,

"Behold, I am setting a plumb line
in the midst of my people Israel;
I will never again pass by them;
the high places of Isaac shall be made desolate,
and the sanctuaries of Israel shall be laid waste,
and I will rise against the house of Jeroboam with the
sword." (Amos 7:7–9)

Amos understood that relenting on the first two acts of destruction was acceptable. But the time had come for God to act, and Amos had to accept the inevitable punishment for the kingdom of Israel.

The lessons Amos teaches about prayer are:

1. Prayer is a simple conversation. Amos does not use any flowery words, preset phrases, doxology, or glowing honorariums. He gets

straight to the point; in fact, many may not realize these are prayers. Remember, Amos is a workingman with just a little education. His prayers reflect his relationship with the Lord, which is God is God and Amos is a sinner like everyone else. But he *knows* God is listening and will respond and act accordingly.

2. Did Amos change God's mind? No, God is sovereign and all knowing. The vision He gave Amos was only one of many possibilities. It caused Amos to work even harder to get the people of the northern kingdom to repent, and some did. We know even today God is waiting for as many people as possible to find Him before He unleashes the Second Coming. Amos's prayer to God is an act of honoring the immense glory of God.

3. Amos's intercessory prayer is an example of how God can change our hearts, just like he changed Amos's heart to be more compassionate toward the kingdom of Israel. He initially was fired up for God to punish all these sinful people, but as he fully comprehends the tragic end for them, he realizes their punishment is not what he wants.

4. We make our case in prayer and leave the actions in the hands of God. Our minds are too small to begin to understand the thinking of God. Amos was praying on behalf of his people; some were his friends or used to be his friends. When we feel compelled to pray, we lay out our thoughts, ideas, and arguments before an all-knowing God and let it go.

I like the story of the mother whose bright young son is going off to college. She prays to God to take care of him and to give him a roommate who is equally bright, moral, trustworthy, and studious. Upon dropping him off at the dorm, she is shocked to find his new roommate to be a somewhat disheveled young man with a history of substance abuse, who had been previously been expelled from school. But this young man is looking for a second chance. She confesses to her son her disappointment that her prayer was not met, and he responds, "Maybe his mom prayed the exact same prayer you prayed." One of the prayers was answered.

Theology

Although I have not discussed theology in detail with any of the other topics, I think it important to cover the theology of prayer before going into what is suitable for praying as a businessperson. My disclaimer for my personal expertise in prayer is in the book of Luke:

> And when he came to the place, he said to them [Jesus's disciples], "Pray that you may not enter into temptation." And he withdrew from them about a stone's throw, and knelt down and prayed … And when he rose from prayer, he came to the disciples and found them sleeping for sorrow, and he said to them, "Why are you sleeping? Rise and pray that you may not enter into temptation." (Luke 22:40–41, 45–46)

We can find comfort in the idea that even Jesus's disciples, when praying at the feet of the Master, still struggled with prayer.

If you are like me, once someone starts using words like justification, sanctification, intercession, experiential, ecclesiastical, ecumenical, and all the "–ology" words, I immediately start wondering how my Kansas City Royals baseball team is doing and if my lawn needs mowing. So I tend to keep my theology discussions simple, short, and to the point. Prayer is nothing more than a conversation with God; prayer is nothing less than a conversation with God. Most civilizations have some form of prayer, and even the Bible acknowledges that the pagan nations surrounding the Israelites prayed to one form of god or another. My favorite is the story told earlier about Elijah challenging the priests of Baal, one of the pagan gods, to a prayer duel to see who could get their god to ignite a fire (1 Kings 18). Even people who have little or no religious connections and find themselves in a difficult situation will resort to a "prayer" for help.

The Bible has surprisingly little direction on how to pray, and this is where the numerous examples become invaluable. Throughout the Bible we see many types of prayers: petition, intercession, adoration, thanksgiving, and confession, to name a few. Prayer is intended to be spontaneous. This is to avoid having any structure or specific form that could become a barrier to our ability to connect with our Lord and Savior. Prayer is a conversation in the same way we converse with our best friend. We do not only talk to our best friend when we have a dire problem, when we are wit's end, or when we have no one else to talk to. We tell our best friend our good news, bad news, concerns, funny things, and sad stories, and complement each other. That is how we are to talk to God. Prayer is an intimate relationship. I am always amazed and disappointed when friends of mine find themselves in trouble, pray to God for the first time in years, do not get what they ask for, and then are angry God did not come through.

Let's examine several scriptures that address prayer.

> And without faith it is impossible to please him, for whoever would draw near to God must believe that he exists and that he rewards those who seek him. (Hebrews 11:6)

This verse has three important components. First is we must have faith. Why would you go to a God you do not believe in, and why would a God that you do not believe in answer your prayer? You need to build a relationship with God. The concept of "please Him" troubles some people. Make no mistake, we are the creation of God and our purpose is to bring Him glory (Isaiah 43:7, 1 Corinthians 10:31). God does not need us or anything we bring. Nevertheless, we are so important to Him that He sent His Son to die on the cross for our sins.

Second, we are to draw near to Him and seek Him. That is the purpose of this book: to make us aware of the vast wealth of knowledge, advice, and help that is available in the Bible. It is not a collection of one-line verses that many spout off to prove they are religious. The Bible is filled, from beginning to end, with great material of which every line is applicable to our lives. We just need to immerse ourselves in the stories and learn how God loves us, how He is waiting for us to come to Him, and how He wants us to start a relationship with Him.

Third and finally, He rewards. He is our best friend and has the power to do whatever He wishes. It is His choice to answer our prayers, and the Bible tells us He will answer our prayers.

I'm not good at praying. I struggle to try to find the right words and the right time, and to understand what God's will is for me.

> Likewise the Spirit helps us in our weakness. For we do not
> know what to pray for as we ought, but the Spirit himself
> intercedes for us with groanings too deep for words. And he
> who searches hearts knows what is the mind of the Spirit,
> because[g] the Spirit intercedes for the saints according to
> the will of God. (Romans 8:26–27)

I do not have to worry about what to say. I need to just say what is in my heart and know the Holy Spirit will intercede on my behalf. It is an interesting paradox that our God is all knowing, yet we are asked to "rejoice always, pray without ceasing, give thanks in all circumstances" (1 Thessalonians 5:16) about the things He already knows and has predetermined. Prayer is our way of acknowledging and worshipping God.

A last verse to cover is one that is often referenced and misused. The question at hand is if God answer all our prayers.

> Truly, truly, I say to you, whoever believes in me will also
> do the works that I do; and greater works than these will
> he do, because I am going to the Father. Whatever you ask
> in my name, this I will do, that the Father may be glorified
> in the Son. If you ask me anything in my name, I will do
> it. (John 14:12–14)

Many people read this verse and remember only "If you ask me anything in my name, I will do it" (John 14:14). Many would like to think if they ask for anything—for healing, a new car, their spouse to change, or their football team to win—and tack on "in Jesus's name," it will be granted. To keep this verse in context, we need to focus on the first sentence that is talking about the works of Christ. What are the works of Christ? Jesus Christ's works are those based on His death, resurrection, and exaltation. It is His work to point to the Gospel to transform lives. So our prayers to God are how we ask God to extend His kingdom here on earth as it is in heaven (Matthew 6:10). As long as our prayer requests are within those parameters, we should expect an answer from God. One point of caution, however, is that "no" is an answer. God's ways are not our ways, and we will never understand or comprehend His thinking (Ecclesiastes 8, Isaiah 55:8–9).

Prayers for and about Work

So let's get right to the point. Your business does not have enough work to keep your designers busy, the traffic in your store is not enough to pay the rent, not enough people are buying and using your app, not enough doctors are using your software to coordinate prescriptions, you're not winning enough construction bids to keep your crews busy—whatever the reason, you are in dire straits and need more business. Can you and should you pray for more business? There are two answers to this question.

Answer Number One

The first answer is by all means go ahead and pray. And by pray, I mean clasp your hands together, get on your knees if you are so inclined, and ask God out loud for help. Be bold and say exactly what is on your mind regardless of whether or not you think it is appropriate. Tell Him your concerns and why you think you are in this situation. Pour your heart out to Him. Remind Him of what you have done and what the impacts will be on your employees whom you think of as an extended family. Ask Him outright to send you more business. Or ask Him for some other inspiration that will generate new business, or to point your steps in another direction to get you out of the jam you're in. All this is just a start, and I need to mention that Christians are just as likely to find themselves in this predicament as non-Christians. No one has a copyright on finding themselves in difficult predicaments in business, whether of their own making or not.

I believe it is okay to ask God for what you want, especially if you are just learning to pray. If you need more business, ask for more business. If you want your alma mater's basketball team to win, ask. If you want to win the lottery, go ahead and ask. By asking, you have started the conversation with God. My observation is your prayer has four possible outcomes:

1. The best of all is God will grant you what you ask. More business will begin to come your way, your team will win, and whatever has been requested will happen. You will not know if it was God's answer, or if you had asked for more, would you have gotten more. But your prayer will have been answered.

2. God will let you know that your request is not part of His plan. How you are told this is based on the depth of your relationship with God. If you are new to praying and following the Christian faith, your prayer is simply not answered. As you mature in your prayer life, you will notice that although your prayer seems unanswered, other options begin to open up, pointing your original prayer request in another direction. God will tell you where He wants you to go if you just learn to listen.

3. God will let you know the timing is not right. Through your prayer life, you feel and learn you are on the right track, you are following what God wants you to do, but your specific request is not going to be answered exactly how you asked it just yet. I know this puts you in a state of confusion and limbo. What do I do now? Keep talking to God and listening for His response. Remember, you are building a dialogue and God will take care of you in His own way. Many of us may spend long periods of time praying, knowing we are doing what God is asking of us, but do not hear instantly if our prayers are answered.

4. And then, when least expected, God answers your prayer in an unanticipated way that is so much more than what you have been asking for. You get a request that is over the top. Maybe you get an inquiry from a potential client that takes you to the next business level, or you receive a long-term order requiring you to grow bigger than expected, or you discover a new application for your software. It might mean you have to work harder, take a few more risks, and hire more people. But it's God working out His plan within you. I'm sure banks do not like to see that on an application, but there is no better business plan than having God as part of it.

The answer to the question "Should I pray for more business?" is asking God if our business is part of His will for us. To find this answer we need to continue to pray. We need to tell God we know He is faithful, loving, and just, and our interest is to submit to His will. God's will is not always obvious, and you may not definitely know God's plans. But if it is part of His plan for your business to flourish, so be it. If His plans are otherwise, ask for knowledge of what those new plans look like. Acknowledge that you are open to new avenues, opportunities, and the changes He might have in store for you. Let Him know you are ready for a change. Let God know He is strongest in your weakness and this might be a time of trial for you to grow. You are asking for His guidance and help (2 Corinthians 12:7–10) because you are a simple servant of God and know everything you have been given is from Him.

Answer Number Two

I mentioned there are two answers to the question "Do we pray for more business?" In the first answer, the businessperson prays and hopes. By praying, waiting, and hoping, the businessperson often attempts to rely on him- or herself and resorts to either drastic or unethical thinking. It is hard to wait and hope and do nothing, especially if you are an entrepreneur. You find yourself waiting for one of four outcomes. It's at this point where the businessperson is most vulnerable. Are you just hoping for more business, or have you sincerely put your trust in God? It's at this point where many fail to trust God and fall to the temptations of our secular society. I am always disappointed to see successful businesspeople caught in criminal activities, such as fraud and theft, or resort to addictions, such as alcohol/drug abuse and spousal abuse.

In the second answer, the businessperson prays, places trust in God, knows there is a reason behind what is going on, and prepares for God's answer, knowing full well it might be a complete change of direction. Peace of mind rules this situation, and the businessperson practices patience (although that may take considerable effort). We surrender ourselves to the grace of God. Finding your way to this answer begins years before the predicament of needing help is encountered. These years are used to build an intimate relationship with God and develop a complete reliance on Him.

In both answers, prudent business practices, such as matching revenues with expenses, evaluating employment agreements, making payroll adjustments, and renegotiating rent, should be used. Just because you are waiting for God's answer is no reason to not act using the God- given business talents you possess.

Fortunately this process of prayer is the same regardless of your circumstances. You are threatened with a lawsuit, a building you designed has a structural failure, a competitor beats you to the development of a superior software product—any major business-threatening event is a time to pray. Of course, you are better off if you laid a strong foundation with God before the threat, but you can go to God anytime and start building that relationship. God will listen even on the way to bankruptcy court.

Major events are not the only time to pray. What about when you are trying to choose between two employment candidates for a key role in your company? Do you think God might have an insight into the qualification of these candidates? The same is true for selecting a new business location, website look, or logo; expanding to a new city; or disciplining an employee—anything that involves a decision. God is your friend, and He is waiting for you to ask Him to help in all circumstances.

In closing, I want to share a prayer from the apostle Paul that I think exhibits how we should pray. I'm not going to break down all the elements of this prayer, but I'd like you to read it and focus on each line and each word. It's a prayer to the church in Colossae, and Paul is expressing his desire for its members to bear "fruit in every good work." What more could we ask.

> And so, from the day we heard, we have not ceased to pray for you, asking that you may be filled with the knowledge of his will in all spiritual wisdom and understanding,[1] so as to walk in a manner worthy of the Lord, fully pleasing to him, bearing fruit in every good work and increasing in the knowledge of God. May you be strengthened with all power, according to his glorious might, for all endurance and patience with joy, giving thanks to the Father, who has qualified you to share in the inheritance of the saints in light. He has delivered us from the domain of darkness and transferred us to the kingdom of his beloved Son, in whom we have redemption, the forgiveness of sins. (Colossians 1:9–12)

Zebedee

Zebedee has an advantage over many of us. He was brought up in a culture that thrived on prayer and made it a part of everything they did. He prayed at sunrise, midafternoon, and sunset. He had a pipeline built to God so strong that no circumstance could be encountered where he was not immediately in contact with God, asking for help, advice, and direction. God had taken away Zebedee's worries, so all he had to focus on was enjoying the gifts he was blessed with.

Summary

1. Amos, the Old Testament prophet, is a remarkable teacher of how and when to pray. He was not trained in what God called him to do, but when called he was passionate about praying for the kingdom of Israel to repent. His prayers were not eloquent and full of biblical passages. He just talked to God about his concerns and fears. And God listened. That worked for Amos, and it will work for us.

2. Our theology of prayer is based on examples from the Bible. Without faith, however, it is impossible to please God (Hebrews 11:6). We need to know God, draw near to Him, and know He *will* respond. We need to build our relationship with Him so our communication link is established long before we need to go to Him with a serious problem or question.

3. Always pray for what you want; be bold and be specific. We do not know the ways of our Lord; His thoughts are higher than ours. But if you do not ask and communicate with Him, you have no chance of getting what you want. But be careful, you may get what you want and much more.

Notes

CHAPTER 13

Zebedee Moves On

Zebedee was alone with his boat and fishing equipment, but he knew he was not alone. Although he was a practicing first-century Jew, who experienced all the legalism Jesus came to correct, he still had an intimate relationship with God. Zebedee and Salome passed on to their sons a passion for a religion different from the Jewish religion of the day. The religion of the established Jewish elite did not mirror the words of the Bible. They knew, as many did during this period in history, what they practiced was not from the Bible. That was what Jesus came to tell the world. Jesus came to fulfill His prophecy and save the world. Are we practicing today a religion that is true to the Bible?

Although I have not openly admitted it until now, the underlying mission of this book is to bring others to believe in and follow Jesus Christ. Being smart businesspeople, I'm sure you figured that out, and I thank you for sticking with me all the way through this book. I strive daily to fulfill what God is instructing me to do, and I can say the results are always more astounding than I could have dreamed. Since I do not want not keep this approach to myself, I'm always looking for creative ways to demonstrate to my friends, acquaintances, and business associates just how Jesus Christ will change their lives if they let Him. I assure you, the business knowledge and personal advice found in the Bible are just the tip of the iceberg of the blessings that come from reading and following the scriptures.

In closing this book, I want to cover one more character found in the Bible who demonstrates the true benefits of relying on God in all circumstances in life. Contrary to most of my other stories, this character is popular and well known. This character is King David, who is the subject of history books, fiction books, biographical books, leadership books, and children's books. He is the topic of made-for-TV and big-screen movies alike. And King David deserves all this attention. Anyone who focuses on just one story of David's life, however, is missing out on the richness that being faithful to God brings to every aspect of one's life. The story of David and Goliath (1 Samuel 17) is a great story, but it was just one small chapter of a bigger story. The same is true of how David became an anointed king (1 Samuel 16), how he broke God's commands and ate the consecrated bread (1 Samuel 21, Matthew 12:4), and how he committed adultery (2 Samuel 11). To appreciate King David, his story must be thought of in terms of his entire life.

Youthful Stage

I see David's life in three stages, the first of which is his youthful stage. David's father, Jesse, was the grandson of Boaz and Ruth, who are the stars of the book of Ruth, the eighth book in the Old Testament. Jesse is an old man when we first meet him in 1 Samuel 15 where he is represented as a small business owner in the sheep production business. In this story, the prophet and judge Samuel was instructed by God to go to Jesse's house where he would find the next king of the House of Judah. Samuel rejected the seven older sons and had David, the youngest, who was out tending the sheep, brought in. Samuel immediately recognized him as the king God had sent him to find. Saul anointed David on the spot, and he became the king-in-waiting.

Circumstances led David to be found bringing his brothers provisions, as they were in King Saul's army and engaged in a battle with the Philistine army. David was twenty years old by this time, and the battle was not a battle between armies but a standoff with a mountain of a man named Goliath of Gath standing between both armies. He was challenging anyone in King Saul's army to fight him one-on-one for all the marbles. His physical description, as found in 1 Samuel 17, is more that little impressive, assuming you can convert cubits and shekels to feet and pounds. If an Israelite could defeat Goliath, the Philistines would become Israelite slaves; if Goliath won, the Israelites would become Philistine slaves. Children's books do a great job of showing how David knocked Goliath down with one small stone thrown from his sling, but they respectfully omit the part about lopping his head off with his own sword and the Israelite army attacking and killing all the surprised Philistines. Because of David's part in this victory, he earned King Saul's gratitude and respect and was taken into his royal family to be one of his advisors.

During these youthful years, David learned to use a sling while protecting his father's sheep and learned the ways of government from King Saul. These were growing and learning times for David. He developed a prowess as a military leader and became commander over King Saul's army. It was also during this time that David's musical talents shone. David was everything everyone wanted. He was intelligent, handsome, eloquent in speech, and respected by the army. He was a national hero on the battlefield and a talented musician. He was loved by all the people, and because of this, King Saul grew to hate and despise David.

Fugitive Years

The second stage of David's life began when King Saul decided out of jealously to kill him. David was now on the run for his life. He found himself the leader of roughly four hundred men.

> And everyone who was in distress, and everyone who was in debt, and everyone who was bitter in soul, gathered to him. And he became commander over them. (1 Samuel 22:2)

David was a fugitive, and King Saul was out searching for him with David's own army. David, however, was not just hiding and fearing for his life. Being an enterprising man, David and his ragtag band of followers earned a nice reputation by fighting for several neighboring nations as long as they were not fighting the Israelites. It's ironic that the Philistine army (remember Goliath) came to rely on David and his men for their military victories. David had been on the run from Saul for over seven years, and on two occasions he had the opportunity to kill King Saul, knowing full well he would become king and his days of running would be over. But David could not bring himself to kill Saul.

> And he came to the sheepfolds by the way, where there was a cave, and Saul went in to relieve himself. Now David and his men were sitting in the innermost parts of the cave. And the men of David said to him, "Here is the day of which the Lord said to you, "Behold, I will give your enemy into your hand, and you shall do to him as it shall seem good to you." Then David arose and stealthily cut off a corner of Saul's robe. And afterward David's heart struck him, because he had cut off a corner of Saul's robe. He said to his men, "The Lord forbid that I should do this thing to my lord, the Lord's anointed, to put out my hand against him, seeing he is the Lord's anointed." So David persuaded his men with these words and did not permit them to attack Saul. And Saul rose up and left the cave and went on his way. (1 Samuel 24:3–7)

Despite being pursued by King Saul and knowing the outcome for David if Saul died, David would not go against the king whom God anointed. Finally, by the time David was roughly thirty years of age, King Saul was killed in a battle on Mount Gilboa between the Israelites and Philistines (1 Samuel 31). David was elsewhere fighting the Amalekites when this happened.

Upon hearing of King Saul's death, David claimed his kingly right. All men of Judea accepted David as king, and he was finally anointed king. But not all Israelites accepted David. One of Saul's sons attempted to unite the other tribes of Israel, and a civil war ensued. David finally prevailed in uniting all twelve tribes of Israel into one nation. Through many successful wars, David succeeded in making Israel an independent state and gained the respect and fear of the surrounding nations. David was able to conquer Jerusalem and make it the political center of the Israelite nation. The ark of the covenant was moved to Jerusalem, and David began making plans for building a permanent temple for the ark and as a place to worship God. There are not many records of all the wars and battles David fought, but as time moved on, life slowly became less of a battle and an easier time for David. Or did it?

Too Easy Years

After David became king, he committed three grievous sins. The first sin began one sunny day when he spied Bathsheba bathing on a nearby rooftop. David was so overcome by her beauty he had her come to his palace and seduced her. The actual story is more lustful, intriguing, and complex than my casual narrative, but the result was Bathsheba became pregnant. When attempts to have her husband appear as the father of the child failed, David had him killed (2 Samuel 11). David sinned by committing adultery and murder, two of the Ten Commandments.

The second sin of David was vanity, which resulted when he ordered a census be taken of the men in his kingdom (2 Chronicles 21). Now I know taking a census sounds too commonplace to be considered a sin, but in Old Testament times, a census was only taken of what belonged to a person. The men of Israel belonged to the Lord God, not King David, and census taking was specifically prohibited by God as detailed in Exodus 30:21.

The third sin, although not technically a sin, was David's lack of attention to his children. One half brother raped a daughter, and that half brother was then killed by another brother. David's only action was to banish the brother, named Absalom, from Jerusalem. Never once did David punish, intervene, counsel, or console his children. When Absalom returned to Jerusalem, he politicked his way into favor with the population to the point they proclaimed him the new king. King David once again was found on the run. Much to King David's dismay, his army fought Absalom's army and Absalom was killed. A grief-stricken King David was finally allowed to return to his throne (2 Samuel 13–19).

During this period David had in his court a prophet named Nathan. Following the episode with Bathsheba and her husband, Nathan forced David to see his sinful ways, whereupon David earnestly asked God for repentance (2 Samuel 12). The child Bathsheba was pregnant with through adultery died, but she had a second child with David after they married.

This was Solomon, King David's successor. Regardless of David asking God for repentance, 2 Samuel 11:27 says, "But the thing that David had done displeased the Lord." David was so sincere in his repentance that God pardoned him, although he knew future penalties would come. "Now therefore the sword shall never depart from your house" (2 Samuel 12:10) let King David know he would not have any periods of peace because of his indiscretion with Bathsheba.

The census brought on a different set of penalties. 2 Samuel 24:10–14 reveals:

> But David's heart struck him after he had numbered the people. And David said to the Lord, "I have sinned greatly in what I have done. But now, O Lord, please take away the iniquity of your servant, for I have done very foolishly." And when David arose in the morning, the word of the Lord came to the prophet Gad, David's seer, saying,[12] "Go and say to David, 'Thus says the Lord Three things I offer you. Choose one of them, that I may do it to you.'" So Gad came to David and told him, and said to him, "Shall three[E] years of famine come to you in your land? Or will you flee three months before your foes while they pursue you? Or shall there be three days' pestilence in your land? Now consider, and decide what answer I shall return to him who sent me." Then David said to Gad, "I am in great distress. Let us fall into the hand of the Lord, for his mercy is great; but let me not fall into the hand of man."

David was given a choice, and he chose pestilence. Seventy thousand people died, and just as the pestilence reached Jerusalem, God provided mercy and stayed the pestilence from killing any more. King David's people paid a heavy price for his sin of vanity.

King David had about ten peaceful years after his son Absalom was killed. In the end, Solomon was named the successor amid much family controversy, and David could design and prepare for the temple to be built by Solomon. David's advice to the new King Solomon was:

And you, Solomon my son, know the God of your father and serve him with a whole heart and with a willing mind, for the Lord searches all hearts and understands every plan and thought. If you seek him, he will be found by you, but if you forsake him, he will cast you off forever. Be careful now, for the Lord has chosen you to build a house for the sanctuary; be strong and do it." (1 Chronicles 28:9–10)

Know God, serve God, and seek God. David's eulogy of sorts is found in 1 Chronicles 29:9: "Then he died at a good age, full of days, riches, and honor."

You and King David

The story of King David's life is full of God's glory; my short narrative does not reflect the complete story as found in 1 Chronicles and in 1 and 2 Samuel. I suggest you take an evening to read his story from beginning to end. The reason I brought you through David's life is I now want you to place yourself in David's place as if it's your business life. Maybe you remember your "youthful stage," or you are currently in that stage where the business world is exhilarating and exciting. You are full of energy and a sponge for knowledge. But are you making lifelong friends in many different circles, or are you so full of self-drive that you forget your friends and acquaintances? Are you considering whether or not these relationships and the reputation you are building will be something you are proud of? David's youthful stage is where he made friends, real friends who spoke the truth to him and were friends for a lifetime.

Do you remember your "fugitive stage"? Or are you in your fugitive stage? Hopefully you are not on the run and hiding out in the crags and crevasses of the wilderness, but in a business sense, you might be fighting for the next rung on the career ladder. Maybe your fugitive stage refers to a challenge to land the next customer or find the next market niche that will buy your new clothing designs or software solutions. Look at David during this stage; you will notice several key elements. First, this was the time David honed his leadership skills. He started with a ragtag army of only four hundred men who all traveled with their families. In David's time, real armies were measured in tens of thousands, not hundreds. Yet he built relationships with neighboring nations so he could help them in their wars and earn their trust (to a certain extent) and respect. These relationships were with armies he had previously defeated on the battlefield. Can you do that with your competitors and peers in your field of business? Yes, you are fighting for business, but are you building a business as well? Are you earning the respect that allows you to go from competitor to strategic partner and back to competitor on a regular basis? Or are you building bridges only to burn them down?

As a fugitive, David found a source of strength that could withstand any trial or disaster. That strength was in God. He built relationships so he could practice all the skills needed to hold people accountable, keep morale up, find new work, and put people in the right seats. David cultivated the practice of prayer and always followed God's directions. When King Saul was out to kill David, David asked God where he should go. God had David hide in the hills of Judea just a few miles from Saul's palace. Instead of running as far as possible, God placed David as near as possible to his enemy. David trusted God with what seemed like bad advice. Is your relationship with God such that you will follow Him even if it seems like bad advice to you? Business is a world of risks, and your decision to take risks depends on the information and advice you receive. Is God one of your advisors? During your fugitive stage, you will be developing and nurturing your relationship with God, as well as learning how to talk to Him and, most importantly, how to listen to Him.

I don't want to talk about the "too easy" stage, but unfortunately we are humans who are cursed with sin. From my observations and personal experience, many people get to a stage where they quit relying on and listening to God and start making decisions contrary to the direction the Bible gives us. I'm not talking about adultery and murder like David experienced. I'm thinking of a stage where we think we have it made, we know everything we need to know, and we have made all the relationships we need. Maybe we think we have sold all the insurance policies we need to and can now just rest on our past, or perhaps we have enough rental apartments to make a nice income without doing any work, or we have built a large enough staff that we can come in late and play golf every afternoon. None of those circumstances are problematic; in fact, they're great. David had won all the wars he needed to win, had a nice reputation, and could work or not work the hours he wanted. But as with David when he was walking on the rooftop balcony one pleasant, sunny afternoon, it is where the too-easy times take you that are the problem. Does your car know the way to the casino, do you drink too much during your afternoon round of golf, or do you become belligerent when your supervisor wants you to make more business calls? Have you taken up expensive hobbies that you cannot afford? Are you finding friends of the opposite sex? Does this too-easy time take away from your family? And most importantly, does this too-easy time take away from your relationship with God?

The story of King David is important because of how he entered and exited each stage, how he made all the mistakes we sinful people make, how he repented to God of his sins, and how he reestablished a stronger relationship with God. Although he made mistakes, he accepted responsibility for them and took the penalty. Isn't that what it is all about? Try to be the best we can, know we are not perfect, ask God to forgive our mistakes, accept the penalty, and move on.

Next Steps

If you have not accepted Jesus as the Lord and Savior of your life, I suggest you start there. This is a simple and easy step, but it is a giant step.

Next, find a great church in which to participate. Some churches talk about joining and attending; that's not enough. You need to participate. Churches are full of sinful people just like hospitals are full of sick people. The difference is when sick people get well, they go home. Not so with churches. Once we understand our sinful nature, our lives get better and better only by taking part in a group of other believers. My suggestion is to find a church that believes in the inerrancy of scripture—that alone will save you the time spent getting over the confusion of what some people think is right and wrong in the Bible.

Third, get a good Bible and be ready to write in it, make notes, and highlight verses; and plan on wearing it out. They will always print more Bibles. The Bible is a sacred book, but that does not mean you cannot keep your personal notes and thoughts in it.

Finally, make some Christian friends and then make time for them.

We all grow together, and there is no end to our growth potential. You don't have to get rid of your old friends; instead introduce them to your new Christian friends. You will be saving their lives.

If you are already a believer, now is the time to introduce your Christian principles into your business, and do not be bashful about where your new guiding principles come from. Be bold and show your faith seven days each week. I'm aware there is a lot of information advising us not to promote our faith in our workplace, but don't let that stop you from using the best business advice book—the Holy Bible—from managing your business to its full potential.

Let me close with a prayer:

> Gracious and loving heavenly Father, You have blessed many of Your people with the gift to manage, operate, and grow businesses in Your created world. We are placed in an environment where the cares and needs of this world intersect Your plan for eternity. We each have partners, employees, coworkers, subconsultants, vendors, and suppliers who rely on us to help them be successful. But not everyone we are yoked with is a believer. Please guide us so our successes in business are matched with Your will. Give us guidance on how to represent You so everyone we come in contact with will know of Your love and grace through our actions. God, we know You love us, look out for us, care for us, and want the best for us, and for that we love and worship you. In Jesus's name, amen.

Notes

1   John R. Erickson, "The Nourishment Business," *World*, https://world.wng. org/2016/07/the_nourishment_business (accessed August 25, 2016).

2   Jim Collins, *Good to Great* (New York: HarperCollins, 2001).

3   Collins, *Good*, 42.

4   Geno Wickman, *Traction: Get a Grip on Your Business* (Dallas: BenBella Books, 2011, 3).

5   Geoff Colvin, *Talent Is Overrated: What Really Separates World-Class Performers from Everybody Else* (New York: Penguin Group, 2010).

6   OakTree Software Inc., Accordance 11: Bible Software 2015.

7   Tony Schwartz, "The Twelve Attributes of a Truly Great Place to Work," *Harvard Business Review*, September 19, 2011, https://hbr.org/2011/09/the-twelve-attributes-of-a-tru.html# (accessed August 23, 2016).

8   John Baldoni, "Employee Engagement Does More than Boost Productivity," *Harvard Business Review*, July 4, 2013, https://hbr.org/2013/07/employee-engagement-does-more/ (accessed August 23, 2016).

9   Patrick Lencioni, "To Grow Your Business, Know Your People," *Inc.*, September 2015, 92.

10 Dan Vander Lugt, *Why Does the Bible Seem to Tolerate the Institution of Slavery?*, 2001, http://www.gospelcom.net/rbc/questions/answer.php?catagory=bible& folder=slavery&topic=Slavery&file=slavery.xml.

11 Louis Ginzberg, *Legends of the Bible* (Philadelphia: Jewish Publication Society of America, 1956) referenced at: http://biblehub.com/commentaries/guzik/ commentaries/1402.htm.

12 Emma Green, "Finding Jesus at Work," *The Atlantic*, February 17, 2016, http://www.theatlantic.com/business/archive/2016/02/work-secularization-chaplaincies/462987/ (accessed July 23, 2016).

13 Henry J. Evans, *Winning with Accountability: the Secret Language of High-Performing Organizations* (Dallas: CornerStone Leadership Institute, 2008).

14 "Accountability," BusinessDictionary.com, Web Finance, Inc. (nd), http://www. businessdictionary.com/definition/accountability.html (accessed July 2416).

15 OakTree Software Inc., Accordance 11:Bible Software 2015.

16 OakTree Software Inc., Accordance 11:Bible Software 2015.

17 OakTree Software Inc., Accordance 11:Bible Software 2015.

18 OakTree Software Inc., Accordance 11:Bible Software 2015.

19 Michael Hyatt, "4 Ways to Boost Your Team Engagement," *Your Virtual Mentor: Win at Work, Succeed at Life* (blog), October 19, 2016, https://michaelhyatt.com/team-engagement.html.

20 Chartered Institute of Marketing, Moor Hall, Cookham, Maidenhead, Berkshire SL6 9QH UK, http://www.cim.co.uk/more/getin2marketing/what-is-marketing/.

21 University Business Magazine, Professional Media Group, 35 Nutmeg Drive, Trumbull, CT, 06611; online at: http://www.universitybusiness.com/article/new-definition-marketing.

22 Seth Godin, *Purple Cow* (New York: Penguin Group, 2009).

23 "Invest," *Oxford English Dictionary*, 2016, Oxford Dictionaries, Web, 29-July-2016.

24 OakTree Software Inc., Accordance 11: Bible Software 2015.

25 "High calling," *Urban Dictionary*, 2016, Urban Dictionary, Web, 29-July-2016.

26 OakTree Software Inc., Accordance 11: Bible Software 2015.

27 Emily Thomsen, "Which Day of the Week?" http://www.sabbathtruth.com/free-resources/article-library/id/912/which-day-of-the-week accessed 16-Jan-2016.

28 R. C. Sproul, "Defining the Debate," Ligonier Ministries, ligonier.org, www.ligonier.org/learn/articles/defining-debate/ (accessed January 15, 2016).

29 Richard M. Ryan, Jessy H Bernstein, and Kirk Warren Brown, "Weekend, Work, and Well-Being: Psychological Needs Satisfactions and Day of the Week Effects on Mood, Vitality, and Physical Symptoms," *Journal of Social and Clinical Psychology*, Vol. 29, No. 1, 2010, 95–122.

30 Ryan, "Weekend," 95–122.

31 Marianna Virtanen, Archana Singh-Manoux, Jane E. Ferrie, David Gimeno, Michael G. Marmot, Marko Elovainio, Markus Jokela, Jussi Vahtera, Mika Kivimäki, "Long Working Hours and Cognitive Function: The Whitehall II Study". *Am J Epidemiol* 2009; 169 (5): 596-605. doi: 10.1093/aje/kwn382, https://academic.oup.com/aje/article/169/5/596/143020/Long-Working-Hours-and-Cognitive-FunctionThe (accessed January 15, 2016).

32 OakTree Software Inc., Accordance 11: Bible Software 2015.

33 OakTree Software Inc., Accordance 11: Bible Software 2015.

34 OakTree Software Inc., Accordance 11: Bible Software 2015.

CPSIA information can be obtained
at www.ICGtesting.com
Printed in the USA
LVOW08*2339050418

572528LV00002B/8/P

9 781512 783353